MEDICINE WOMEN, *CURANDERAS*, AND WOMEN DOCTORS

By
**Bobette Perrone
H. Henrietta Stockel
Victoria Krueger**

UNIVERSITY OF OKLAHOMA PRESS : NORMAN

OTHER BOOKS BY H. HENRIETTA STOCKEL

Women of the Apache Nation: Voices of Truth (Reno, 1991)
Survival of the Spirit: The Chiricahua Apaches in Captivity (Reno, 1993)

Library of Congress Cataloging-in-Publication Data

Perrone, Bobette, 1927–
    Medicine women, curanderas, and women doctors / by Bobette
Perrone, H. Henrietta Stockel, Victoria Krueger.
        p.   cm.
    Bibliography: p. 239
    Includes index.
        1. Women healers—Cross-cultural studies.   2. Women physicians—
Cross-cultural studies.   3. Medical anthropology.   4. Indians of
North America—Medicine.   I. Stockel, H. Henrietta, 1938–   .
II. Krueger, Victoria, 1942–   . III. Title.
R692.P47   1989
610'.82—dc20   89-4901

    ISBN: 978-0-8061-2512-1 (paper)

9   10   11   12

MEDICINE WOMEN,
CURANDERAS,
AND
WOMEN DOCTORS

To the Great Spirit—
in all its voices

CONTENTS

viii

ILLUSTRATIONS

PREFACE

Why did we write this book? As one author puts it: "I had been hurt. I had experienced a head-on collision with life forces in one grand crash. I thought I was getting lazy the day I called my office to say I'd make it by 10 o'clock, not 8:00 A.M. When I went into an emergency room where the male doctor kept me waiting in the foyer, gowned in a paper top, with my woman's hips and ass and thighs cold and exposed to passersby, I sat with humiliation on a stainless-steel stool. I suggested stress. He said, 'Indigestion,' adding, 'There are no women executives.' I was referred to Dr. Futaba Matsumoto, whose English I could barely comprehend but whose tone I understood as caring. She ordered an EKG, seeing that I was experiencing a heart attack at that very moment.

"My physical life was saved by the intelligence and insight and humanity of a woman doctor. The first woman to doctor me. It was strange. It was also strange to me to not be healthy and strong. So I plunged back into work, and had another heart attack. Professionals and friends all gave one message: 'Quit or die.' It's what I call my window-pane decision. Having reached the power position of having a windowed office, calfskin attache case, new car with payments, I looked through the window overlooking a prestigious parking lot and said, 'No. I will not die for this.' The illness cost me every integral part of my life at that time.

"Gradually, I became physically stronger but I also discovered that AMA medicine didn't heal my woundedness, didn't heal my pain. I, a strong and vital woman, was in need of some greater healing. And I set out upon a journey to find it and to reclaim it.

"The process of healing included a return to the Santa Fe of child-hood years and memories and the curing influences of the Gonzales family, as poor as we, who shared trout caught from the Pecos River, and of the Taos Indian woman who traded her coffee for my grandmother's sugar. It was the humanity, the sense of community that called me back and that helped give birth to this book. I would not then have called it spirituality. I would not then have called it healing. I do now."

Why did we write this book? Another author states: "Forty years ago in a grade-school classroom, I excitedly opened a new reader. Books always thrilled me, but I was unable to comprehend the odd attraction I felt as I read a child's story about the Atchison, Topeka, and Santa Fe Railroad. The name 'Santa Fe' was intriguing; I whispered it aloud again and again. It sounded like magic to me.

"Twenty-five years after that moment, I could wait no longer. Finally and deliberately, I concluded my life in the east and moved to Santa Fe with two cats, one suitcase, and with a heart ready to cooperate with my destiny. Whatever that was, I knew it was in Santa Fe.

"Now, having experienced the awesome wonder of the Southwest for fourteen years, I am still a novice at understanding destiny, but through this book I have learned the enormous power of women's beliefs, an essential segment of their unique connection with the Creator. Sharing this knowledge respectfully is my personal contribution to the universe in honor of the spirituality, ever new, that I first felt as a youngster and that led me, ultimately, to Santa Fe to participate in the writing of *Medicine Women*, Curanderas, *and Women Doctors*."

Why was this book written? Yet another author believes "that the Great Spirit, God, the All, Higher Intelligence, or Higher Power (whatever word one chooses) wants sharing, cooperation, and a global consciousness as the directions in which the world needs to move. In that spirit was this book written."

A few words about how this book was written. To obtain the information presented, medicine women and *curanderas* who would speak to us first had to be found. The search was arduous and limited because of the declining number of traditional Native American women healers and the cultural disapproval they frequently face when discussing the sacred aspects of Native American healing with "outsiders." *Curanderas* also are aging, and few replacements are coming along. In addition, we also encountered resistance from practitioners in each culture, including doctors who feared "breaking rank" within the American Medical Association (AMA).

To reach an honest exchange with medicine women and *curanderas* especially, one that culminated in a welcome to observe and record the ancient and present beliefs and sacred rituals, it was necessary for us first to assure the potential teachers that they would be viewed through their cultures' perspectives, not our own. We also promised that the integrity of their ways of life would be preserved and that their stories would be told as they reported them, not as we writers interpreted them. All in all, it took more than five years to record the work—a period of time during which an atmosphere of credibility and responsibility was created.

Carte blanche from informants was not easily forthcoming, and we were not automatically granted permission for publication. In most cases, stipulations were required. For example, Dhyani Ywahoo objected strongly to a brief history of the Cherokee people written with the use of academic sources as references. She insisted that the portrayal of her people's history was not accurate and was biased from a white, Anglo educational system's point of view. Accordingly, the segment about Cherokee history has been deleted from this text. Interviewees asked for and received review permission. What we, in turn, asked for and received was permission from them to use the material in this book. Although more interpretation of the information might be wished for, it could not be achieved without substantial risk of losing permissions—and the information is invaluable. It was a challenge to present useful comparisons and contrasts within a framework of attempting to remain faithful to the women and to the material presented—not intruding or interpreting.

Similarly, the lack of women physicians who were willing to be candid, and the large number who refused publication permission, was a surprise to us. A number of doctors who had already been interviewed withdrew from the project after reading a transcript of their own words, because of second thoughts about the reaction of the medical community to their forthright statements. It is interesting that many were as protective of not breaking rank with their profession and culture as were the traditional healers from other cultures.

The privilege of trust was extended by many, however, and all of us are indeed the richer for the encounters. We were stretched from who we were before we learned, to who we are now. We are very grateful to those who placed enough trust in us to share themselves and their cultural beliefs with us, and subsequently with you, the readers.

We have incorporated the usage or nonusage of accent marks as utilized by the speakers themselves. For example, José accents his first name but deletes the tilde in Pino. We honor the preferences of each individual.

Lastly, when we use terms such as "southwestern Hispanic traditions," "Southwest Native Americans," or "American Medical Association (AMA) physicians," we are summarizing a variety of attitudes found among various subsets of these groups rather than speaking for all members of such named groups. The terms encompass vast diversities. The Apache belief system, for example, is different from the Navajo, which in turn is different from the Pueblo of the Rio Grande. Similarly, the Mexican-Americans of Texas are different from the Chicanos of Los Angeles, who, in turn, are different from the northern New Mexico village residents who are direct descendants of two to three hundred years of Spanish lineage. There are equally divergent values and attitudes within the Western Hemisphere's scientific medicine, a discipline which, for easy readability, we are referring to as "AMA medicine."

We have condensed these widely disparate subgroups into three major cultural thrusts, knowing that we do not give full justice to their diversity, but aspiring to make comparisons and contrasts apparent, rather than getting bogged down in detail. Therefore, we have selected the prevailing attitudes, the primary stance, to condense an otherwise unwieldy amount of information.

The majority of readers will probably come to this book with more information about "modern scientific" medicine than about southwestern Native American or traditional southwestern Hispanic healing practices. Our intent is not to slight "modern" medicine by not elaborating on it in equal detail but rather to add information not generally available to most readers. In this regard, we have strongly addressed in the introduction biases and assumptions likely to be held by this same majority toward "traditional" versus "modern" medicine. Readers are asked to take these considerations into serious account.

This book was written to assist the movement to provide the most comprehensive healing available through the use of an additive (and-and) model rather than an adversarial, or exclusive, (either-or) model of medicine. Drawing on various cultures and women's healing and attitudes can result in major contributions to modern medicine.

We have always appreciated advice friends give us about reading a book—comments like, "Read this from back to front," or, "The premise of this book is on page x, the conclusion is on page y, and the juicy parts are in chapter z." With such information, we read according to mood. If we wish to stroll leisurely through the garden, we can sniff each flower and each *bon mot* along the way, relishing each turn of phrase. If we are on a data-gathering mission, racing along like a Maserati, we gather rosebuds—quickly.

Our suggestions for reading this book are as follows: If you wish to read only the stories of women healers, the table of contents demarcates them clearly. If you wish to read assumptions and premises encapsulated, read the introductory and interpretative material at the beginning of each section. In other words, the data presented are separated from the interpretations.

The writers of this book are as disparate as the practitioners in each culture. Part five continues the format begun in the segments about medicine women, *curanderas*, and women doctors; each author speaks in her own voice and style about her observations, experiences, and the notions generated.

For the full experience, read the book in its entirety, adding your own questions and feelings. In whatever way you read this book, however, we hope you enjoy it and gain from it.

BOBETTE PERRONE
Santa Fe, New Mexico   H. HENRIETTA STOCKEL
VICTORIA KRUEGER

ACKNOWLEDGMENTS

Writing this book has occupied six years. We have met hundreds of people, and our gratitude is due to all who have given their time in discussing the book, in working with us, and in generally facilitating the final product. For the ubiquitous reason of space, we can list only certain contributors, but we wish that all who helped will accept our warm thanks, appreciation, and acknowledgment of indebtedness for unique and invaluable contributions.

For inspiration and process we, first and foremost, lovingly thank the medicine women, *curanderas,* and women doctors who so generously gave of themselves so that this book might be written. In the course of working on it, we have been cheered by spending time, leisurely healing time, with tough, gentle, and interesting women. We also thank their families and loved ones who added support and information, especially those families in the Navajo Nation who invited us into their homes and camps and allowed us to participate in their ceremonies, sings, and dances.

To our own families we extend special feelings for meaningful contributions: to a son, Joshua Phillips, a man with his own sons now, who has had a more profound effect than he can ever know and who always has—know, forever, that your reflections have always mattered; to Laurie, for the loving and respectful appreciation of the roles as we define and blend them and the learning that comes, and for saving writings for grandsons, Stryker and Nicholas, classes of 2000 and 2004—a delight in who you are and in the stories we shall share around our own campfires; to parents, James and Catherine Skidmore, who taught intellectual curiosity and warmth; to Kathy Krueger, a daughter of the heart, a legacy of strength.

xviii

Heartfelt thanks also go to our family of friends, for physical, emotional, and spiritual sustenance. To coauthors who were tough but hung in for six years of amazement and discovery about creative collaboration; to a dearest friend and companion, gratitude for other kinds of stories shared and lifetime's questions openly asked, openly answered; to Judy Kraul, who kept the flame to our feet and gave warmth to our hearts; to Helen Lyons, who brought us kicking and screaming into the cosmos of computers with her arts of teaching and friendship; to Sally and Chester Wright for years of kindness and helpfulness. We are thankful for the unfailing support and understanding of Beatrice R. Martinez, who was present at the creation, and to Louise d'A. Fairchild, who has been ever present; to Donald R. Bealer, Bernice E. Kennedy, Cecilia M. Bachicha, Teressa S. Matousek and her family; and to Jane H. Cotter for her honest and gentle criticisms. To Dennis Dunnum, Bart and Mark Kaltenbach, Ren Greene, David Thorp, and Jason Frederick, who have cussed, discussed, dissented, and agreed through six years of process, we are grateful, and we have affection for each.

To Lili Tomlin and Jane Wagner, for their insights into creative processes, we are indebted. To Adrienne Rich we are indebted also for her public courage.

We lovingly thank Tom Radko, our editor, our own Maxwell Perkins, and our friend, and the University of Oklahoma Press—a true helper in the development of this book.

For research and writing we thank: Peggy Scott, former director of cultural research at the Navajo Community College, Navajo Nation, Tsalie, Arizona; Brook Medicine Eagle; Norma Cordell; Caryn Miles, Ph.D., Wabun of the Bear Tribe; the LAMA Foundation; Helen Fragua, R.N.; Joan Ellen Price; Barbara Du Bois, dean of Sunray School of Sacred Studies; Tlo Lowry; Diane Stein, of the *Los Artesanos* bookstore in Las Vegas, New Mexico; and Rain Parish, former curator of the Wheelwright Museum in Santa Fe.

We especially thank Professor Susan Lang-McMonagle, who established the original contacts with the Navajo Nation, and who has given constant friendship, knowledge, and encouragement; and Roz Eisenberg, Elizabeth Cooley, Ph.D., and Sheila Namir, Ph.D., for sharing every referral at their disposal.

For editing assistance, we thank everyone who added, deleted, commented, and blue-penciled, but especially Sue-Ellen Jacobs, Ph.D., Judy Kraul, Susan Lang-McMonagle, Elizabeth Cooley, Ph.D., and Sheila Namir, Ph.D.; and Becky Staples and Elizabeth Shaw.

For proofreading, a tedious task at best, we thank Judy Kraul, Louise d'A. Fairchild, Pat Williams, and Bernice E. Kennedy.

For photography, photographic processes, and artwork, thanks to Tom Nibblick, Donald R. Bealer, Louise d'A. Fairchild, Jack Mills, José Ortiz y Pino, III, and Bart Kaltenbach.

B.P.
H.H.S.
V.K.

MEDICINE WOMEN, *CURANDERAS,* AND WOMEN DOCTORS

CHAPTER 1

BRIDGES

An Introduction

There are bridges in geography
        . . . from Manhattan to Brooklyn
There are bridges in music
        . . . from B flat to C
There are bridges in life
        . . . birth
        . . . graduation
        . . . marriage
        . . . death
There are bridges
        . . . between genders
        . . . between cultures
        . . . between philosophies of healing

The first premise of this book is that each of the different cultural approaches to healing presented in this volume has something to contribute to the goal of wellness. Western, scientific, or what we will call "AMA medicine" (medicine as practiced by members of the American Medical Association) has provided surgery, x-rays, lasers, antibiotics, vaccines, and many more procedures and products that have extended the lifespan of most Americans into their seventies. It must be acknowledged, however, that there is a growing and uncomfortable realization within the realms of AMA medicine about healing practices. Doctors themselves are criticizing some areas within their profession that they now believe require and even demand change. Medical journals have spoken out and acknowledged the serious difficulties in the delivery of health care. And the consumer-patient is voicing similar objections, both verbally and in the form of malpractice suits. The medical profession has been put on notice.

What is needed to correct the problems? Many elements missing in AMA medicine can be found in the cultures we present here, and in the women we studied. The traditional and contemporary ways of healing are not in conflict with each other, not antagonistic; rather, they can be complementary, and they can work together toward a single purpose of curing the patient. The model for healing can be a syncretic model, a fusion or union of originally differing and even conflicting components. The either-or position is an adversarial model. One of the main arguments of this book is that the traditional healing practitioner uses techniques and a pharmacopoeia (herbs and other sources of medicine) that are the foundation of modern medical practices. Such contributions have been valuable, and more can be learned from them than has been to date.

Assumptions and values about healing can be reevaluated and perhaps incorporated as well. For example, traditional cultures demonstrate a partnership, a connectedness between the healer and the patient. In contrast, if satisfying healing by a physician consisted solely of an examination and then a prescription for the correct medication, the vanishing of a doctor-patient relationship would not be so loudly decried. The best from each of the three cultures should be studied, with the insights and information obtained incorporated productively into the delivery of health care. This synergistic vision is the authors' first premise and a worthy goal.

The second premise is that women have particular characteristics (not necessarily unique to women) that make important contributions to healing. They bring skills such as touching, hugging, talking, and paying attention to the "other" (the patient), and they are good at verbal and nonverbal communication. They bring empathy and attention and a sense of connectedness, caring, and community. Psychologist Judith Jordan, of Harvard Medical School, states that "studies of sex differences in empathy show that while both sexes are equally good at noticing and labeling affective states in others, women are more motivated to respond."[1] Carol Tarvis and Carole Offir summarize the classic experiments of Bem in which subjects were asked to listen to apparently spontaneous conversations of another person (who was actually a confederate of the experimenters delivering a memorized script regarding personal problems). In the results, "it turned out that . . . women reacted with more concern than did men."[2] Robert Rosenthal and his associates found that "women excel at decoding nonverbal signs of other people's feelings."[3] M. Hoffman states, "There is some evidence . . . that girls are more likely to share in the emotions of others—to feel happy when others are happy, distressed when they are distressed."[4] Rosenthal's study on nonverbal cues and their relationship to empathy points to the need of women to attend accurately to an infant's nonverbal communication: "If women, as well as other oppressed groups, must 'read' the expressions of others with great accuracy in order to advance or even survive, then they could become nonverbally sensitive at an early age . . . when one is powerless, one must be subtle."[5]

Summarizing the issue of empathy, Jordan states: "Empathy is a complex process that relies on a high level of ego strength and development and involves a balance of thought and feeling. Men and women differ in their ability to respond empathetically. Men tend to have difficulty with surrender and the act of temporarily joining with one another. It implies for them passivity, loss of objectivity and loss of control. Women, on the other hand, are conditioned to be more empathetic."[6] Thus research substantiates differences in male and female empathy and nurturing, showing that women possess these characteristics and attributes, making them especially skilled healers.

The stories of women healers have rarely been told and need to be. Carol Christ says:

> Women live in a world where women's stories have rarely been told from their own perspectives. The stories celebrated in culture are told of self and world, and their most profound stories orient them to what they perceive as the great powers of the universe. But since women have not been told their own stories, they have not actively shaped their experiences of self and world or named the great powers from their own perspectives.[7]

The female-oriented approach to problem solving has not been adequately explored, examined, or incorporated. Important studies are now being done that may change this. One purpose of this book is to contribute to a broad spectrum of investigations of the benefits of a female-oriented approach to healing. We hear many things about medicine men; what do we hear about medicine women? Moreover, we ask you to examine your own choice of a male or female physician. Relevant questions about male and female healers may reveal much about gender assumptions. Culturally, the same questions apply. Whom would you choose? A medical doctor, an herbalist, a midwife, a Native American medicine person? What are your assumptions and what are your reasons?

Every system of operations makes assumptions, and healing is no exception. Sometimes these assumptions are overt, sometimes covert; sometimes a culture is conscious of the assumptions, but most of the time it is not. Before we can understand the healing systems of the Native American, Southwest Hispanic, and Anglo cultures, we must understand the assumptions on which they are based.

AMA medicine, the dominant method of Western healing for many decades, assumes that physical illnesses are the result of physical causes only (viruses, organ malfunctions, bacteria, genetics, and biochemical agents). Although Western medicine has increasingly recognized psychological factors as contributing to the cause of ailments (e.g., stress as the cause of ulcers), the primary assumption still is that the basic causes of physical illnesses are, in fact, physical.

In contrast, a Navajo medicine woman might say that a person has become ill from looking upon the face of a dead one; a Hispanic healer (*la curandera*) will say that illness is frequently a matter of chance and that "chance" is somehow associated with the will of God. One fundamental assumption in both Native American and Southwest Hispanic cultures is that physical diseases can be caused by the violation of spiritual or religious laws. A spiritual dimension or concept of bewitchment (such as the Hispanic theory of *embrujada*) as an active source of some illnesses is a foreign idea to Western medical practitioners and is not given much credibility by those who believe truth resides in a microscope. When one seeks to discern why healers approach the task of healing so differently, it is crucial to understand such cultural differences. A Navajo medicine sing, for instance, makes little sense as a curative procedure if one assumes that only bacteria and viruses cause diseases.

To understand the healing practices of other cultures, the reader is asked to consider unfamiliar healing assumptions with an open mind (even though they differ a great deal from the premises of Western medicine) and to weed out unconscious bias. We are asking the reader to suspend assumptions just as we as authors had to suspend our own standard language and training. A difficult task is presented. How does one weed out unconscious bias when, by definition, "unconscious" means that one is not aware. This approach is suggested: practice free association. What do you, the reader, feel when you experience any of the following: a Harvard degree hanging on your doctor's office wall; the smell of alcohol or antiseptic; the hum of the x-ray machine; the sting of a hypodermic needle or the burn of iodine; the wooden taste of a tongue depressor. For most people accustomed to Western medicine, these experiences create a sense of trust and belief that the doctors know what they are doing and will impart health. These procedures or experiences foster an assurance that the physicians using them have access to the "truth" of healing. Actually, these are learned responses, evidence of one's unconscious, automatic biases and assumptions about "science" and "medicine."

Do you believe that all doctors are equally competent any more than you believe that all plumbers or all auto mechanics or all secretaries are equally competent? If you have been brought up in scientific, Anglo, academic cultures, you may assume that physicians are equally competent, whereas you would view as ludicrous the idea that all electricians are equally skilled. Why this discrepancy? Do we think as we walk into the doctor's office, "Aha, I smell antiseptic, therefore I trust this professional?" Is that not an assumption? Is that not a belief system? It has nothing to do with truth. This doctor could be totally inept. Yet, we tend to trust because of the familiar smells and sights in the doctor's office.

If, however, one says, "I am not that trusting, I am always careful, and I always get a second opinion," then first, one is not in the majority. Many Americans believe that entering a doctor's office will automatically provide them the best healing or treatment available. Even when a second opinion is sought, however, if two doctors (both trained in the same principles) reach the same diagnosis, are they not most often believed? This assumption that two similar opinions represent the "truth" could also be a bias. Someone who does not believe in medicine women or *curanderas*, for example, would not consider even ten similar or identical opinions to constitute the truth.

Imagine looking back from a vantage point of one thousand years in the future, retrospectively evaluating our current, "sophisticated" medical and scientific procedures. One might see today's physician waving laser beams over a patient's body as a primitive, archaic, and incomprehensible healing technique, just as from some perspectives a medicine woman waving eagle feathers, or a *curandera* holding a crucifix over a patient, is viewed by some as archaic. The similarities are striking and compelling. Future generations may lose touch with the major assumptions underpinning contemporary western medicine, just as many of us have now lost touch with the assumptions integral to older cultures that continue to practice the ancient healing ways. Forgetting the assumptions on which a procedure is based may make the procedure incomprehensible, but it does not make it invalid.

Most readers make assumptions about the concept of objectivity. It is an assumption that one can be objective. Yet, the mere choice of selecting what will be observed is a bias. As viewed by Hager, "objectivity" is a myth because it is simply another system of belief, in this instance the system adhered to by scientists. It is not *the* truth, although it is assumed by many to be so and is no longer a questioned assumption.[8] A dilemma arises when scientists delude themselves into believing that their own opinions and beliefs play no role in their pursuit of objectivity.

One example of nonobjectivity (bias) is sexism in science. States Londa Schiebinger, "Scientific knowledge cannot be neutral because it is structured by power relations—and they examine the masculinist values practiced within the context of the norms of scientific inquiry."[9] The vast majority of research studies, for example, have been based on white, male choices of the topic, male selection of subjects, male interpretation of the data, the establishment of norms based on those interpretations—and the subsequent application of those norms to the entire population. Carol Gilligan states, "There's been a sort of coming forward from other researchers who've told me about studies where women were dropped from the sample because their responses were complicating the situation." [10] These reports indicate that there are good grounds for challenging the myth and assumption of objectivity in science.

In addition to sexism, "scientism" is a bias. For example, a 1980s television show host kicked off a discussion by physicians of assumptions in medicine with the question "Are hospitals killing us?" Dr. Robert Mendelsohn replied: "I refer to hospitals as the temples of the religion of modern medicine because modern medicine isn't a science, it's really a belief system. There's practically no science in medicine." [11] In other words, modern medicine and science are a belief system based on the myth of objectivity.

In contrast to the assumption of objectivity, consider the premises other cultures have long held about the connection between spirituality and healing. In the practice of Western scientific medicine, the ability to heal is earthly, but in traditional Indian and Hispanic cultures, the power to heal is divine. A medicine woman's power comes through her spirituality, evidenced in the healing ceremonies she performs. A *curandera*'s power comes from her religion and her deep belief that God has selected her to heal on earth. These are very different assumptions about healing from that of "scientific objectivity." Where do such assumptions come from?

The assumptions of a culture have their foundation in cultural myths. Myths are any body of stories and information believed to explain how things work or how they happened. Western science uses the myth of objectivity as one of its founding principles. In contrast, when asked, "What connection has the Biblical creation myth to healing?" a docent at liturgy in Santa Fe, New Mexico, said, "Everything." She talked about the perfection of Adam and Eve, "created in God's image." She stated that when Adam and Eve, having been perfect according to the myth, "were cast out of Paradise, they became mortal and hence, they fell heir to the ills of the flesh and to the ills of the world." [12] Thus, illness came into being because of original sin. This is an assumption about what causes illness, based on Biblical myth.

In addition to myths defining causes of illness, myths are related to healing as well. Healing in the Catholic Southwest Hispanic culture is related to getting out of a state of sin. Therefore, healing often includes the process of confession, asking forgiveness and penance, which puts one back in compliance with the rules of the God-given myths and opens the way for saints or God to grant healing.

Myths are also related to healing in many traditional Native American societies where a basic assumption about illness is that it can be caused by being in disharmony with the gods, community, neighbors, family, and the environment. Therefore, the healer, knowing the myth-given rules governing society and ascertaining how an individual has violated these rules, determines how to heal the ailment by putting the person back in total harmony with the society.

Myths are also related to healing because they contribute to a patient's faith and confidence. The stories and myths one has been told (and has believed), and familiar, comforting rituals, prompt the recipient to be more open to healing, be it in the form of a laser beam, an eagle feather, or a crucifix. Creating faith is an essential function of the myth, and it occurs cross-culturally: faith in the healer, faith in the power of a cure. Belief in a cure is enhanced by hearing stories about the usefulness of that cure for other people. There is a strong belief that going to the Mayo Clinic will accomplish something favorable for the sojourner, and patients more willingly undergo radiation treatment for cancer when told by physician, friends, and media that radiation is effective in curing that kind of cancer. Faith in myths and stories allays fears and doubts and builds and accelerates trust. Hearing from others, whether family or strangers, or knowing of a study recounting that many contemporaries have been healed by a particular pill, a medicine sing, a ritual, a trip to Lourdes, or a new surgical process, an ailing individual can feel hope and the sense of not being alone. Therein is built the expectation of success and the lessening of anxiety, which are in and of themselves health giving.

If one accepts the premise that faith is involved in a workable cure, then a patient's faith that radiation will help does in fact enhance the curative effect of the treatment. Faith in this sense is not just spiritual; it is faith that the system, whatever it is, will work. And faith does not automatically imply supernatural forces. Physicians and therapists have long been aware that once the appointment for consultation is made, frequently the patient's severe discomfort is tremendously ameliorated. This phenomenon has a name: the "waiting-list effect." An AMA equivalent of faith is the placebo effect. Experiments show that belief in a pill's efficacy will cure an ailment in many situations. At the University of California, San Francisco, Dr. John Levine, an internist and pain researcher, and D. Howard Fields, associate professor of neurology and physiology, administered a saline solution to some volunteer subjects who had wisdom teeth extracted and expected to suffer intense pain. Others were given painkillers. One-third of the patients given the saline solution found the pain significantly reduced.

Dr. Arthur Shapiro, professor of psychiatry at Mount Sinai Medical Center, in New York City, says: "This remarkable tendency to respond to belief and suggestion in such dramatic fashion has helped convince many researchers that all of us are potential placebo-responders. I think it's part of our genetic inheritance as human beings. . . . The placebo effect, it appears, has a definite basis in the chemistry of the brain." [13] Whether one believes that placebos, blessings, prayers, and even hexes or curses are "really real" or are the psychological effects of faith, depends on the assumptions one makes about what is real.

On the following pages are some "realities," some assumptions, concepts, premises, which are crucial to understanding the particular cultural healing methods described.

In many Native American cultures, it is assumed that a person is composed of a physical body, a psychological component, and a spiritual being with a connectedness to the earth and to other spirits/souls. Disruption of any of these parts can cause illness. It is assumed that the spiritual being has definite relationships with the earth, with other spirits (living and dead), and with powers both animate and inanimate. These powers take the forms of animals, deities, elements of nature, objects, one's relatives, and one's relationship to all of these entities. Within many Native American traditions such relationships are real, powerful, crucial, and *as* important as the tangible, physical world is to the Western medical mind. The Native American concept of existing powers, not tangible or visual, but having tremendous impact on one's physical well-being is difficult for many people to grasp and accept. Indeed, much Anglo-

American education rests on the assumption that the realm of physical matter is the only level of reality and essentially, therefore, the only cause of illness.

In the Hispanic, Roman Catholic religious tradition there is the assumption that an active, efficacious power to heal emanates from God and the saints. It is akin to the Native American tradition in that, once again, dimensions other than the physical are influential factors in causing and curing illnesses. Because it is assumed that power and energy come from a spiritual dimension, both Hispanic and Native American traditions view certain spiritually identified objects as having power. In the Hispanic Catholic usage, these frequently are relics of saints, their bones, clothing, personal possessions, or pieces of wood from their coffins. In the Native American tradition, feathers, rattles, and animal skins, parts, teeth, and claws are viewed as power objects. In both traditions, these objects not only have symbolic power (symbolized meaning) but are thought to have actual efficacious power of their own; their equivalents in Western medicine are antibiotics, a laser beam, or radiation therapy. These agents are seen as having actual efficacious power by their very nature. They are primary power sources that, when used properly, can heal.

The converse of the above is also true. Power objects can be used to damage. Just as misdirected or too much radiation can maim or kill a person, so too the power emanating from various objects or situations in the Native American and Hispanic systems can be destructive—the inhalation of corpse powder, for example, or being cursed by a witch. Regardless of whether power is used for healing or for hexing, however, the basic assumption is that some objects themselves have inherent power. Thus, both the Native American and Hispanic cultures add the spiritual dimension to the physical as a cause of illness and a source for cures.

Both the Southwest Native American and Hispanic Catholic traditions assume that interpersonal relationships can be both a cause of illness and a source of healing. Curses are considered a potential source of illness because the power to harm is real and is possessed by certain persons. On the positive side, good communal energy— good thoughts, prayers from well-wishers, plus the intervention of priests, saints, and the Trinity—is trusted to bring healing. This idea (that people can cause sickness with a curse or bring health with a prayer) is perhaps one of the most difficult for AMA medicine to accept or understand. Nevertheless, the assumption is that the prayers of people in the community have power or are efficacious; the more prayers said in one's behalf, the more likely one is to be healed and the more effective the healing will be. The notion of great community involvement is important. For example, a young man from a southern Colorado Indian tribe was seriously wounded in Vietnam and lay close to death in a hospital far from home. When his mother was notified, she called a group together, and they prayed and performed certain rituals. The soldier lived and appeared on public television in 1982 to tell his story. He gave tribute to the tribal ritual of communal prayer and credited the group and its healing energy with responsibility for his recovery.

In contrast, the AMA approach sees and treats illness and healing solely as an individualistic experience (with the exceptions of genetic and contagious diseases). If community resources are even lined up to help a patient, it is generally with an eye toward the mechanics of recuperation (who goes to the grocery store, helps the patient up the steps, pushes the wheelchair, changes the bandage). Little attention, if any, is paid to the psychological gains of having loving caretakers surrounding the patient. Hospitalized patients are frequently not allowed the attention of those they may need most, for example, friends, playmates, lovers, teachers, medicine people, and other trusted ones. Restrictive policy based on social labeling allows only husbands or wives and blood relatives at the patient's side and then only during the hours that are most convenient for the medical personnel.

To soften this picture of familiar, Western-scientific medicine, it must be noted that increasing numbers of doctors are taking emotional and interpersonal factors into consideration as both causes of illness and as healing potentials. For example, growing numbers of physicians view divorce, job-related tension, and economic and peer pressure as causative factors in illness. On the healing side, many physicians are encouraging support networks of friends and neighbors and other community agents. Nevertheless, change comes slowly.

We may legitimately compare the communal focus of native or

tribal ceremonies to the small amount of "community" or connectedness found in AMA medicine's beliefs. In scientific medicine, if the right machine can be plugged into the patient, or the right pill administered, the doctor's personal involvement (except diagnostically and prescriptively) is limited. A cure might even occur in the physician's absence if a patient is knowledgeable enough to take the correct dosage of leftovers in the medicine cabinet, whereas in the other, more traditional cultures, the medicine person's or the priest's presence is an essential ingredient to healing.

The inclusion of psychological and spiritual forces in healing is a major shift from the AMA model, which disregards the spiritual-social factors involved in the causes and cures of illnesses. But even this combined concept is still incomplete for understanding of Native American and Southwest Hispanic healing. Having three agents (the physical, psychological, and spiritual) that can affect an individual, the equilibrium or harmony or balance among these components emerges as yet another source of health or illness.

Most Native Americans believe that when the connection between one's own energy system and outside energy is out of balance, malfunctions of the body occur. Since relationships with other people, in many traditions, are part of being in harmony with one's surroundings, members of the tribe participate in ceremonies to restore balance and symmetry to the ailing patient.

Harmony has meaning at both the literal and the symbolic levels. At the literal level, one Native American traditional concept describing what constitutes health is that when the gods create a bit of matter, each piece (including body organs) is set to vibrate at a particular frequency for proper functioning, and illness occurs when an organ is not vibrating at the proper frequency. As an analogy, a radio station must be tuned to the right frequency to receive sound waves clearly. If the dial drifts, the radio does not clearly receive the energy being sent from the transmitter. Communication becomes distorted, static interferences occur. That is exactly what happens to a body organ when its frequency goes out of tune and it does not function properly—the signals are out of harmony. Many Native American cultures believe organs in the body function properly when they vibrate in conjunction with, or are in harmony with, the other organs in the body. Illness occurs when organs are out of such harmony or out of vibrational tune; curing occurs when these vibrations and harmonies are reestablished via community chanting and sings, which reestablish proper harmony and balance. The chants and songs (an integral part of most Native American healing ceremonies) are designed to change the frequency of a vibration within the malfunctioning organ via rhythm and sound.

To understand this concept at a subjective, emotional level (not a judgmental level), think about the effect you feel when you listen to "hard rock" as opposed to "mood music." Or recall the sound of a breeze through a pine bough and compare it to the honking of horns in peak commuter traffic. You then have a subjective sense of what research has found to be the impact of rhythm and sound on the emotions and even on the physical condition of individuals and groups. Gregorian chants, used extensively in the Catholic tradition (including the Hispanic), serve the same function of creating a particular vibrational harmonic within the individual that helps attune the listener to both spiritual understanding and healing.

Harmony and balance in the symbolic sense occur when one views illness as an affliction visited by God in punishment for some sin, original or current. Psychologically, the effect is, "I've broken a spiritual law; I am being punished by the deity (as I define it); I need to do penance; then I will be forgiven and my affliction will be lifted." Here the notion is of illness caused by a disharmonious relationship with other people and god(s), and the prayerful curing ceremony is utilized to correct the imbalance. Still another demonstration of harmony and balance is the southwestern Hispanic Catholic concept that while God places ailments on earth, so too does God give humans a naturally growing plant to cure each illness. This is the assumption on which herbalists rely.

Systems other than science that can contribute to healing are worthy of respectful exploration, especially those that provide connectedness—connectedness between the healer and the healed, connectedness with compassion and empathy, connectedness with one's own feelings, and connectedness with spirituality, with the universe and the higher powers. The psychological issue of connectedness has been missing from healing in recent years. This gap between scientific objectivity and connectedness is beginning to narrow, even within the boundaries of AMA medicine.

Progressive medical schools have instituted programs on "how to deal with the patient, the patient's family, and his/her whole life, rather than 'the third bed on the left with the coronary.'" [14] Similarly, an article in the *New England Journal of Medicine* stated, "There is continuing debate about the best method in selecting medical students, and it is agreed that there should be as much emphasis in the medical schools on the need to develop right attitudes toward patients as on acquiring knowledge and skills." [15]

Treating a patient holistically is nothing new. It is a resurgence of the way medicine was practiced many decades ago by country doctors who treated patients in their homes or in one-room offices in small towns across the length and breadth of a young nation. It is also a validation of the healing beliefs held by ancient Native American and Hispanic cultures, certainties clung to doggedly despite the changing times in medicine.

American medicine is growing and changing. There is a movement toward noninvasive surgery and techniques: sonic evaluation of fetuses, arthroscopic surgery on joints, laser removal of diseased tissues, chemotherapy, radiation, less trauma, less blood—more understanding of the emotional impact of putting a body "under the knife."

We ask you to suspend belief in the system to which you currently subscribe, just as you do when you go to the movies and allow yourself to become totally immersed in the reality presented on the screen. Approach these concepts of healing in the same manner. Permit yourself to become caught up in the internal consistency of each culture's system. This is what the authors have done in researching and writing this book. To gain understanding of healing approaches that were not immediately congenial to our own base of assumptions, we put aside our biases. We found the reward was worth the effort. We gained the knowledge that a syncretic approach in health-seeking behavior—an approach combining traditional techniques and pharmacopoeia; elements of spirituality; women's values, attitudes, and attributes; and AMA medicine—can increase healing and well-being.

Although they are very different from one another, all of the women interviewed for this book have commonality; they are tough and gentle women. They are tough in that each sets limits and can take command. They have long periods of rigorous training by established practitioners from within their cultures. They also have in common a desire or "calling" to become healers, frequently combining this role with other community (or family) roles. They have had to tolerate social disapproval. Each also has profound gentleness. Current medical practice can profit from the stories, values, attitudes, and attributes of these women.

PART ONE

MEDICINE WOMEN

CHAPTER 2

INTRODUCTION

In the 1970s and 80s there has been a renewal of interest in Native American culture, medicine, and healing. It includes the belated acknowledgment of contributions to healings made by Native Americans in the past and a growing dissatisfaction with the impersonality (and perhaps incompleteness) of Western, scientifically based medicine.

The history of contributions by Native American cultures (hundreds of them) to modern healing techniques and knowledge has not been widely known. For example, many tribes have long used willow, which contains salicin, one of the chemical bases of aspirin. Coca was employed as a pain reducer/killer centuries before cocaine was heavily used in 1884 by Western physicians. Stoneseed (*Lithosperum ruderale*), utilized by some Nevada tribes to suppress ovulation or promote temporary sterility, has been tested in modern medical laboratories in the search for contraceptives and has been found effective.

These are but a few examples of the pharmacological array used in Native American healing that has paved the way for modern "advances." Two hundred indigenous drugs attributed to Native American origins have been introduced into the United States Pharmacopoeia (USP) since it first appeared in 1820, or into the National Formulary (NF) since its introduction in 1888. In terms of medical implements and treatments, "Native Americans are credited with the invention of the syringe (using an animal bladder as bulb and hollow bone or quill as applicator), recognizing the necessity of drainage and irrigation of deep wounds, and paving the way for the discovery of insulin and the birth control pill."[1]

The same author quoted above also relates that "many laypersons and doctors agree that at the time the Europeans arrived on American shores, the average Indian-on-the-plains or in-the-woods knew more about anatomy and the treatment of trauma and illness than the average European, and in some respects, more than European physicians. Large-scale bleeding, for instance, very much in vogue among white doctors until the late 1800s for almost any ailment, was a bewildering and senseless practice in the eyes of most tribes, though Native Americans would occasionally use superficial letting of blood in cases of inflammation. Native American understanding and treatment of wounds was far superior to that of whites in the seventeenth, eighteenth, and even nineteenth centuries, and countless observers during those years remarked on the fact that few cripples or amputees were seen among the natives."[2]

Native Americans render medical treatment in a caring manner. Virtually all Native American cultures include the concept of harmony with nature, harmony with community, and harmony with the spiritual realm. Such values are quite different from those held by middle-class Anglo-Americans. The following list compares traditional Navajo values with Anglo-American values.

Conflicts in Cultural Values

Anglo-American Middle-Class Values	Navajo Indian Traditional Values
1. Mastery over nature—to control, subjugate, and overcome.	1. Harmony with nature—to be compatible, to maintain natural state.
2. Scheduled living.	2. Non-scheduled living.
3. Future-oriented.	3. Present-oriented.
4. Competitive Individualism—"Always win first place."	4. Non-competitive — Deference to group needs. "Win once; let others win."
5. Acceptance of others possible on basis of roles and status.	5. Acceptance of others on basis of demonstrated personal integrity.

6. Punishment related to guilt.

7. Representative democracy.

8. Individuality, fame, and recognition emphasized.

9. Cultural aspiration to achieve at a level higher than parents—"Climb the ladder of success."

10. Save for the future.

6. Punishment related to shame.

7. Face-to-face government—traditionally little tribal leadership.

8. Anonymity and humility stressed.

9. Cultural aspiration to follow in the ways of the old people.

10. Share resources and wealth with those who need it today.[3]

The recent attention to Native American ways has brought difficulties as well as useful exposure, however. Native Americans are critical of the way in which their sacred knowledge has been exploited by educators, anthropologists, clergy, and the myriad of others who had early access to information through contacts with tribal members.

Many Native American people feel acutely that they have suffered from what they believe was done throughout history by outside cultures, politicians, anthropologists, and fashionable writers. They are sick of being studied under the anthropological microscope and sick of discussing their heritage with academicians whom they believe will take the information and force it into predesigned molds that warp their cultural truths. Richard Twostrike writes, "As an Indian, I am . . . concerned about the public's view of Indian medicine and spirituality."[4] Twostrike criticizes that "overgeneralized erroneous conclusions about Indians claim to apply to all Indians of all tribes. . . . This is sad, especially sad when authentic native healers and doctors are now trying to gain recognition as valid therapists . . . this is the epitome of exploitation and of capitalizing on the sacred things of indigenous peoples."[5]

Cheyenne-Arapaho medicine man John Redtail Freesoul, author of *Breath of the Invisible*, has concern for the Native American spiritual path, or the traditional Red Road. He is disturbed about what he considers abuse of spirituality. He has said that "Indians in [Lynn] Andrews' books are portrayed as powerful, mystical shamans, and that like similar books by Carlos Castaneda, they contain an 'overdose of spiritual fireworks and hoopla that has nothing to do with real spiritual growth and behavior change.'"[6] Freesoul is also disturbed about

> what Native Americans perceive to be a spreading and dangerous misuse and exploitation of traditional Native American spirituality . . . for many decades Native American spiritual practices were shrouded in secrecy; but that in recent years (partly as fulfillment of prophecy) many native elders and medicine people have become more open about such practices—some of them even sharing their knowledge of the Red Road with those of other races and religions in hopes of helping the Earth and its people through a time of intense purification. But it has become apparent . . . that some of that trust was misplaced.[7]

Because of alleged misuse of confidences by some current writers, "there's a tightening up . . . among leaders now . . . this makes it more difficult. We have to be more careful . . . Stanley Looking Horse, a highly respected pipe carrier among Native Americans, is now talking with the pipe holders of many groups and societies, telling them to be careful just who and how they instruct."[8] Freesoul states that such abuses create a "backlash . . . in which many traditional natives who were once willing to serve as respectful 'bridges' . . . are now becoming reluctant to share anything at all."[9]

Consequently, there was a long period of time in which no information was forthcoming, and now, once again, the doors are carefully opening. Obtaining the information presented here was an arduous task. First, knowledgeable respondents had to be found. The search was limited both by the declining numbers of traditional Indian women healers and by the cultural sanctions the healers face when discussing the sacred aspects of Native American healing with non-native seekers. Each woman we interviewed made her own decision about talking with us. Decisions were based on, among other criteria, comprehension, respect, and acknowledgment afforded the healer and her culture. We have followed the instructions and wishes of these women healers and truly hope that these accounts and interviews reflect an attitude of respect and integrity.

In this book, the authors have sought carefully to avoid further slights, distortions, or abuse of the information that has been graciously shared by the medicine women interviewed. We agreed to maintain the communal and contextual spirit of the knowledge (a remarkable concept by itself) shared with us. The medicine women who were our respondents insisted upon this demonstration of our respect for their culture as a condition of talking with us. To accurately convey both the content and the style of the women who talked while we listened, we selected a varied format for presenting the material as authentically as possible. For example, Dhyani Ywahoo extracted the commitment that her segment would be written exactly as she spoke—word for word—without an interpretation that is inherently fostered through the American educational system.

Regardless of the individual reasons for studying the traditions of American Indian medicine, the learner must approach the subject with respect and tabula rasa, a clean slate upon which no other cultural bias has been indelibly written. Only when this is accomplished will the seeker discover the full richness of ancient ceremonies that challenge, baffle, enchant, and prohibit instant interpretation.

Clara Sue Kidwell has been a professor of Native American Studies at the University of California, Berkeley, for thirteen years. She says: "Native American people have a very pragmatic attitude toward things: if it works, you use it. Obviously certain things that the Public Health Service uses work, and certain things that traditional healers use work, and people have no qualms about mixing various kinds of healing ceremonies. They derive benefits from Western drugs and treatments as well as from a sense of community and balance that Native American curing ceremonies bring about."[10]

It is suggested that the reader adopt, however tenuously, a similar attitude toward Native American healing. The traditions have many hundreds of years of data gathering behind them: data on herbs, on minerals, and on human interactions among the uncountable possibilities. Such data can be useful in an integrated approach to healing. It is this harmony that joins all the many aspects of Native American healing into a sacred medicine circle that connects the medicine women to each other, to their spirits, and to their traditions.

The three medicine women presented are each different in their focus and in their specialties, and yet they all have similarities. Annie

Kahn, a Navajo, lives in a hogan in Arizona; she teaches, herds sheep, and heals people, and through the path of Nizhoni, Five Fingers, has recently introduced the concept of Navajo Cultural Weekends to the reservation. Tu Moonwalker, an Apache, lives in a trailer near Santa Fe, New Mexico, with nearly fifty animals; she makes beautiful, holy baskets, she teaches, and she heals. Dhyani Ywahoo, a Cherokee, is director of the Sunray Meditation Society, in Vermont (an international spiritual center dedicated to world peace); she uses crystals, teaches, and heals.

They are all tough and gentle women. They all can be unrelenting. They each heal. Each woman teaches, using personal methods and individual style. Annie Kahn of the Water Clan teaches toughness and gentleness. Her medicine gift is the source of *hozhooji*, the Navajo blessing of harmony and eternity, and her tutelage is loving and knowledgeable; the stories about her are endless. She teaches respect for all things: plants and animals (another Nation, she calls them) and human beings. She introduced us to her Great Spirit, to the Spirits of the Universe, to Grandfather Dawn, and to White Buffalo. She is a Firereader—and she showed us how she reads the smoke. Knowing her was never easy. It still is not. But it has always been full of wonder. And consequence. Always rewarding. Whether at the Navajo Community College or in an isolated hogan on the desert, hers is a medicine name that is repeated with awe, affection, and tremendous respect. Every encounter is unforgettable.

Tu Moonwalker shows the universe in miniaturized microcosm: ordered, in harmony, tidy. She weaves emotion, caring, healing, and love into every basket. If one is aesthetically aware, one then sees the metaphor of basket-and-universe. If one is emotionally aware, one feels the gift. Either way, healing comes from her baskets, which are her power objects and are infused with the energy of a woman wishing to heal. She comes from a distinguished Apache lineage and has the fierceness of her warrior clan. Her educational degree links biochemistry with the herbs she puts in a medicine pouch. She weaves in both worlds.

Dhanyi Ywahoo teaches meditation, spirituality, and healing across the country and internationally. She has royal lineage, currently being the "Keeper of the Priestcraft" of the Cherokee Nation. Precise in her wording and gentle of voice and spirit, she conveys information in a quiet, steady, sure, and calming manner. Using her own peace, her own centeredness, she anchors others as she heals with crystals.

Here, then, are their stories—told in their words and in their ways and through experiences shared with them.

Annie Kahn: Navajo Medicine Woman (Photo by Bobette Perrone)

CHAPTER 3

ANNIE KAHN
The Flower That Speaks in a Pollen Way

There is a Navajo medicine woman of the Water Clan who lives near
Lukachukai, Arizona, on the Navajo Reservation. She calls her
home place Nizhoni, meaning "It is beautiful." Her name is Annie
Kahn, and she is known as the Flower That Speaks in a Pollen Way.
"Kahn" is the Americanized name selected by the family at the time
of the infamous Long Walk of brutality and incredible cruelty, when
the United States Army rounded up the Navajo and marched them
across the desert to a prison camp. At that time, Annie's family's
name changed from the original Navajo to "Kahn" due to the mandate imposed on Indian names by the United States because Americans thought Indian designations too bothersome. "Kahn" replaced
the Indian name forever because, in the eyes of the army, it was more
pronounceable. It is a tough background she is descended from, but
one in keeping with this character of a woman with whom our first
encounter was nearly our last.

We were told she had the only telephone in the district. So we
called. We called for an interview. She said, simply, "No!" and
hung up.[1]

Stunned, we called back. She listened. She said, "You want to
turn me upside down and empty me out." "No," we said, "we want
to learn. We respect your courage—and our own." She said nothing
at first. At length she said, "You write and tell me who you are." We
said, "What do you want to know?" She answered, "You figure it
out."[2] She again abruptly hung up the telephone.

We wrote. We talked about ourselves. We talked about healing.
We talked about learning. Two weeks later, a letter arrived, and the
Flower That Speaks in a Pollen Way wrote: "Ya'at'eeh, greetings.

The only way I can do justice to the subject of Navajo medicine, the best way for understanding one another, is to sit down together and talk." We called. She was very gracious. She asked us to send a list of questions in advance. We set a date. We all said we'd look forward to our meeting. She said, "You will be welcome in my home."

We drove from Santa Fe, New Mexico, to northern Arizona and found the red dust road that vaguely separated desert space and vastness. Before us were the hogans, little mud and log pinpoints beneath a massive purple escarpment looming over the valley.

Annie Kahn greeted us. She wore a beautiful Navajo-style skirt and blouse of lovely calico in a pattern of tiny flowers. She laughed about the dress, saying that blues, greens, and purples were her favorites, that because they were such tiny specks of flowers, it made people come closer to her—and she liked that. The skirt had voluminous gathers allowing barely a glimpse of doeskin moccasins. Around her neck she wore a turquoise necklace, and her strong wrists held many bracelets. She was beautiful, fiftyish, stylish, happy, serious, and impishly mischievous. She introduced her three dogs: Blackie, Brownie, and Whitey.

She presented her daughters, Nez Bah and Charlotte, in their twenties and in their blue jeans. Their black hair sent off blue sparks in the sunlight. She shook hands with us, holding each of ours with both of hers, holding firmly beyond prescribed time. She laughed gustily, turned to her daughters, and said, "These ladies are welcome. Their turquoise is beautiful." She looked at the sun and said, "It's just right."[3]

Annie did not invite us into her home but, instead, directed us toward one of the two hogans. She told us to drive clockwise around it. Our instructions were explicit: drive and walk clockwise around *everything*, repeating the pathway of the sun. We entered the first hogan, the residential one that had windows, a composition roof, a cast-iron wood stove located just east of center (nearer the small doorway), and a closed-in smokehole through which the stovepipe extended. We were not invited into the ceremonial hogan, some one hundred yards beyond, until much later in the friendship. The floor was hard-packed deep, deep, red dirt, "to keep closer to the earth,"[4] Annie said. Outside, the logs were painted red, the cracks between them chinked or filled with white-painted mortar. The house and the two hogans stretched out as lonely, single-file sentinels toward the Lukachukai Wash, a grassland that abutted multicolored cliffs, vividly pink at morn, dusty rose by afternoon, vermillion at sunset.

It was a cold January morning, and the steam of beings breathing was visible as three Indian women and two white women gathered in a warming circle outside the hogan. The air was still, the morning quiet. In preparation for the trip, we had not known whether to dress "up" or "down." As true Santa Feans, we did both. We wore our best-fitting jeans, spiffiest boots, our finest turquoise, and most colorful ribbon-shirts. Straightforward as always, Annie approved, saying matter-of-factly, "We like pretty people." We said, "Thank you," and meant it.

Annie ushered us into the fire-warmed hogan, where we followed the clockwise pattern. We were instructed to shake the hand of everyone present within a hogan whenever entering or departing.

The policy of payment to the medicine woman was always to do so prior to services rendered—sometimes a rabbit, a piece of jewelry. In this case, we had agreed upon a fee, but had not discussed the mode of payment. Annie asked us for cash, saying the nearest bank was one hundred miles south. Startled by the unexpected request, we scrounged in our pockets and wallets and even pooled coins. We paid and were left with twenty-eight cents between us—as well as some apprehension about what other surprises awaited us. (We later reflected on the parallel of an Indian walking into a doctor's office for the first time, with no knowledge about insurance or Medicare.)

Having surmounted the payment situation, we each located a place to sit. Peremptorily, the medicine woman advised us that only one could stay in the hogan; the other would have to leave. It was the coldest month of winter. We looked blankly into one another's faces. Annie turned to one of us selected as Talker. She said, "You called. You stay." She was decisive. She was also pleasant. We had come a long way. This was, we learned, yet another testing.

One of us rose, indicating we understood, and quietly walked out into the cold. Annie stood by the open entryway saying nothing. She watched. Outside, the lone woman stepped paces into the desert, found a rock to sit upon, and sat, her back to Annie. Annie watched the woman view the mountain range, watched her touch the winter plants around her, watched her adjust her body to the rock. She observed the woman who remained alone in the hogan as well. She observed her, scrutinizing her to ascertain how solid was that personhood sitting alone in the hogan's center without her companion, surrounded by the Navajo women. Annie had taken a chair as the woman outside walked alone. Now, she rose, walked to the doorway, beckoned the woman to return to the hogan's warm interior. "You can stay," she called. Pointing at the one who had remained, she said, "But only you can talk. You called. You talk. Too many people talking and asking questions make distractions."

We began to comprehend what we had heard, that medicine people repeatedly test for one's sincerity and seriousness about professed desire for learning. We had not really believed it. Inwardly, we grumbled at ourselves for not recognizing what was taking place and at Annie for requiring an eight-hundred-mile trip for the privilege.

The Flower That Speaks in a Pollen Way sat on a wooden chair close to the fire. Her daughters were to her left on a bed, leaning their backs against the wall, forming the beginning of a tight circle. One white woman sat on a second bed, continuing the circle, the second on a chair facing Annie. The mother directed the daughter to bring coffee from the main house. Nez Bah carried back a small blue-splatter porcelain pot and placed it on the edge of the wood stove. The medicine woman did not offer her coffee to anyone else in the room, even though it was cold and relatively early in the morning. And we wanted coffee.

We took our assigned positions within the circle and the Talker was again instructed to walk clockwise around the hogan, approach the medicine woman, and state what was wanted, asking that payment be accepted. The medicine woman opened a briefcase, withdrawing a sheath of typed papers obviously prepared with extensive care. She said: "I want you to know that I went over your questions. I have read the message carefully. You are after information regarding Navajo Medicine and Navajo Medicine Women. Make sure that you understand when you leave here." Her extensively written answers to our questions were presented to us. We do not know of any university professor or any physician who would have taken as much interest and effort. It softened the edges of our disgruntledness at being tested so much, and somehow it all made perfect sense.

Obviously prepared, Annie Kahn was thorough and open. Annie Kahn does very little that she does not intend to do. She is precise, thoughtful, says only what she means to say, and does not share when she chooses not to do so. Time with her demonstrated that she is a very funny lady, easy, generous, fun-loving, and very, very knowledgeable. But she calls the shots. And, though she lets one enter, there are barriers as to how far. Respect, earned respect, was the hallmark of that first trip and visit. And loads of information.

Annie never, never began her answers with "well," comma, pause. She always knew what she wanted to say and how she wanted to say it. She knew when she did not wish to answer, as well. Silence was her respected companion.

We wanted to know how a medicine person is selected, and so Annie described the aspect of inherited lineage. She told us that many parents of medicine people are themselves medicine bearers, but a child that does not have the necessary characteristics will not be trained. If, however, a child is born into a nonmedicine family and demonstrates attributes indicating promise, the child can be trained by others. "There are a thousand roads to medicine," said Annie.

Talker asked, "How old were you when you began your education as a medicine woman?"

"Before birth," Annie replied. She told us a Blessingway ceremony had been held by a medicine person praying over her pregnant mother and Annie, the unborn child. The parents had requested it. "I was blessed in the Blessingway before I was born," she stated. "The Blessingway is a Ph.D. in my culture. Before birth," Annie said, "the child is not yet speaking. That is the time the parents speak, care, and teach so that the child will be born with it." She talked about the parents preparing the medicine child for birth by connecting her and themselves with nature and harmony within.

Her parents' preparation for their child's birth was "medicine," said Annie. "They talked medicine. There are stories of the plants that were here before my grandmother was born. The Spirits tell stories. They are the ones that molded me, made my toes, made my heart. And my parents talked medicine. They went out there to touch and talk and pace and shake it in their ear. They prepared."

"When I was sleeping inside her, in my mother's womb, I was

dreaming of coming. When I arrived, I was introduced to my environment. I said, 'Who's here? Who's living here?' 'I am,' they all
said, the plants, the spirits, the seasons. That is why, I'm using 'I
found' the universe and the sky and the earth. When I was born,
these, too, are my parents. When the child gets here, there is going
to be a million things to do. It is very hard for a person once they
arrive. There's their grandmother, all the relatives. They all want to
hold the baby. They all want to kiss the baby. And the child looks at
them and likes all of them!"

Annie explained that when the parents so request, a second
Blessingway ceremony is held for the child within thirty days after
birth, and the same medicine person officiates at both ceremonies.
The child is then assigned to her parents to be taught the Blessingway. Her medicine woman education and training begins.

Both parents take turns in teaching, as do the grandparents, who
have particularly revered roles, and all the relatives take responsibility, using the cycle of nature to teach. "To observe the daytime,"
Annie said, "the child uses all five senses to be in touch with nature,
to ask questions. The child is asked, 'What do you see, what do you
smell, hear? What are you tasting? Touching?' She is asked what
those things mean to her. She is in training." When the dark de-
scends, the family sits around a fire and learns about the night.
There are stars in the universe to be learned. They have names
and functions. The importance of that instruction is indispensable,
Charlotte (Annie's daughter) later told us. She and her sisters were
shepherding the lambs one day when the fog descended so rapidly as
to engulf them, obliterating landmarks and causing disorientation.
As the fog would momentarily lift, the girls would rely upon the
stars to navigate home.

In early training, the parents instruct the child about each of the
four seasons, and periodically ask the youngster questions to determine what she is learning, and how rapidly. "By memory," Annie
emphasized, pointing to our tape recorder. "Right now, that's your
memory. For the person trained to become a medicine being, it must
come from within." The child becomes educated in the ways of nature by breaking open a flower, for example, eating it, and recognizing her connection to it. Annie demonstrated in mime. "Mmmm.
Sweet. And the child says, 'That sweet is in me. That sweet was in

my mother.' This is Blessingway education. Sweet education. It tells
you that the mother, the parents, are dedicated. They are walking
with her."

Annie stressed the use of nature in teaching a child to concentrate,
to establish communication between what one is and what one is
doing. She talked about her childhood caring for the sheep, horses,
cattle, dogs and cats, and her learning of human sexual behavior
by caring for these animals. She talked of the relatedness among
animals and humans, the day and the night, the seasons and the
interactions of the elements on animals and plants alike, and the
inextricable fabric-bonding of the whole of life's texture.

When Annie talked about her formal education, she talked about
her grandmother. "My grandmother was a medicine woman," she
said, "a counseling medicine woman, more, much more than a psychologist. The only reason my grandmother put me in school was
because she worried about your people—the ones that did not speak
Navajo. My grandmother said, 'The people are coming. Now, go to
school. Pick up their language.'" Annie reflected, "I couldn't have
done it myself. You can't do things by yourself. You are dependent
upon something."

Annie's incorporation of both worlds continues with her six children, the eldest of whom, a daughter, was recently graduated from
the University of California at Berkeley law school. Her son attends
Stanford University, studying electrical engineering. Two of her
daughters attend Navajo Community College, on the reservation; a
fourth is married, has a job, and has children (her newborn had a tee
shirt that read, "I am a woman"); and the youngest daughter is at
home, deciding what to do with her life.

We asked Annie to describe her specialty. She said, "I am best
known as the Flower That Speaks in a Pollen Way. I am the ex-
plainer of the ceremonies. My specialty is teaching. Notice that I
am not shaking a feather over you, nor am I feeding you herbs."
(Though, in later ceremonies, she did precisely that—for the purpose and intent of the particular ceremony.) She stated that she
taught in the Blessingway "Hózhóní. Blessingway. My toes, my
bones, my flesh, my juice, my blood, my cells, and my tears, my
hair, and my taste. Winter stories. Tell you summer stories, fall
stories. This is what it is—life. Hózhóní. Blessingway. This kind of

teacher is a medicine woman in a Blessingway. The Blessingway is your Ph.D.," she repeated.

The medicine teacher said it was necessary first to talk about concepts of illness before she could talk about how healing is done. "You are sick," she said, "when you develop the habit of excluding. Therefore, you are off balance. You're out of harmony. Everything that interferes with living makes illness. The mind and the body interaction during physical illness causes friction and lack of cooperation. The mind is to tell the body what to do. But if the mind is either too fast or too slow, the body may describe and reveal what the mind is doing." She had spoken of physical illness. She had spoken of stress. She had talked about disharmony.

She said, "I want to live. I get hungry, but I do not eat. It makes me sick. In healing," she continued, "one must understand that it is normal to be hungry. Not accepting causes illness. Causes delay. Therefore, there is friction causing greater illness. To heal, one must be in balance. Must understand. Must accept. This very act causes healing. Poverty made me sick. I had no shoes to wear. No warm clothes. I kept on patching. It made me sick because I had to throw it away. Lack of sleep made me sick. If I do not have spiritual power, it makes me sick. There is a shiny crust on some people, like locusts leave. A shell. That is the worst kind of poverty we have. Emptiness. It is illness at its worst. It is best when my heart moves, your heart moves. Immediately, we are together. When we do not communicate, we are ill."

Having laid the foundation, Annie proceeded with a discussion of how healing takes place. She incorporated six basic agents, or conditions, that bring about the result of healing: (1) consciousness-raising; (2) organization and order; (3) obedience and faith; (4) power and spirituality; (5) preparation for the ceremony; and (6) the selected ceremony itself.

We had become aware of a consistent rhythm to Annie's voice, the tenor, tone, and measured flow of her words. The cadence of the delivery, combined with the caring, affected us; our breathing patterns changed, became more even, slower. Body movement was more fluid, speech less strident, less hurried. Even our skin texture was softer. Observing our behavior, the medicine woman held her necklace in both hands. She said, "When you hire a medicine person,

they always wear a necklace of some kind to show you a very peace-
ful, quiet manner. To show you beauty. To feel it themselves. That is
making medicine. That's how I raise consciousness. Not only my
consciousness, but the earth and the plants." The connection with
the earth and sky, the universe, was a vital and repeated theme. We
were instructed to consciously hold sky and earth images within our
mental vision and by doing so to become aware of what our eyes do
not behold, to begin to "see" with our eyes closed. "The rest will
come slowly," Annie said, "and, most likely, it will come to you in
your dreams. When this happens, do what I do. Wake at five o'clock
in the morning. Not at sunrise—before sunrise. Take a shower. Take
a bath. Move slowly, consciously. Consciousness raising. *Know* what
you are doing. Touch things. Taste things. What is, *is*. It cannot be
seen with the eyes. It is present. In order to be in touch with that,
you have to be consciously aware of *right now*. Train yourself. Do not
just zero in on a schedule and zero out. Know what you are doing.
You came here, zoooom, you know. But the trees were looking for
you because I told them to. Because they are of me. The mountains
were looking for you. The flowers. They knew you were coming.
There were clouds over there, and sunlight, and there was night.
They knew you were coming. But you did not relate to them. *Those*
are the ones that do the healing. No medicine woman, no medicine
man. They are wild. They refuse to be caught. How do you catch a
wild horse with a rope?"

    "Of course," she said, "chants raise consciousness for conscious-
ness is an order of organization." Chants have order, she told us, and
language has order. "It is a matter of organization, the same order as
the earth and the universe, as the four seasons. Spring comes before
summer. It will never change. There is order. The traditional chants
also have order—and consciousness. I accomplish this with language. Navajo language. Like a heartbeat. Boom, boom, boom.
Your body moves with it. Your soul moves with it. You found me. It
is all well arranged."

    The link between order and obedience and obedience and faith,
according to Annie, is a natural consequence. If one is obedient,
trusting, and has faith, whatever is not presently understood will be
revealed by the very act of obedience.

    Throughout the discussion of healing, Annie emphasized the attitude of the patient. Imperative in the process toward health, she told us, are obedience and discipline. Obedience is translated by Annie as a "willingness to obey, a submission to the laws of order, while discipline is the self-control and efficiency that enforces obedience. There is always a maturity of attitude involved and it is continuous. Like a diet. It is personal, gentle, peaceful. And private! If we say, 'I walk in beauty,' it is beauty that we begin to walk with. It can be trusted. It will be revealed to you in your dreams, or you will see it yourself, your ears will hear it. You will be guided to understand."

Events are ordered, organized, for us. "Obviously, at the time knowledge is being revealed, not all people present will help you. Somebody else that is to be your helper is not yet there. But whatever it is that is being revealed to you cannot wait. We women do not give birth like that. We have to measure time. It's a matter of order. Time makes the difference. The time when a person is revealing to you may be all the time that person has with you. It may be all the time they have before they leave here."

Annie stressed that the role of faith in healing is to establish sincerity, dedication, trust, and, foremost, obedience. Obedience and prayer is, for a Navajo person: *I walk in beauty*. To walk in beauty is obedience. Obedience, furthermore, is law. It is doing things in the right way at the right time. It is order. It is the spring before summer. We reflect that order. It is harmony. It is interaction with one's environment. It is respect for nature. It is respect for self, because self is nature, is harmonious with the universe.

Healing is also a matter of acceptance, organization, respect, and work. Nourishment was an example given. One is hungry. The body requires food. There is a choice. Good food will fight off disease. Healing occurs. Sleep. It's important. Don't sleep when it's time to work, but "sleep at night when you're supposed to." The order is recognition, acceptance, respect, and work.

To prepare herself for a ceremony, "authenticity in education, in medicine making," Annie says, "I wash my hair. I want my head to be cool and alert so that my thinking power will be cool and alert. I am sure I am free from menstrual period. I collect plants. I use and do a little research to determine how much consciousness raising I want to do. I determine which chants to use. I get up at five o'clock in the morning when I have an appointment. I tell the earth and the sky who is coming. I say, 'you welcome these people, and I will arrange seats for them.' I say, 'I want to reflect you, the sky, and you, the earth. You do the teaching. I will arrange the seats.' Organization is flowing right now from the earth through me, through you. It's like this: you go outside in the morning. Your car won't start. So, you ask your neighbor, whose car is already running, to come over and start the car for you. I'm the jumper cable. Our connection is the earth and the sky. What the medicine woman does before the patient enters is of the earth—the whole earth. When we're talking about healing, we have to find the healing in me. We have to find the healing in you. Two people coming together make medicine."

Annie told us that her preparation includes her own and a projected consciousness raising for those about to arrive. She does not stop there. Washing her hair with yucca root, fresh from the desert soil, she relates with the ancients, with those who have gone before, tapping into their consciousness, their knowledge. "People do die," she says, "but they don't stop there. They keep on living. I am very positive that they are keeping on. When I'm doing the consciousness raising, preparing, I feel it."

Her preparation complete, the patient having arrived, the medicine woman begins the process of diagnosis. She observes what the patient reflects. She asks, "Why is he sick? What does he eat? What does he hide from himself? What does he fail to tell the doctor, and how does the doctor know she is not getting the full information?"

She says, "The patient may move too fast, too quick. The body will describe and reveal what the mind is doing. The patient may have question after question, trying to drown you out. The medicine maker listens. By asking so many questions, the patient tells what is needed. He wants you to know what he is searching for." The medicine maker knows where to make an opening amongst the queries, for they are "a family of questions." A clear channel must be found and one of the inquiries will locate the clear path. "One of those questions, and *my* question, will open that channel. The rest forms in line. Forms in line of a circle. A line that's supposed to be straight. But I don't see it that way. Through this we make medicine, by putting the questions in order. The line becomes a circle and holds us all. That's making medicine."

Annie seeks to motivate the patient to engage and interact with her as the "jumper cable" that consequently connects the patient to insight into self, and hence to the harmony of the world around self.

Annie also consults "white doctors that help us determine what seems to be the problem." Cuts that need to be stitched are taken to them because "traditional healers do not stitch." For the added benefit of use of their equipment, AMA doctors are consulted. "They consult me when they know they can't do any more, when they have come to a dead end. Sometimes I go to them [about a patient], sometimes they come to me, especially the mental health workers. Especially Navajo mental health workers. They are afraid because mental illness is growing. Very afraid. They are concerned about healing medicine."

A "prescription in the Blessingway" is personal. For example, a medicine woman who specializes in herbal medicine is hired. A diagnosis is made. The medicine woman collects specialized herbs, medicine prescribed for the particular remedy. "The patient is told something of the medicine. Herb medicine is a collection of herbs that are right only for *that* person." Only one medicine plant is left with the patient, "who shall learn the name of it, hold it, see it. It must be precisely tasted by itself—to learn the flavor of it." Patient recovery is assisted, Annie said, "from inside." The amount is prescribed. "Use all of the plant, or just taste it. The herbal medicine is given for that person at that time, one particular flavor—like questions. A member of that flavor tribe. The plant goes after that person and brings back all the flavors. Invites them all back in. That is the reason you learn *one* of them. Because you can't handle all of them."

When Annie Kahn, the Flower That Speaks in a Pollen Way, talked about power, she said, "Without exception, spirituality is inherent in healing. Spirituality *is* healing. Spirituality *is* power. No medicine woman will say that she has power because the power belongs to the Great Spirit. It is not hers! Everybody has a certain amount of power. You have power. All of us have power. A medicine woman may use a particular object, such as corn pollen, to make things happen for her. My power is hidden in my prayers. I say 'hidden' because you can't see it. My prayers have names. The names I call upon will assist me—just as you would if I were to call upon you by your name and ask you for your help. You will naturally want to help me. These prayer names might be the Everlasting One, *sa anaaghei* (pronounced sah-a-no-RAY), or the Unbreakable One, *doog odo meejii* (pronounced doe-chigl-NAY-he).

"The medicine woman who is doing the healing ceremony will be assisted by the buffalo who has a sacred name. The buffalo is the international language between Native American cultures. It is the White Buffalo. The White Buffalo exists all the time. Because white is neutral. It's also easy to absorb in the horizon. The White Buffalo I'm speaking of is transparent. And White Buffalo *is* healing power. The White Buffalo is its ordinary name. But it is a very powerful name. By my Navajo language, the White Buffalo has a sacred name. Any Native Americans—say, Kiowa—have a white buffalo or a sacred bull in their rites. I agree with them. In their language, they have a sacred name. What makes a medicine woman a medicine woman? The White Buffalo. Go. Read more about the White Buffalo. Underline and dream about it, see who she is. Who is she?"

Annie would say no more about the White Buffalo, about the sacred name. Asked many ways and many times, she simply shrugged her shoulders, smiled knowingly, and terminated the topic with, "Like I said—prepare and watch. And dream. It will be very clear. You won't be asleep when you're dreaming. Your eyes will be open. You'll see that it's real."

One of our questions to Annie read: Are modern influences interfering with spiritual and religious aspects of traditional healing practices? Annie, well organized and most articulate, always answered each question directed to her with accuracy and proper lengthiness. To the above question, she said, "I just put down 'No'!"

Obedient to herself, Annie told us what she deemed important for us to know. She elaborated. Her disciplined self said, "My role in the world is to not waste time. It is to save the natural beauty of the earth. I am part of the outside world. Only when I am hired do I participate in my profession. I keep my Navajoness. At the same time, I function in the dominant society. The modern medicine woman has excellent spiritual qualities. Through practice, she keeps them polished and active. Her soul is spiritual and it is selfless and it is based on tradition. A modern medicine woman speaks three languages fluently: the Indian language, the English language, and the spiritual language. She chooses to read quality books. She knows her language and she can call on an ancient beauty by name to make

things happen to her. For her. Believing in the ancient beauty allows
her continual life after death. Being a modern medicine woman, she
has to work twice as hard to make connections between Indian, or
Navajo, in particular, and the English-speaking society.

"I see my culture is very beautiful. I see that it is to be preserved
for my grandchildren. I see my children speaking both languages
and I see my children working very hard in both cultures."

Speaking of her Navajo legacy, Annie said, "I accept my history
the way it was, the way my grandmother was, the way her mother
was, the way we were before. The way we are now."

Annie said, "Learn to accept things in life that will help you. If
you are schooled, your approach may be using modern medicine.
If you are a traditional Indian person, you may use all that which is
available to you: prayer power, herbal medicine, ceremony.

"I can speak two languages now. Before I was born, my grandmother spoke two languages. One was spiritual language and one
was everyday language. Anybody that went outside was called 'modern.' Balance. The only difference is that now, it's written. Before, it
wasn't. So we ignore it because it's not on record. Before that, it
didn't exist? Not true. It's really difficult for people to see."

In describing the impact of modern culture on other Navajos,
Annie loosely divided her culture into three groups in their approach
to healing, believing that a small percentage have never left the traditional ways. A second, larger group of people who had knowledge
and belief in traditional healing left but have returned to Navajo
pathways. Yet another group assimilates the "modern approach to
medicine" in totality, rejecting Navajo practices.

The folly of rejecting traditional practices can be seen in the following vignette: On one of the visits, while we lived with Annie
Kahn, a woman psychologist from Chicago arrived. She was seeking
assistance from Annie because she had been suffering severe stroke-
induced headaches that numerous physicians had been unable to
control with medication. Following Annie Kahn's diagnostic assess-
ment, the woman Ph.D. was given the root of a plant and a series of
instructions: soak the plant root in water until the root turns white,
until the juice of the root becomes dark red; then drink the juice.

We were also present sometime later when the woman reported
the results. She noted improvement in the headaches, both in their

frequency and their intensity. Being of scientific bent, she had given the tuber to her physician and requested a laboratory analysis. The analysis revealed ibuprofen, a relatively new drug in the modern medical marketplace, recently (1985) hailed as a wonder drug. The woman's own physician eventually began prescribing pain relievers containing ibuprofen for the control of her headaches. This is an example of "primitive" herbalism having knowledge now being used in "modern" medicine.

Annie Kahn rejects nothing. A medicine woman of great renown in her own culture, she is firmly rooted in traditional Navajo ways, teaching those ways to students at the Navajo Community College, not as a faculty member but as a Navajo medicine woman and cultural expert. She is also a woman of the twentieth century, a seeker and a liaison between the Navajo and the non-Navajo. "Because I want to be understood, I have to work twice as hard. This is ancient beauty itself. I know the earth and the mountains. I'm also glad that your society put up some kind of school and gave me a piece of paper and a pencil to write. In the days of old, the medicine women also had to work twice as hard because they had to work without the help of science, without the help of hospitals, transportation, modern goods. You could not have come [here] without the transportation. You could not have made a schedule with me without a telephone.

"I am a teacher in the Navajo way. I am the one who explains who we are as a *person*. As a *people*. I guide the people to learn more of themselves, and to determine where we think we are going. I am a counselor in mental health to help people think good of themselves, capable of living. In the course of my education, I have learned that white man's education, his medicine, and his science is learned by exploring—by trial and error. This later led me to believe that my children and their children's children would need both cultures—the western and the Native American medicine."

There were two things left to ask Annie Kahn before we departed. Talker asked Annie to summarize illness, then healing. The medicine woman clapped her hands and knees together in one grand gesture. "What causes sickness? Anything that interferes with living! Being in balance creates healing."

Talker then said, "An Apache medicine woman is making a medicine pouch for each of us. We are instructed to collect for our medicine

pouch only that which is truly important to us. May we take some of
the red dirt from the hogan floor?"

"Sure," said the Navajo medicine woman.

Funneling handfuls of red earth into our pockets, Talker thanked
the Water Clan woman, who sat silently in her wooden chair, watching. Then the Flower That Speaks in a Pollen Way rose. She said a
prayer in Navajo. A lengthy prayer. She said, "It means you will return many times. I will one day come to your home in Santa Fe—
when the order is correct. Meanwhile, take some more dirt."[5]

Tu Moonwalker: Apache Medicine Woman and Basketmaker (Photo by
Bobette Perrone)

CHAPTER 4

TU MOONWALKER
Apache Weaver of Healing

Tu Moonwalker said firmly, "I have power."[1] She kept talking as heads turned in her direction. "You will never have as much power as I have," she added, waving her right hand and extending her palm upward. Five of us were sitting and chatting in an office in Santa Fe, at a hub of a meeting place we could all reach in winter. By then, several meetings with Tu had occurred, and we realized that she was a cauldron of contradictions, a woman who felt she had to battle fiercely, albeit quietly, for her superiority. But we had never heard her speak so definitively. Apparently she was beginning to trust us.

She was the first of the Native American medicine women who agreed to talk with us, and the first to let us enter a medicine world unknown to us; the first to allow us foolish and sometimes naive questions, telling us, "There is no silly question. Only silly answers." She was the first to test us; the first to share with us her medicine way. Coming to our house to make enchiladas for us, she suggested that we become family by committing ourselves to spend time monthly with one another.

Recollections of Tu Moonwalker are balanced in an unbalanced manner. She gave of herself generously, making beaded medicine pouches for each of us, time-consuming, delicate, beautiful. She directed us to choose carefully our own selected objects to place in the pouch, at the same time admonishing us as she placed in strands of her own hair, that *her* presence within the custard-colored deerskin would have power *over* us. She informed us that there would need to be five years of annual ritual ceremony before the doeskin pouch carried power-releasing potencies for us; that without her Apache medicine-power granting permission, the pouches would not work.

Tu Moonwalker had arrived at the house with cheese and chili and talk of "dark things" on the road. She spoke of the "evil presence" in the mountains around us, desisting only when the homeowner refused the fear, adding that it "probably came from a far ancient time." [2]

Moonwalker lives in the mountains and carries forty-pound sacks of dog food and grain on her shoulders on bitter winter days so that her animals can eat. Moonwalker loves her horses, goats, cats, dogs, and chickens—and her Toyota pickup truck. Moonwalker is heart-hurt that her white neighbors with four-wheel-drive vehicles refuse to work on the sloshy snow-mudded road to help others who cannot reach their homes.

Tu Moonwalker wants! Tu Moonwalker of the exquisite baskets. Lacy, ironlike reeds of striking mastery woven into ancient design by a woman of ancient heritage and torn affection. Tu Moonwalker wants. Family. Things well done. Fine baskets. Fine art. Good medicine. Strong medicine. Healing for others. Friends. Animals robust, plants vigorous. Her baskets, beautiful and powerful, are always a tribute to her grandmother and her nation. She wants family. Tu Moonwalker, rooted forever in the medicine ways of her people, is now a nomad from her kinfolk, returning to them only on rare occasions. Tu Moonwalker is sometimes saddened, frequently lonely, living in the world of an old Apache enemy, the "white eyes." [3] This is her story.

Tu Moonwalker, Apache medicine basket maker, knows the inside story of the Apache people, the real story, told to her by her grandmother, Dorothy Naiche. And Dorothy, Tu adds with respect, should know because she was the granddaughter of Cochise.

Before Cochise, however, there was Mangas Coloradas, an early defender of the Apache people's right to be free. As a young warrior, Cochise married Mangas's daughter, and one of their sons was Naiche, a coleader with Geronimo of the last Apache band to surrender. Naiche married six women and fathered several children. Dorothy Naiche, a petite woman, was one of his youngest children, and very much a traditional and loyal Apache. Until the day she died, at almost ninety years of age, Dorothy refused to speak the English language—although she had been educated at Carlisle School, a Pennsylvania military institution where captured Apache children had been sent. Dorothy later married Chino Alchise, the grandson of a skilled Apache scout, and their son, Carl Moonwalker, became Tu's father.

Throughout the history of Tu Moonwalker's family, one pathway prevails: medicine. Cochise was a medicine man, Naiche was a medicine man, Dorothy Naiche was a medicine woman, Carl Moonwalker was a medicine man, the scout Alchise was a medicine man, and his son, Bonito Alchise (Tu's grandfather), was a medicine man. And Tu Moonwalker has been trained to be a medicine woman.

"You have to have some special characteristic from birth," Tu said, in describing the Apache selection process that leads a youngster into the medicine way. Her large brown eyes, closely resembling old U.S. Army photos of Naiche's eyes, looked directly into ours. "I showed great personal fortitude and, because of my family background, I was immediately put into the category of 'one we're going to watch and see.'"[4] The elders observed and saw promise, especially when Tu passed the ancient tests that were part of her puberty rites.

"One week down in the desert and one week up in the mountains—by yourself," said Tu. When she was a child, the elders took her to Mount Turnbull on the San Carlos Reservation and left her alone with no nourishment, no water, and only a knife for company. She was expected to find her way back within a week, using her weapon to obtain food and to protect herself—directing the sum total of her twelve and one-half years' experience on earth to survive her vision quest, one of the ancient tests.

Fortunately, Dorothy Naiche and Carl Moonwalker had taken a decided interest in teaching Tu about the healing plants and herbs that grew in their area of Arizona. Also, because Tu had been selected to be a medicine woman, Apache tradition called for her to be reared androgynously—to learn the traits of both genders, qualities that she would need to put to use on Mount Turnbull just to survive.

Tu's experiences as a much younger child were of great benefit to her during her vision quest. Six years before her test on the mountain, Tu had been released from an iron lung, where she had spent her first years fighting for life against infantile paralysis. Part of her recuperation included walking for miles with her grandmother in search of herbal remedies that medicine woman Dorothy Naiche used to heal other patients. The child listened carefully to the descriptions of plants and their uses, then repeated the information as she sat at her grandmother's knee and watched the old woman weave baskets. Dorothy Naiche, perhaps the most skilled Apache basket weaver of all time, patiently taught Tu the arts of basketmaking and healing. Later, Tu would combine both in a style of traditional healing that was uniquely her own.

Up on the mountain during her puberty rites, Tu's thoughts were not about baskets. "There was a big rainstorm," she recalled, her long fingers gesturing gracefully, "and I was going up the side of a cliff. I slipped trying to get over it and fell about fifty feet, rolled, and landed in a cactus patch." Injured and bleeding, but remembering the lessons from Dorothy, the little girl knew exactly which herb to place directly on the lacerations. The herb was nowhere in sight. However, Tu had a feeling it was nearby and, closing her eyes, envisioned a field where the herb grew plentifully. She walked two miles in the right direction until she found it, and then used it as she had been taught to stop the bleeding.

That night, she had a dream. She awakened in a cold sweat. "I looked up and there was this huge bird, standing, and it talked to me in my own native language," she recalled. "He asked me if I thought I'd earned the right to be on the vision quest, and I answered 'No.' He told me I would by the time I'd finished with the walk because 'I leave you with the instincts of survival.' That was the first gift during the vision quest."

During the rest of the trial, various animals came to her and the legendary "Gray Ghost," a revered Apache symbol, appeared. The ghost is a man of great power who presents himself only to people who are meant to be leaders. On the last day of her vision quest, the Gray Ghost told her, "You have succeeded, you will go forward, you will do good, and you will have the patience to succeed, and you will have the patience to learn and understand."

Tu continued, "Once you're chosen and decide to follow, it is very rough to keep up. There are times when it's very lonely, and it's very hard because you're human. You are to help those in need and never falter in helping. Sometimes you might get stepped on, and you might be abused because you are a kind, gentle, giving person. But, in the long run, you've done what you're supposed to do, which is to help with whatever it is that you do so well."

The "whatever it is . . ." leads, interestingly, to a commonality between traditional Apache medicine and Western scientific medicine: specialization. Dorothy Naiche was an herbalist; Tu considers this the highest position on the hierarchal ladder of healing. Another prestigious person is a social medicine person, one akin to today's psychiatrist. Cochise himself, the leader of the Apache people until 1874, was a social medicine man. According to Tu, the remainder of the specialties "sort of run together." There are medicine women who specialize in psychic readings, others who are midwives.

In classifying herself, Tu adopts a modest position. "I can't consider myself anything other than a person who wants to see another one happy. Yes, I've had the label of 'medicine person' put on me and I can live with that. But, I don't feel it is a label one should put on me, although a lot of people do. I'm basically a teacher more than anything else.

"If someone comes to me and has an emotional problem, I can use the herbs to calm them down and then use the psychology I learned to help them talk about it. Then my teaching will tell them what to do, what to learn, what to look for and how to avoid it again."

When Tu speaks of psychology, there is a double-edged reference—one to all that she has learned within the tribe and another to her formal education outside the Apache circle. She refers to the bachelor of arts degree in anthropology, received at California State University in Sacramento, and a bachelor of science degree in biochemistry from the University of California at Davis. She continued her education, she says, by taking two advanced degrees at Texas Tech, in Lubbock, an M.A. in museum science and an M.S. in geology. While her formal, Anglo-oriented education stopped there, she continued learning the Indian ways. "Indian culture is very psychically oriented," she says. "The medicine people have to be trained in psychic feelings. They have to be trained to deal with psychic phenomena." Tu herself has had psychic experiences, one of which she recalls having when she was only four years old and in the hospital because of poliomyelitis. Her father was late for his visit, and Tu told her grandmother that he was having trouble with "men on a machine with two wheels that made a lot of noise." Later, they learned that Carl Moonwalker was injured by a group of Hell's Angels, the notorious motorcycle group. Tu claims that her psychic ability is still with her. "Half of medicine is psychic," she says. "You know immediately what's wrong with someone. They won't tell you. Their soul will."

Tu believes that a medicine woman is very quiet, reserved, almost withdrawn. Medicine people are known, according to Tu, "only by word of mouth. If you're going to answer to somebody, you answer to the faith, and you answer to the ultimate spirit." Tu Moonwalker is not well known among the Apache people as a medicine woman for reasons that she freely discusses. "Because I've lived out here so long, they doubt my sincerity. I'm suspect because they feel I'm tainted by the white man's world. [To go back] I'd have to prove myself all the time and, finally after being [on the reservation] for several years and proving that I haven't changed one iota, I'm accepted again. . . . But I do better not doing that. I help not only my own people, but the Indian people in general, by what I'm doing . . . by my art, by my lectures, and by just being me as an example."

The world-renowned Indian Market, an annual event held on the plaza at Santa Fe, New Mexico, is where invited artists display and sell the absolute best of Indian arts and crafts. It was there, while Tu Moonwalker was selling her baskets, that she helped an older woman recover from sunstroke. "A little bit of psychic healing just got the body stabilized . . . and that's what the emergency people do," Tu says, describing how she helped her customer.

There is yet another aspect of Tu's healing, one that does not require actual relief of medical symptoms but involves her beloved art of basketmaking. Through her knowledge of Apache history, Tu looks back in time to an era when her ancestors gathered willow, wild grasses, and sedge to weave their baskets. She speaks with authority when she describes the wildflowers her grandmother used as dye and the way she worked with the materials. "The whole process of gathering had a ceremony, no matter what you were using. There are proper ways to be observed in the preparation of the materials. I'm extremely grateful that my grandmother showed me these things, because with basketmaking, you really have to feel the whole connection in your soul."[5]

In that statement, Tu reveals her own medicine way: joining her soul with her baskets. "Basketry teaches you to be harmonious with yourself—because once you start the stitchwork, you find yourself

doing it in a rhythm, a natural rhythm that belongs solely to you . . .
It's sort of like self-hypnosis."[6] In the Apache way, harmony and
healing go hand in hand.

The harmony in Tu's baskets gives them a presence, an individuality that conveys the healing traditions of the Apache people.
Each of Tu's miniature baskets—she weaves no other kind—whether
woven from willow or strawberry runners, whether beaded or feath-
ered, is uniquely different from all of the others. Each tells a separate tale of Indian life. "The figures of people and of animals [part of
the basket] come from everyday life and normally, they tell a story.
Sometimes the reader can put his own story on a basket."[7]

The owner of one of Tu Moonwalker's baskets may be unaware of
the healing spirit placed in the basket, but it is present just as surely
as is her style of healing conveyed with her lectures about basket
weaving. She shares her knowledge "by my art, by my lectures, and
by just being me. We [the Apache people] are very much a group-
oriented society. Everything is shared; greed is not tolerated . . . You
are trained as a medicine person, but the training is for the ultimate
goal of the community. You are trained to be outstanding at what you
do, but you are outstanding for the benefit of the community." By
sharing her artistry in basketmaking, Tu practices healing in a totally
different way from most traditional cultural healers, but it is healing
nonetheless.

Tu Moonwalker lives her healing ways high atop a ridge outside of
Santa Fe, New Mexico. Surrounded by a menagerie of animals and
birds, she takes the time each morning to ride her horse among the
forest trees growing on her hilltop land. During her wanderings, she
finds within herself the harmony that is necessary to again begin the
weaving of the baskets—work that awaits her return to the mobile
home she shares with her devoted companion. Tu's reputation as a
skilled basket maker is growing nationally, and the orders for her
wares accumulate faster than she can accommodate them.

Modestly, she talks about one of the most important aspects of her
art, an event that has nothing to do with introducing her baskets to a
wide market. In the spring of 1984, Tu Moonwalker was invited
back to Arizona to teach a troup of young Indians the art of basketmaking. She showed the children how to gather the reeds and fibers,
as her grandmother had shown her, as all of the grandmothers of

time have shown the granddaughters of time. She showed the children how to weave her beloved baskets. She returned them to their lost art.

Traveling is nothing new to Tu Moonwalker. In the last few years, she has had one-woman shows in Fort Worth, Texas, in Florida, and (by special invitation) at the Gallup Intertribal Ceremonial, an elite all-Indian spectacle held annually in New Mexico. Additionally, her work appears in museums, private collections, trading posts throughout the Southwest, and at the famous Indian Market in Santa Fe, where she has been awarded a variety of prizes for her skill. The competition at Indian Market is intense, but time and time again, her basketry has won "Best of Division" and many other trophies. World collectors usually buy her out by midmorning of the first day.

Tu's grandmother, Dorothy Naiche, is always present in spirit. Tu keeps her in her mind and speaks of her freely. She speaks of Dorothy's abiding influence on her life, her teachings, her words, and her enduring love. Each basket that Tu makes holds among its fibers a special memory of a beloved grandmother, a woman who is Tu's link to her unique heritage, a woman from whom Tu learned the age-old healing secrets of the Apache people. Each basket that Tu sells bring to its new owner the spirit of Apache healing—indeed, an uncommon way to cure. By doing it her way, by "just being me,"[8] Tu Moonwalker is a vivid example of one of the many paths to healing that traditional medicine offers in this modern world.

Dhyani Ywahoo: Priestcraft Holder of the Ani Gadoah Clan, Tsalagi (Cherokee) Nation (Photo courtesy Ywahoo collection)

CHAPTER 5

DHYANI YWAHOO
Priestcraft Holder of the Ani Gadoah Clan, Tsalagi (Cherokee) Nation

Who is Dhyani Ywahoo, Keeper of the Priestcraft of the Cherokee Indian Nation, the woman "whose ancestors have for twenty-seven generations been the keepers of the sacred fire and crystals."?[1] She is a medicine woman and her people are "those who are descended from the sun."[2]

In 1976, Dhyani was graduated from New York University, having studied chemistry, music, and philosophy. She began teaching comparative philosophy at the university. "It was a powerful time," she says, "an opportunity to begin to think and understand the streams of many worlds and how people interpret information that is given to them. [I] also realized that cosmology, the philosophy that was shared with me through the old people of my clan, and my relatives, was far more deep and beautiful and satisfying to my spirit than anything that I could see from any part of the world."

Dhyani Ywahoo is the founder and director of the Sunray Meditation Society in Vermont, "which has grown out of the traditions of Native American Indians. Offering programs in meditation, music, dance, and the healing arts, Sunray's focus is on acknowledging the sacred flow within as a key to evolving consciousness."[3] There is much to be said about Dhyani Ywahoo, as a delegate to the United Nations in Geneva in 1981, as a woman involved in the Native American sovereignty issue, as founder of Sunray, as the Priestcraft Lineage Holder of the Ani Gadoah Clan of the Tsalagi [Cherokee] Nation, and as a healer in the broadest terms. No one is more eloquent than Dhyani herself when she speaks of healing—self, nation, a planet—and when she shares the ancient wisdom of the elders.

For three years we talked with Dhyani herself and with Dhyani's associates, and we corresponded. We asked questions and questions and more questions. Dhyani answered them on the condition that her responses be quoted word for word, without interpretation. The question and answer format that follows adheres most faithfully to Dhyani's wishes. It is also the basis for her permission to share this information.

We thought about and reflected upon what she shared, and that sharing is important. Read her words carefully. She selected them for a reason. We take our cue from Dhyani, sharing with others what she has shared with us. This is what Dhyani said, and this is how she said it.

Question: What does your name mean?

Response: How did I come by my name? My grandparents always called me Dhyani. They said it meant 'a gift for the people, a gift of light, a gift from the fire.' I somehow knew as a child I had to grow into it and that I wasn't fully that person yet.

Dhy [the gift for the] ani [people from the light of the fire] is the name given by the grandparents, who were incredibly intuitive people. As I grow older I appreciate more and more the special gifts they had. Over a time . . . I felt the full power of that name and the desire to be a gift and to share for the good of the people . . . as a continuation of the teaching that my elders taught me. My name is a title. It means a certain attainment of consciousness. To be able to manifest from the light, gifts for the people. And Ywahoo is an old name in my family. It means "great mystery" when you trace its roots through the Algonquian language group. The lineage is passed through the female in our family tradition . . . I am tracing my roots to my grandmother's heart, to her sacred fire, and also acknowledging the great mystery that she and my great-grandmother and my grandfather, and so many of the older people, have given me.

Question: Do you describe yourself as a medicine woman? Is that the right term?

Response: It is a word that is made up by other people. I am a keeper of the "priestcraft tradition," which is an ancient tradition. Medicine is an outside word to describe a holy power that makes things well. The people. The land. It calls forth the wellness. The closer translation is really "holy power." To be a holy person is more the true meaning of one who can bring someone again to their remembrance of their true nature. To say "medicine" is really an attempt to be in both worlds at the same time. That is how others have described it, the holy people who have lived and walked in holy ways. The idea of a medicine person is really an anthropologist's concept. There has always been a very developed, a very beautiful, and very complete cosmology religion of native people. Very complete. You are taught from the moment you are born, and you have levels of initiation and study in the sacred societies of your family of what is right. These [levels] were not shared after a time with the settlers or those of European mind, because it became apparent that they could not or would not respect [them]. Also, in hindsight, one can see that when the settlers first came, the tradition of healing with herbs, just sharing the natural gifts that the earth has to offer, was very readily shared with whomever came and asked for it. In fact, most of the pharmacopoeia of the world today comes from native tradition.

The priestcraft tradition is a continuing means of maintaining the Tsalagi [Cherokee] world view. Those who are priests have the duty of keeping the sacred crystal, which is shown to all the people once yearly. In the crystal individuals may view the possible future shaped by their thinking. If one should see oneself lying down in the crystal, then one would fast and pray to correct their relationship with the creative forces so that one might walk yet another year. Those who are priests study the stars and moon so the ceremonial cycle can be maintained for the benefit of all beings. Sacred hymns, songs of healing, knowledge of healing through scratching [like acupuncture] and healing herbs are studied. The priest must have a prodigious memory to recall creation stories, tracing our roots to the Pleiades star system, and must be well versed in the law as given by Eonalegi— the consciousness of the priest or priestcraft [is important] . . . everyone has a spiritual duty. We are all in communion with the universe. The priest is someone who makes a willing commitment of their whole life to maintaining the idea of complementary resolution. Someone who chooses to see the whole and not to separate any part thereof, nor to bring about a separation—always to see the reconciliation of the people in harmony.

Question: How do you define illness and health?

Response: It's a thought form, an idea of discord that causes one to be ill. One comes out of phase with the pulse of the earth and that can bring famine to all of the people. One person can become lonely, feeling emotionally deprived. And if the family, the clan, and the nation, don't come quickly to see that person in the circle again and invite that person to realize the seed of thought that has given them the feeling of being without, then the anxiety, through the pulsing of the earth and the break in continuity of family, nation, and clan consciousness, can bring about a famine or a drought. The relationship of human consciousness is always very real to the native people.

No, it is not a metaphor. If your heart is feeling empty, and your clan does not see a way to show its fullness to you, then there is a danger that the whole clan may suffer a failure of their corn. Or the animals may go away. Or the rivers may dry up. Or forest fires may come. In the Indian mind, everything is related. You have a relationship with the spirit of every tree, and with the spirit of the sea, and with every creature that walks, crawls, swims, flies, walks on two legs, four legs, a hundred legs. Each one of us has a relationship. Somehow, being out of phase in that cycle of relationships, either with ourselves, our family, is going to have an effect on the individual's health and, ultimately, on the whole planet.

From the native perspective, the concept of wholeness is to recognize one's holiness, to realize that one's thoughts and actions are very closely interwoven with the physical world around, that one's thoughts bring about a tangible reality in ease and harmony, or dis-ease and discord, according to the quality of those thoughts and actions.

Question: When one has reached, or realized, the state of wholeness, how is this characterized?

Response: By good humor! Good humor most of all and also the ability to bring others to the remembrance of their strength and the lightness of their minds. Also by a certain relationship with the natural world where the animals and people feel comfort, and being in the presence of someone who remembers themselves as holy. It reminds others that they, too, are holy beings.

Question: How were you chosen, or did you choose to become a healer?

Response: They spoke of dreams before I was born, indicating that I would come, that I'd be a girl child, although in my consciousness they referred to me as "the old man." How is it that I was chosen to receive the teaching from my elders? They said they dreamt of me, and I can remember myself as a child, looking at my cousins who always seemed to be making a lot of noise and jumping about, feeling that I was pretty different. There was always the need to be quiet and to be still. I would always watch, and some people would say, "Hey, please don't bring her because when she's around, we say what we mean," which was always causing havoc with some of my relatives. Whenever I came, they'd say whatever they really meant to each other. They didn't always like that! Whether I chose them, or they chose me . . . I feel very much that they *grasped* me. They gathered me from the realm of potential and helped shape me. They actually shaped me. [In] some of the ceremonies there is a lot of massaging and pulling and tugging so that the bones can hold their energy. We used to have ceremonies like that when young women came of age, when they began to menstruate, too. These began very young, when they were pulling and pushing. I understand now that those massages were so that I could hold the energy that they chose to pass on to me so that I could do the sacred movements in the dances.

Yes, it was very clear. The first time that I was taken away from my mother to be with the old people, I was two years old. At that time, I was really excited by it. I would always get so close to the fire that my hair would burn. I did that regularly. My mother, of course, would be a nervous wreck about me near a stove. But these people would let me near the big [ceremonial] fire! Which I really was happy about. They understood that I wasn't going to hurt myself, or that I wouldn't be hurt, and they let me know that the fire was something sacred. They could see that I loved the fire and that the fire loved me. My Aunt Hattie said, "Oh, you can talk to the fire and the fire talks to you." She actually gave me the first lesson talking to the fire and feeling it, and making it rise and fall. So I had a sense that I was—I was very obviously singled out from innumerable grand-children and great-grandchildren.

The people who are trained from birth [within the priestcraft have] certain signs of character . . . certain staunchness or straightness of eyes, sometimes being born with a veil over the face, and communication of the spirit to its relatives before it comes. In that process, one says, "Oh, perhaps there is one who will make that commitment." No one really puts it on the child. It's always a choice that the young person can make.

One always chooses their parents, you know. I remember asking this question to my grandparents and my great-grandparents and my great-grandfather at least ten different ways. I'd say, "Well, if I choose my parents, which I know I did because I can remember it, then in the choosing, that means I was alive before." Then my great-grandfather would say, "Yes, and you are alive now, and in the past, the present, and the future are this moment." The choice we call to ourselves through emotional needs, through mental purpose.

Question: How does one become Keeper of the Lineage?

Response: Through empowerment of elders who keep the teachings. One becomes Keeper of the Lineage by the passing of instructions in rites, demonstrated by being given charge of the sacred bundles and songs for their care. The purpose of the training is to ensure that the songs and rituals which maintain the harmony of people and land will continue for the good of all beings. The songs and dances, through bio-resonance, interact with the earth and stars, keeping a harmonious balance, ensuring good relations between people and abundant crops.

Becoming the Keeper of the Lineage is derived most importantly through the inner development of communion with all of the relatives on the earth and the universe. To sense one's thought as a stream [and] to realize that our thinking is weaving a dream consciousness. As a child within our family, when we awoke we would tell each other our dreams in the mornings, and those are some of my fondest memories.

Dhyani started very young in her pathway of learning the medicine way. She said, "I remember being two years old and hiding under a table, looking at people who came to get medicine from my grandfather. He was making comments. My grandmother was commenting to me about why and how they were doing certain things. When I was four, there was a ceremony. The whole cabin was darkened throughout the day for observation of the natural world and people's actions—a means of mindful respect for life's interactions. Also, observation enables one to see effects of thought and action."

She spoke of the ceremony. "It was very powerful. I felt the wind come into the room and in the space between my great-grandfather's and grandfather's hands I saw, first, a fox playing and then the whole woods, and the whole planet and the whole solar system. The purpose of ceremony is to create an atmosphere of communion with the elemental forces of life, which through interaction shape a people's destiny. This particular ceremony was an initiation into a spiritual society. In the old days every child was initiated as a matter of course. I was told that I was 'being taken into' a spiritual society that I might know the wisdom of the 'Old Ones.' They had a very keen insight and an ability to show it."

Question: Being so young, how did you interpret that powerful experience?

Response: I thought I was the wind! They laughed because I took everything rather stoically. I never showed fear to them [the elders] or uneasiness. I would just sit or stand there and watch them. They indicated that watching was important.

Question: Do you feel that courage is synonymous with healing?

Response: I think it takes courage to realize that we are whole. Basically, in the medicine of the Ani Gadoah people, we come from the premise that one is whole. It is only through incorrect thought or relation of thought and action that one manifests illness, either individually or in the group or the whole society. The basic concept of right action and spiritual duty to all relations is inherent in all of the Indian teachings that I've met throughout the years.

Question: In your case the lineage skipped a generation. Is this common?

Response: No, it doesn't always skip a generation. It is for someone to be willing because there are certain individual sacrifices that one may make. When you really make a commitment for carrying the seeds of wisdom, of healing traditions, and keeping sacred fires as well as practices with crystals, . . . It was a choice they made because no one in the generation before mine wanted to. My grandfather must have waited a long time because he lived to be 127 years, and I was fourteen when he passed on. About fourteen.

Question: Who gives you sanction?

Response: The elders who pass it on. It's always to be used the way they instructed—that has empowered me to teach certain things to people. The empowerment comes after demonstration of songs and rituals and is concluded by the passing of a sacred bundle to one who has been taught their care. The elders pass such bundles to be sure the wisdom continues for the good of the people. If someone wants to be involved in medicine, I ask them, "Why?" Because there are great powers that are released. If someone says, "I want to be like somebody," that's not it. The "why" to become a medicine person is to realize that one has the gift to share and has an inherently great capacity for carrying energy and that energy may be positive for the benefit of the people one chooses to walk the medicine way. And it chooses *you.*

Question: It chooses you, and then you choose to accept it?

Response: It seems to happen simultaneously. Why be a medicine person when it means giving up a great deal of your personal life and time? Because you are committed to maintaining an energy field for a whole people, and the "why" is because you can. It is a duty.

When one is chosen, it is because one has the means to manifest that beauteous way. When one does not heed the call, one loses the very sustenance of life itself. I've been told of a person who was called in a vision and met with all of the twelve grandfathers, and chose not to heed that vision; instead, chose to return to the mines to dig and plunder the earth. Within a few months of that vision, and not heeding its call, that person lost their life. Because your vision is your life. How we see the world, how we see each other, calls forth our future. After being called, one must affirm that they will, and then one must observe the world around and observe most deeply the innermost secrets of one's own heart, and be aware of the way in which one responds to the sound of the tree and the voice of another, to be sure that the heart responds from the moment, and truly hears the wisdom of another. One also develops the eye of discriminating wisdom so that one can see what is happening without making a judgment with its finality.

As one is called to the path, one puts aside a lack of faith in one's own power. As one is called to the path, one is aware of the power of mind. One is aware of the power of the voice to create what is good. As one steps on the path, one realizes they cannot step off. To begin the road is to again come into the stream of your knowing and, like the salmon, to return to your source. So, to become a holy person, to be called as a healer, to be called as a voice of truth for the people, to be called as a politician—requires forethought, certainty to speak the truth, to put aside anger and doubt, to recognize the inherent beauty that is within everyone, to energetically keep your heart and your feet aware of the end of the road, and to recognize the many towns, villages that arise along the road, but to know they are not the final destination.

They did say to me when I was young that I would deal with many people of all races and all nationalities, and that that was something that none of them chose to do. Nor had to do. That's what people used to call me in New York: the Ambassador.

Question: How is a healer trained and what are fundamental importances in that training?

Response: The most important thing, as the old people told me, was the power of our thought and our voice. Always it is better to look beyond what was apparently ugly or discordant, to the beauty that was certainly within it. That was most important, because all manifestations of disease, whether they occur in an individual or a nation, are seated in the mind. It is a thought before it becomes an answer. The idea of empowerment is really the idea of training or studying.

There are many initiations, and for some of the people who are in the priestcraft, it began in their infancy with a special guide. They had a particular purpose. The whole focus was to hold the thought of abundance, or to relate especially to the concept of peace for the nation. [The focus is to be] responsible for holding the thought of peace, for holding the thought of the well-being, the health, and the abundance of the nation, the people—through the waking voice of the fifth generation; that is my age group. [The responsibility] is also to rekindle the light of the truth in the hearts of people of other races, as well.

I've seen and heard the dances and the sacred ceremonies so now I know [them]. We realize that there is a whole process of preparation. There is a cycle of passing the medicine bundle from one to another. At a certain time, I was given the medicine bag of one grandfather, of one grandmother, of another grandfather, and my great-grandfather.

These meant different things as I was given those bundles and they came at different stages of my life. In my training, they meant: She has now understood this.

I wish to clarify something in terms of initiations. Not everyone goes through the complete cycle. Some, for special circumstances, may quickly go through many initiations. Because of the time confines of the life span of my great-grandfather, my grandmother, my grandfather, and their concern with our passing things before they left the flesh, because they really were the last who knew these things, many things were told to me before the time. [Therefore] the initiations were taken before the time. I am not fifty-one years old yet but I have received those chants, those rituals, that understanding.

From the teachings of the elders, Dhyani learned the legacy as the keeper of the lineage and her life pathway. The essence of her teaching came from her grandmother, grandfather, and grandmother's father "who was a most remarkable man. The most remarkable thing about all three of them, which really showed me about the difference between whole and compartmentalized people, is they always knew what they or any of their relatives was doing. If I spoke to one, the others knew what I had said. There was a continuity of consciousness that was really very clear. I never saw those faces show anger, fear, jealousy, or annoyance. No matter what."

Dhyani recounted an incident in her childhood which, by its example, demonstrated the compassionate qualities needed by healers. "In the Carolinas," she said, "people were pretty racist. Occasionally, we would encounter that on the way to town. Nothing ever distracted them [the elders]. They'd say, 'You pray for those persons.' One person, in fact, was particularly awful. It was a woman. My sister and I were dressed up with pinafore dresses. We were with my grandfather going into town, standing outside the general store. A lady came over and said, 'Oh, how beautiful,' and her friend said, 'Hey, don't talk to them. Can't you see them is red niggers?' My grandfather came out, looked at them and said, 'Don't be upset. They just don't know their hearts.' Two weeks later, that woman came to him seeking help. I understand what he meant about not being cruel or returning people's ignorance. Often they don't know how to contact you and they fail to reach their higher selves. All beings seek to communicate. Some have forgotten how."

Asked if she had ever experienced a struggle with anger, jealousy, or envy in her lifetime, Dhyani answered, "Energies change through transformation and non-attachment. I don't resonate to anything that is not whole. People may have such feelings, but that doesn't require my participation. I have a very good life. Those emotions pass and one works on creating good relations.

"For me, the dream and the vision is the same process because even when the body's asleep, there is a consciousness. The actual *vision quest* has been going on all my life. At four, I was left alone for a day and a half in the woods in the Smokies and it was very beautiful to me. My particular responsibility was to look into the eyes of a deer. So I had to wait for one. I learned a great deal and I saw that we are all communicating, that language is beyond the verbalization, and that through my thoughts, I could create a field of energy of peace and comfort around me, and even inspire animals to keep the child warm."

Dhyani related that she had been invited to travel to Turkey and India and said that "the people in Turkey had dreamed of meeting me before we came together. During that trip to India, coming very close to death by standing on the tail of a cobra, I realized, 'Oh, yes, one can be a gift,' as that serpent showed me, or told me [about the] option of choosing life and death by meeting the life force with respect rather than confrontation." She began to understand the depth of wisdom taught by her elders.

"Also," she said, "I was kind of silly because I believed them when they said snakes don't bite Indians. Somehow, as I was standing there very close to the snake, I realized that, of course, this is going to be okay—snakes don't bite Indians. That's just a reminder of the profound effect their words and their teaching had upon me. In every aspect of my life, every situation I've met as an adult, always their words come back as a reminder. Their words always remind me of the larger truth that we are all relatives to what is occurring. The meeting with the serpent, the sacred snake, was a teaching—that the cobra taught me something. Every creature, every being, is a relative of one's own. You see, the snake is very powerful to us. Not as a symbol of evil, but as a symbol of vibration. The eternal vibration. The eternal consciousness. In itself, it has no consciousness: it *is*. It is the symbol of integration, and my grandparents said that [is] one of the tricks used to enslave people's minds, to give people the idea that the serpent moving on the sand or the soil represented evil when it is only in people's minds that evil is generated. Every vibration moves in a wave. So, it really wasn't until 1976 that I truly felt that I was a gift to the people."

Question: What happened in 1976?
Response: It was the accumulation of the grand testing which didn't occur in this country. I can tell you a bit about it. That occurred in the Himalayas. I was really moved—by a mynah bird, actually—although there were students traveling with me from Israel and Turkey (which was one of my early attempts to bring the children of Abraham back together). It was really kind of difficult, so I just went off for a while up the mountain by myself. A few of the sherpas, when they realized I was a woman, didn't want to come. I had trained for a whole year before that very strenuously. [They] couldn't really tell that I was a woman. People thought I was a boy. Anyway, only one sherpa came with me and I was determined to get to this temple by nightfall. There were huge boulders falling. There was an earthquake—all kinds of things were happening. But this one sherpa was really inclined—he understood that I had to do that. It was one of the visions that I had seen in the fire in our place of study when I was a child. I was getting a little distracted by the students and their political arguments, and a mynah bird came and said, "You'd better leave them. Remember what we taught you. Remember what we taught you." My grandparents knew this would happen. In fact, my grandmother, even though she'd been dead, called me on the telephone when I was getting ready to fly out of New York. You know, it really was quite remarkable! She told me she's a planet now. I believe it, too. I learned constantly from the elders. Even now, because by our tradition, you're not really manifest as an adult until you're fifty-one.

Question: And what happens at age fifty-one?
Response: [Women] are usually beyond individual family bearing at age fifty-one and able to be mother for all things.

Question: So you have your initial responsibility to your immediate family and and then to the humanity family?

Response: Yes. With the Cherokee, the healer or any person is not an adult until fifty-one. We don't make sexual distinctions. In terms of female body or male body, and/or one being more appropriate than another, because she does have children, the light aura of a female body has some opening in it. That makes it more of a challenge. That's why it is considered a greater sacrifice [for women]—and one of the reasons the women are so revered in our society. That open space in the aura also means you are constantly giving not only to your children (which usually cause the open space) but to all living things. It takes a very clear focus to close that space. That's really when you become a medicine person. Then one may give with clear intention. My aura has always been sealed.

Question: Where are there differences between the medicine way as your elders practiced and the way you practice?

Response: There is no difference other than the fact that I deal with many nationalities.

Question: Yours is a broader base?

Response: Which was their purpose. There was a period of darkness that descended on the people, which I think began around 1820, when the Indians were very severely harassed, murdered, and sent from their homeland in the Carolinas, and because of that, the earth would become quite polluted and unstable. They [the elders] felt that we of the fifth generation, after darkness descended on the people, would hold our voice until the proper time as the darkness was ready to be dispelled, and come out and work with people all over the world. My great-grandfather even showed me places I'd go in the Himalayas and other parts of the world, visions seen in the sacred fire and within crystals. In my child's mind, I said, "Huh? What makes him think all of this is going to happen?" But everything they pointed out to me has come to pass, even to the people that I meet.

Question: What is your personal preparation prior to a healing ceremony?

Response: Quiet and sometimes fasting for three or four days, although there are times when there is no water available. And deep contemplation, the gathering of the particular frequencies. In the human body, you know, every organ vibrates to a certain song, a certain pitch. Discord of the mind upsets that pitch and causes organ systems to become ill. So, in the time before a passing bundle ceremony, there is a great preparation of quiet and listening to the sounds and tuning one's own voice [to] . . . resonate . . . [with] the tones of other people.

Question: Is there any difference between a natural healer and one who is trained?

Response: The one who is trained is usually trained because they have the natural gift. The natural healer may do things intuitively; that is, one who has not had any particular training. The one who knows what they are doing has observed themselves very carefully, and has observed the relationship of the elements, the herbs, the touch of one's hand upon another's body, the power of the voice on another's body, and has recognized certain principles and operates within those principles. It is the difference between being civilized and not. Civilized, uncivilized; that word is more a joke because the greatest civilization is the person who demonstrates the highest qualities of civilization. [It] is the one who lives in greatest harmony with their environment. It is not necessary to create large edifices of material. It is necessary to recognize oneself within the large edifice of the wheel of life.

Question: How would you discriminate between one who follows the medicine way, one who is a true healer, and one who claims to be?

Response: There are some very definite things that happen. In the process of watching the priest or the priestess grow, there are certain changes that occur in the head. One of them is that a little fluid comes out of the top of the head. In the testing of me, sometimes they'd ask me to light up or hold a thought. You are tested.

Question: How does the Native American healer, or you as the carrier of the priestcraft, assist others in realizing holiness?

Response: Through a resonating, a song, so that one can feel themselves—like the strings of the guitar being tuned—coming again to the right note of their true expression. Everyone has a song of power. It is the spiritual purpose. It is a psalm that weaves all of their relationships. [It] is the integrity of their organ systems in harmonious relationship as health. The holy person, the medicine person, the healer, calls people to remembering their songs, and resonates that clear note so that others may come again to be in tune with the great voice of truth in themselves. The voice is our greatest medicine. We say herbs are a part of our healing, but the greatest of healers has no tools at all. We also use [bone] needles to scratch . . . the skin, working very much on the meridians to balance energy. Yet, the greatest physician has no tools.

Question: Are the sounds and the chants the tuning forks? Are the chants different from the songs? Do symmetry and the chants elicit healing?

Response: Yes. Because they are so old. In other parts of the world there are similar chants, yet no one really knows what they mean. They are songs, but language has evolved beyond. The sounds in themselves have such a symmetry that they bring about a healing in the body. It is through the symmetry of particular tones and tonal relationships . . . that they are corrected, that bring about the right toning of the organ systems which have become ill through discord . . . not vibrating at the right frequency. It is a very exact science. When I saw the science being taught at the universities, I realized it was very limited in comparison to that [ancient] wisdom.

There is always the idea of the shaman, the priest, the holy woman, whether she's the honored woman of the Cherokees or whether she's the Virgin Mary. This means there is an ideal, and the individual acts upon those key thoughts, acts upon those ideals, and seeks to bring them into manifestation in their own life. You can recognize the system that has it already outlined for you, and allow your mind to become it. The most dynamic energy that comes for one's manifesting their ideal, comes with the power of the voice. The power song, the chanting, the praying. That really brings life-force into your body and your life so that you can put aside those patterns that lead nowhere. This is the whole process of purification.

Or you can do it like the Indian of the Americas. You can say, "I will. I am going to sit here in a hole for four days, not eating or drinking, and listen to the true voice within my heart." That is diligence and will. Or, you can say, "I will put aside that which appears rootless and I will trace the roots of my own consciousness within myself, and from there I will find a road that enables me to bring forth the holiness of myself and others." It is for the individual, the group, the nation, the planet, to realize which thoughts are fruitless and to recognize which thoughts and actions will bring forth what is good for the people. [One must] perceive those thoughts which will ultimately lead to creative endeavor. That is a choice everyone must make. The "how" is in looking at yourself, recognizing your relationship with the elements around you, to realize that those elements are consciousness. The denial of the fire of truth in yourself is going to be the denial of your heart's beat—maybe make your arteries get hard or something like that. It's all interrelated.

The priestcraft lineage holders are people who are keepers of the tradition and the rituals, the preparation of seeds for planting, the gleaning of information and guidance for the whole nation, and also who have learned a great deal about the relationship of sound and vibration. We work with quartz crystals. You know, the quartz crystal is very much a part of our technological age—the televisions, radios, telephones, for carrying messages. Through a certain attunement of the consciousness, one is able to perceive the possible future that the people's actions are taking and thereby help them guide and come to a right decision about proper action that would be fitting even seven generations from now. It is the same principle as a tuning fork. We actually use a tuning crystal. And manifest that crystal within our own being.

Question: You said that you feel the crystals are alive. Could you talk about that?

Response: Yes, they have consciousness. Everything vibrating is consciousness, is thought. To hold a form, it is vibrating along a certain symmetry. It holds the idea of that symmetry, that it can continue.

Question: Would the same be true of a rock?

Response: Yes, although a rock, in terms of intelligence, is not as refined as the intelligence of the crystal because its lines of symmetry run in many directions. A crystal has a particular shape. All of the atoms line up according to that shape. A sedimentary rock has variations of atomic alignment within it, which would be various currents of thinking, whereas the quartz crystal, which attunes us to many worlds and creation, is all aligned along a certain direction. A quartz crystal always taxes a hexagonal shape. It has intelligence to carry its form.

An important part of Dhyani's work is with quartz crystals, which she says have remarkable qualities of holding and magnifying energy.

Because crystals are perhaps the least known tool for healing presented in this book, a brief elaboration may be useful. Crystals resemble meticulously cut gems. A clear quartz crystal is perfectly six-sided, with each side parallel to the side opposite. The adjoining sides make precise 120-degree angles. Quartz crystals have been used from ancient times to the present as a source of light and energy by healers, spiritual leaders, and scientists. The mystique created by crystals has been evident throughout history in legends and tales from Merlin in King Arthur's court to Changing Woman of the Navajo to C. G. Jung to computers.

Crystal properties include vibrating at a high, exact rate of speed and storing, amplifying, and transforming energy and vibrations. Hence their use in healing by some Native Americans for centuries as well as in modern computers. Indeed, crystals are unique gems, and the mystery surrounding them complements the mysteries of healing.

Dhyani explains that there are crystals buried throughout North America that have been "programmed" to speed the process of evolution, and anyone who is living here is touched by the vibration. Dhyani, through her chemistry studies at New York University, believes that "there are many levels to crystal work—and various degrees of understanding. Crystals communicate. They amplify and pick up particular frequencies and set into motion—like a tuning fork. There is a physical integrity within the planet—which has effect upon the crystal. The crystal gets discorded because it is a living being sharing in the dream as well as in the mineral kingdom. There is a biophysical level creating a production of negative ions and the attraction of rain clouds and lightning which sets up a field of energy: therefore, a biofeedback. Within the crystal, it becomes vivified. Within the spiritual level, the crystal beauty comes again. The crystal is the exterior expression of a clear mind. It is symbolic of the clear mind in everything.

"Also, it is the realization of teachings that come over a hundred thousand years. I said twenty-seven generations of people have kept this particular information of the crystals, and the sounds that my family has taught me [are] now being shared with many people. The exercises are very deep so that one can maintain the pulse of the earth. That understanding of the pulse of the earth is very significant in terms of our sacred ceremonies and how [we] align the crystals—how those crystals call forth the holiness for all the people.

"The healing is to bring again the right resonance, the right frequencies, to the organ system, and it is first to make clear the aspects of consciousness that have caused the discord. Always, this is a participatory exercise. One who comes to us for healing also must take responsibility for their own process. The person who is being healed is very much involved in the process. The whole Indian medicine way is that nothing is done for you except what you create. Basically, you help a person recreate the tones of their harmony."

Question: At what point would you refer someone to a medical doctor? Western medicine?

Response: When it became apparent that discord was so deeply entrenched in the body and that the will to be well was lost. . . . Allopathic medicine does not deal with the whole—it deals with the parts. And therein is its weakness. I considered being an allopathic physician. Then I saw that the training was not even one one-hundredth as clear and wise and beneficial as what my grandparents taught me. Western medicine concentrates on the problem, although I am careful about making generalizations because there are two state presidents of two different state AMA organizations that have studied with me, so I wouldn't say that it is the "AMA mind." It's just a habit of thinking, to think that there are problems. A problem is a state of mind. People have created problems through the affirmation of them. When someone visits a physician just to get the shots for a passport, they are asked, "Have you any problems?" That's not the Indian way to heal. That's really no way to heal. The science of the Ani Gadoah priestcraft is a wisdom, a science that I have found in my travels shared by other cultures. The Tibetans have a remarkably similar practice and their physiological concept of the human body is much the same in terms of five airs coming in through the navel and stars—energy centers—above the body as well as within it. The Chinese ancient Taoist philosophy is also very similar. Although I am the caretaker and the holder of the lineage of the Ani Gadoah people, over the years in my travels I realize the one truth of what is right is in the heart of many people.

The only one who was really a whole man in psychology and talked about the mind was Jung. The others talk about problems and feeding illness and feeding thought-forms of limitation. We've got some people in our advanced study group who are heads of psychology departments in very prestigious universities. When I say what psychology's process appears to be, they are dumbfounded and crestfallen. Then they say, "Oh, yeah—there is a way to see the wholeness of the person." And to know, most importantly, that our words give power. If we are focusing on what went wrong, how are we going to see what's right? There is a need to integrate experiences of the past, and we have rituals and spiritual exercises to do, as well as physical, and just everyday affirmation. Some people have been really brutalized by parents or the educational system and they need an opportunity to restructure. The restructuring should not place blame. It's just thought regenerating, bringing together the left, the right, and the middle brain.

Question: The middle brain?

Response: We call that snake or turtle mind. That's very important. That is the balance of our whole nature . . . In the creation process, we say it's the emptiness that everything comes from, and it manifests through three fires. One is will. One is wisdom. The other is active intelligence. [It] is for the human being to rebuild—the rebuilding of the rainbow bridges to make the connection between those hemispheres on the brain. And the foundation is the serpent's mind. Yes, that midbrain function is very significant to the survival of the species. It is the seat of survival.

Question: Can you recall for us, in detail, one of your most fulfilling experiences in healing?

Response: There are so many. One that was very dramatic was when a person came here in a wheelchair. I have trained many people, most of whom are already health care professionals of very high caliber and heads of departments in various universities. It was at one of those training sessions that the woman in a wheelchair came. We were dancing, so I told her, "Come on. Get up and dance."

I went over and took her hand. She forgot that she had disempowered herself to weakness and in the moment of my saying, "Come, let's dance," [she] remembered the power and she got up. She is without that wheelchair today.

Question: Disempowered herself with her weakness?

Response: Yes. The idea of self-empowerment, which is really what vision quest is, [is] to realize your power. The medicine person's search is to realize this special gift, here in the world. In these times, most people are disempowered, and have abdicated their right to wholeness, abdicated their voice to saying what is correct—to a system that says, "Well, somebody's going to have to give up their opinion"—because there's always a minority view rather than an integrated view. Therefore, the parts of the whole are in an antagonistic opposition rather than being in a flow. Many human beings, particularly of western mind (meaning European-trained), are particularly disenfranchised in their sense of spiritual continuity. Because there are hormones within the brain that in themselves can overcome depression: just with a simple exercise, one [can] begin to secrete those endorphins and overcome depression. Yet, people are somehow caught. The idea of self-empowerment is to realize that you make choices in your life, and those choices are the result of your thought and your actions. What comes back to you from your actions is your whole life. One needs to very carefully consider their own vision of self. An example is thinking, "Oh, I'm fat and ugly." To say that over and over again is going to change one's metabolism to such a degree that you will become fat and ugly. Do you understand?

Question: You are saying that, for example, in a state of depression, one can change their own hormones by positive thought, by their own self-empowerment rather than by resorting to medication?

Response: Yes. There are certain neurons in your brain that will never fire unless you have muscles moving in opposition or [in] spiral motion. To introduce someone to those exercises, which was the dance for this woman—she'd been doing them in the chair—just to introduce someone to those exercises begins to open and awaken the flow of energy in the entire body. Also, the very same endorphins that help you feel good relieve pain. So, the more one moves, the better health. That's a very clear view for someone who has felt,

"Oh, I can't do it myself." When you take them gently through a few shoulder spirals, finger and wrist spirals, they feel a greater amount of energy in themselves. "Oh, I see!" And that phrase, "Oh, I see," is very important in the medicine.

There have been other healings that have been loving and wondrous. One was a mother who somehow had a dream to get in touch with me. She was from Jamaica, and I wasn't able—the child had Hodgkin's disease—to visit them. I asked for the child's birthdate and I was able to make a song that would harmonize the system. The child has been quite well and off drugs for years, now. Hodgkin's disease is rather easy to treat in terms of spiritual healing because it is really to bring the person's mind-view and immunological system to come into a compatible existence.

Question: Is the issue of faith of the receiver in healing primarily one of responsibility?

Response: Right. It is one of consciousness.

Question: How do you start your day?

Response: I start my day by praying.

Question: And what is your prayer?

Response: Creator, the sun has arisen, and may on this day the people realize the light in their hearts. . . . These days, my morning prayer and all of the prayers very much focus on transforming the planetary thought of scarcity and aggression so that nations can realize themselves as a planetary family. That is very important at this time.

Question: What do you do after your morning prayer?

Response: Exercise. Do a dance to the four directions. Then, preparation of food, eggs, cornbread, cornmeal. Lots of fruit and nuts, especially dried fruits in the winter.

Question: What are the special experiences during your day that you enjoy?

Response: Ahh, when I see people light up. When people get something clear in their minds, about their holiness, their relationship to life. That adds another star to the beauty of the day. Especially in working with students—when I see that—that is very blessing. Also, when I see a particular project of planetary education is being manifest; that, too, is very joyous.

Every interview, every record of an interview with Dhyani is rich, mind-expanding, thoughtful, and empowering. She wishes to join the All and to be joined with and by everyone in the healing of the Earth. In an article entitled, "Ancient Wisdom for a Re-Awakening World," she said: "The Earth has cried out; her cry began early this century. The *form* of thought generated by human beings was one of such discordant nature that the elements could not respond to Her will and Her lifeblood could not move. So a call was put out to bring more of the Old Ones back to Earth—those who have what we call Mother-Father consciousness, who are full beings with no desire to be on Earth but who are servers—to come back this time in Indian bodies but also to be able to communicate with people of other cultures. So you see us now, walking throughout the world, some talking in the vein of politics and expressing the pain and horror of a race almost decimated, and a few of us who come to speak only of the spirit."[4]

In an interview with us, Dhanyi added: "It is only now that some people are being stirred, and also through a recognition that the prevailing mind-set of industrial man is only going to lead to death of the planet and everyone, that has brought people again to consider and look with curiosity (and some with respect) to the native practice. It is very orderly. Everything is planned. There is a reason for every movement. A reason for everything. And it has been so for many generations.

"Initially, people did share their wisdom with all those who came, but they saw that it was abused. So a decision was made in council to no longer share the information, until such time as it became absolutely necessary for the well-being of the earth and the future generations. Because we are in such a critical time, it is now necessary for us, as human beings, to call all of our relatives to become correct with the earth. It is the wisdom to see and to experience the continuity of thought—to realize that our thought generates actions. Each one of us is bringing into manifestation through our thought, word, and deed the very quality of our life. We have a responsibility that our thoughts, our words, and our actions as individuals, as family, as a clan, as a nation, must be in harmony for the good of people seven generations down the road.

"Yes, there is an inherent power in the legacy. It seems to be a very clear relationship with animals and people and a sense of comforting attitude. Wherever or whatever country I'm in, the people think I came from there, and I'm one of their relatives. I feel that.

"I think that it is important for people to know we are in the final stages of purification. Purifying the planetary body. That is the transmutation of everyone's consciousness that we must transform as human beings to come again to the sacred hoop of life, and each one [must] take responsibility for the dreams we weave and [that] our actions make a scene of beauty and light."

Question: Where is that similar or different from the Christian ethic?

Response: The Christian ethic—you know, Jesus does it for you. People use Jesus like a doormat. I know His mother didn't sacrifice for Him to be used like that. The difference is, we don't depend upon somebody else to do it. We really know it has to be done in our hearts and in our relations with one another ourselves.

You know the earth has meridian systems—just as the human person does. We call them lightning. The way the people think, and act, and what is done to the earth has an effect on the health and the level of vitality of the human people. We are living in this age at a time of devitalization, where the amount of negative ions per cubic centimeter in the average place is far below what it was, say, 25 years ago. There is a direct relationship between those negative ions and brain hormonal function. So the digging in the earth and the release of pollutants in the earth is, first, an expression of people's own abdication of empowerment. It's a disrespect for life in the future generations as well as the present. On a deeper level, it is devitalizing the whole course of life for all people. That is how medicine is perceived by the Ani Gadoah. It's not just the individual. It is a whole process. We all have a responsibility in maintaining the balance and harmony of the planet.

"Our book," we said, "is about medicine women, *curanderas,* and women doctors. What do you feel the spirit guides would want to see in this book?"

Dhyani spoke thoughtfully. She said that the spirit guides would want "people to know that there is an opportunity to turn aside the cycle of planetary and human destruction, and come again to right relation with all of our relatives through affirmation of what is good in ourselves and others." She said that "the qualities of women are not in opposition to the qualities of men. Because everything together, mother and father, is necessary for the form to manifest at all. Be it a rock, a tree, or a human being.

"One of the gifts to humanity [is] the variation of consciousness that comes with the body. Basically, the woman's medicine is very expansive and nonintrusive, whereas my grandfather would put his hand in someone and take something out. That is something more commonly seen with male practitioners, whereas the woman makes the changes in the light body. Sometimes the male practitioners do also, because the higher a medicine person has really integrated both mother and father within themselves, those distinctions then are no longer important. But we place a great emphasis on the role of the honored woman in our culture. That is the woman who holds dear the thought of family and turns aside whatever enmity there may be in the community and transforms it to love, and that is very much the power of mother's energy.

"What is significant in the energy of the female healer, holy lady, honored woman—so many ways to describe what is significant in wearing the female form—is that one is able to nurture. One is able to nurture the seed of good and pure mind within everyone. One is able to feed the ideal that comes from the realms of Angawi—the realm of ideal form, so that it can be actualized for the good of the people. To be a woman in this time is a great blessing. Also [it] is a great challenge. Sometimes I am asked a question, 'Well, does the male medicine man do it differently?' And, yes, he does. He does do it differently. Because it is his purpose sometimes to *scare* the sickness out. If any of you have seen one of my cousins, Rolling Thunder, well, he does something to make somebody better. He can scream and yell frightfully to scare the bad thinking out. The person becomes so concerned by that unexpected noise that they forget to hold the form that was making them feel ill at ease. Whereas the female, myself included, when working with one who is thinking ill, it is my intention to let that person feel like a child again; to comfort them, to nurture them, so that they can recognize that whole being within, that holy kid who remembers how to dance around the sacred hoop. And that is the real power of the woman in this time.

"And every woman has a duty to call the male again to see the beauty in himself. It is up to every mother to remind her son that he has in his hands the ability to create, and that tearing down the sweat lodge with the change of the season is good and necessary so that what was purified can be returned to the earth. But most importantly, he needs to be reminded that he also rebuilds the sweat lodge each season. And here we are, coming in the change of seasons from one world to the next, and we are preparing for the season of most great peace. So the son's thoughts of ignorance, which was manifest as a great industrial society, crisscrossing wires across the land and upsetting the voice of Mother Earth, and interfering with the flow of the lightning bird, now the son must realize [it is time] to take down some of the wires and those edifices, and allow the natural current of life and love to flow, so that we can truly be the dignified human beings that we are. So it is.

"In these times, much of the power of the female voice comes in reaction to the ignorance of the man, so it is an empowerment through anger. In the matrilineal society of the Ani Gadoah people there hasn't been that opportunity for such an angry separation to occur, because the woman always realized her power and spoke it. It was never an issue. Female rights—male rights. Female sensitivity group—male sensitivity group. Even when the women have a medicine circle, and it is called a woman's circle, still there would be men there. If the men have a meeting, still they would require or call on the presence of some female energy. There is a bit more integration, perhaps because it is a matrilineal society, rooted in the land. The people were able to maintain a balance of consciousness around the issue of sexual identification.

"When I was young, in many of the ceremonies that the old people did, which were part of the education process for me, in many of the ceremonies they would call me the 'old man.' It never occurred to me to question it—only that somehow some aspect of the inner nature was being reflected that had nothing to do with the little girl's body that I wore.

"The idea that has stirred and awakened many women to the

power of their voices as the mother, or has brought women to speak out against the ignorance of the time is a real ideal. We have the duty as females to speak out about what is incorrect, and to show the means of right relationship. What is most important as our function is one of nurturing, as our gift is one of nurturing. It is most important to remember that the empowerment of the voice cannot come from anger. It comes from the certainty of the gentle power within ourselves. It comes from the certainty that nurturing, giving, receiving, also requires a fierceness to see that the children grow. What is more fierce than the mother protecting her child? To be a woman and to recognize her gentle nature is also to recognize her strength and power, to speak from our hearts, to act from our hearts, to know that the seed of holiness, wholeness, is inherent in everyone and that it requires the gentle rains of the woman. The female rains, we call it, bring forth the corn. If it rains too hard, if the voice is too strong and thunderous, then the tended plants are knocked down. When the rain is gentle and warm, then the seeds take root and they flourish. Let our words be strong and at the same time gentle. Let our planting be planting seeds of certainty. Let our voices call our relatives to right relation and good action. And let us point to what is good and show the means of its manifestation.

"Thank you for the opportunity to speak these things. May you be surrounded ever in the light of wisdom and joy, and may this book you are writing bring many women again to the certainty of their gifts, and may the men who read it realize the mother within, and may we all realize ourselves in the circle of light."

PART TWO

LAS CURANDERAS

CHAPTER 6

INTRODUCTION

Traditional Hispanic women healers are known as *curanderas*, a term that is as varied within the Hispanic culture as are the methods these women use to cure. Despite fundamental cultural similarities, the techniques and properties applied in healing by *curanderas* in northern New Mexico are not necessarily the same as those preferred by *curanderas* in the neighboring state of Texas or in the canyons of New York's Spanish Harlem, where the healers are influenced by a Puerto Rican background. Too, there are *curanderas* curing the sick in Florida using procedures that were effective in Cuba but would be foreign to *curanderas* practicing in East Los Angeles.

Regardless of regional differences, however, these Hispanic women healers are all descendants of immigrants who arrived in America from Spain or one of its colonies. Modern *curanderas* may be the last generation to be acutely aware of the Spanish colonial culture and its influences, including various designations used to describe ethnicity: Spanish-American, Mexican-American, or Chicana. A culture, as Judy Grahn states, "does not exist as one big puddle into which everything flows indiscriminately. Like vast oceans, cultures have their own geography, currents and tides, pools and backwaters. The separate streams of a culture flow together in multiple currents of classes, age groups, regions, and . . . backgrounds, each adding a very specific variety to the whole swirl of life."[1] For purposes of uniformity and clarification, however, certain basic terms will be explained.

Hispanic is a term used to identify "the more traditional type of Spanish-American who settled in the Southwest over 300 years ago," said Arturo Pineda, an official in New Mexico's state government who is, in the late 80s, responsible for the design of social programs that specifically benefit the underprivileged. According to Pineda, 90 percent of New Mexico's poor are Hispanic. "That designation," he says,

> is similar to "Hispano," which can be heard in different songs, *dichos* [sayings], and the folklore of the past. The age group that comprises Hispanos is usually forty years old and over and has strong ties to the culture, its language and values. In the 1970s and 1980s, a new type of Hispano began to emerge—the Chicano. The younger group differed greatly from the Hispanic in many ways: their Spanish language became poor to non-existent in usage, traditional religious and family values were traded for more contemporary values. These Chicanos are the children of the Hispanos, but they have changed to fit more comfortably within society and changed to be able to compete more vigorously within the socio-economic strata. Back in college days I was a Chicano, but now I'm more Hispano than anything else. "Chicano," to me, is a political rather than a cultural designation. Some Chicanos I know can't even speak Spanish.[2]

Beatrice Roybal Martinez, a direct descendant of one of the earliest conquistadors to arrive in the Southwest, considered herself neither Chicana nor Hispano. "I am an American woman of Spanish descent," she told us in 1981. However, the term *Hispanic* will be used here because it encompasses the many separate streams possible within a culture; the specific definition of Hispanic used in this book is "a person of Spanish descent native to the American Southwest."[3]

The definition of *curanderismo* is similarly diverse. The specific techniques comprising *curanderismo* vary geographically and have different labels attached: Mexican-American healing practices, rural folkloric medicine, and so on. For our purposes, the following definition of *curanderismo* is applicable: "*Curanderismo* consists of a set of folk medical beliefs, rituals, and practices that seem to address the psychological, spiritual, and social needs of traditional . . . people. It is a complex system of folk medicine with its own theoretical, diagnostic, and therapeutic aspects. *Curanderismo* is conceptually holistic in nature; no separation is made between the mind and the body, as in western medicine and psychology."[4] *Curanderismo*, simply, is the art of Hispanic healing.

Lastly, when referring to a higher power, the *curanderas* used the phrase "the Lord" more frequently than they used any of the other designations available (for example, God, Jesus, or Our Saviour). References have been kept intact when quoting the *curanderas*.

Curanderismo begins inside each family, where there is one woman who assumes the role of a "Key Family Member,"[5] someone who has obtained rudimentary medical knowledge. When a family member becomes ill, the key family member is the first person the patient contacts to find the right *remedios* to cure the ailment. By seeking help within the extended family, the patient contributes to the culture's self-containment; it is not even necessary to step outside for medical care.

If the key family member's remedies fail and the ailment becomes more acute, the patient then seeks the help of a *curandera*, a healer who may be outside the family circle but who is still within the bounds of the culture. The *curandera* treats the patient with remedies that have helped generations of ancestors. Both patient and healer, by their actions, perpetuate cultural values and convey new legitimacy upon the ethnic healing norms that have been such a steadfast part of the traditional Hispanic folkways.

Curanderas believe that if they are successful and their patient recovers, it is God's will. If they cannot cure their patient, it is God's will that the patient go elsewhere for care. The patient knows this too—that the *curandera* has been chosen by God to heal. Patients may also believe that sickness is a result of the devil gaining a foothold in their lives, causing an internal imbalance between good and evil. They hope the *curandera*, representing the healing graces of God, will bring equilibrium back into their lives through God's will, thus evincing a cure. If the *curandera* cannot help, the patient will enter the mainstream of scientific medical care, but only after all avenues of cultural, familial, and religious healing methods have failed.

A comprehension of the healing rituals of the southwestern Hispanic New Mexico folk culture requires a look behind contemporary values and standards, a look into the distant past to another time in history. In putting aside learned attitudes and biases, one can begin to understand and appreciate the healing folkways of a culture that, in many aspects, still remains distinctly apart from the American melting pot.

Curanderismo came to the Southwest with the Spanish and Mexican pioneers. It was carried across an ocean, then overland by conquistadors, Franciscan friars, and the women healers, *curanderas,* who were part of the vast caravans traveling north to settle the land in the name of cross and crown.

Along the way, Catholic priests and friars functioned as the medics of their time, removing cactus thorns from children's fingers, stitching lacerations with stringy fiber from the century plant, or cooling a feverish brow. When they were at a loss to treat more serious, unexpected ills, the clergy relied on the *curanderas* for assistance. These women were the repository of ancient folk-healing knowledge and seemed to know exactly how to treat complicated afflictions by using a variety of herbs and healing plants they carried with them.

Their basic knowledge of healing herbs was enhanced upon their arrival in North America by the new varieties of herbs they found growing in the new land. With teaching from various Indian tribes, the healers discovered that the indigenous plants had properties different from those of the ones found in Spain or Mexico.

The colonists, most of whom were devout and pious Christians, had a substantial background in Catholic theology, the religion that produced sincere trust in the representatives of the God who surrounded them—the Franciscan friars. All of the travelers, especially the *curanderas,* shared the same beliefs about cultural healing techniques, some of which called upon certain saints to aid in recovery from ailments. And so, when a friar or a *curandera* invoked the name of a saint to intercede with God on the patient's behalf, everyone understood the role the saints played in healing.

Because they have been chosen by God and have proven themselves worthy, the saints are considered holy by the Catholic Church— worthy of veneration and able, through God's grace, to intercede on behalf of mortals seeking blessings from above. The church teaches that the saints present petitions to God. Invoking the saints, asking them to intercede, does not supplant prayer directly to God, but it reinforces it and gives intentions more meaning, as when one asks a friend for help in trying to make a good impression on another. The saints are friends, and by way of their friendship, they help *curanderas* and other folk healers cure the ailments of their patients. *Curanderas* also believe they have a special task, a mission sanctioned from above: to do God's healing on earth.

Part of what makes a good healer, *curandera* Juanita Sedillo said in

a 1982 issue of *New Mexico Magazine*,[6] is a mutual faith in God between the healer and the healed, and her firm conviction that God
put the *remedios* on earth as cures for ailments. Mrs. Sedillo saw
many things in her life—cures she considered to be routine and
others she thought could be brought about only through *milagrosos*
(miracles), all of which were part of a *curandera's* faith in her own
ability to heal.

Eighty-seven years old when interviewed in 1982, Mrs. Sedillo
recalled a time when Hispanic women healers made house calls,
much like country doctors. Juanita Sedillo learned *curanderismo*
from her grandmother and began treating patients herself when she
was twenty-two years old, just about the time a few medical doctors
first roamed the hills of northern New Mexico on horseback and in
buggies. *Curanderas* at that time were not numerous, and they traveled for miles to treat their patients. One can imagine that *curandera*
and physician occasionally met on the road, in town, or even at the
home of a patient. Language barriers may have prevented a detailed
discussion between the two healers, but there is no doubt that communication of sorts was established.

Broken bones were a common affliction in those days, and Mrs.
Sedillo's treatment included the use of warm horse manure; the patient's fever was lowered with "a combination of potatoes, vinegar,
and mud."[7] Mrs. Sedillo also worked as a *partera*, delivering thousands of babies and often staying awake night and day until the
birthing process was over. She would be gone from her home for
days, but folks would find her when they needed her. In something
resembling a doctor's kit, she carried a diploma certifying her abilities in midwifery. Herbal remedies were there too, to be prepared
when needed to speed the baby's journey into another reality. Children thought she carried babies in her case, and when she left a new
mother with a baby, they were convinced. Later, when women began going to hospitals to deliver their children, so did Mrs. Sedillo
on occasion, quite often in the middle of the night, and always with
the permission of the medical staff. How she assisted in the delivery
room was kept a secret, but it is certain that her attendance was reassuring to the mother-to-be.

Recently, James Jaramillo, M.D., a Hispanic physician in Albuquerque, New Mexico, described various types of traditional His-

panic healers, all of whom take their names from *curandera*, a generic designation akin to a physician, who can also be a specialist, e.g., surgeon, psychiatrist, or opthalmologist. A *curandera total* holds the highest position on the hierarchal Hispanic ladder of healing, so Jaramillo found it easy to understand why most traditional healers prefer to be known as *curanderas total*.[8] This designation includes all the various subspecialties: herbs, midwifery, massage, and spiritual techniques. Only the most powerful of healers call themselves *curanderas total*, and then only after careful consideration.

One legendary *curandera total* was Josephita Ortiz y Davis. "*Curanderas total* utilize ritualism and symbolism in their art and are able to move in and out of dimensions not bound to earth—the spiritual and the mystical," declared José Ortiz y Pino III, a former New Mexico government elected official and a *curandero* (male Hispanic healer) who has written and spoken extensively about his family background. "My great-grandmother Josephita Ortiz y Davis," he recalls, "was a powerful woman who healed in a dark room full of power objects."[9] That chamber today (1988) is roped off inside the family *hacienda*, left as it was the day Josephita died. Whatever agents of healing she used are still there, preserved intact in the places she put them. Hanging from the *vigas* (ceiling beams made from peeled tree trunks) were numerous bundles of dry, brittle plants and vegetables that had long since lost their aroma and potency. We saw the outline of a *mano y metate*, the Spanish equivalent of a mortar and pestle, resting in a shadowed corner, long unused and smothered by decades of spider webs. Also offering silent testimony to Josephita's healing skills were a stuffed raven, a coiled snake, a bear's head, and a large, crystal globe. Whatever other things *la curandera total* needed for healing were there as well, covered by the dust of a century. We could only imagine what they were.

"Medicinal plants are powerful, but the *curandera* tunes into the essence of the plant itself to appreciate its healing properties," Ortiz y Pino explained. "Some plants reach their highest potency at night, some during rainy weather, others in the morning or during bright sunshine. A *curandera* knows each plant individually, understands its celestial, lunar, and seasonal cycles, its periods of greatest strength and declining potency."[10]

Drying Room of *yerbas y remedios* (Photo by Bobette Perrone)

While *curanderas total* are analogous to general practitioners and have the highest status, there are others, specialists in discrete areas of healing, who technically are not *curanderas total*. A *yerbera* (herbalist) works with herbs alone and does not put her hands on patients, but she may, nevertheless, be called a *curandera*. A *partera* is a midwife, but she may also use herbs during the course of prenatal care; she may be a *yerbera* and a *curandera* as well. Additionally, labels attached to traditional healers may vary from village to village or town to town, so that a woman who is called a *curandera* in one location may be called a *medica* in another.

Dr. Jaramillo discussed one genre of healer called a *sobardora*, who is a specialist in massage therapy, especially as it applies to the stomach and digestive tract. *Sobardoras* heal with their hands and supplement their efforts with herbal medications when appropriate, he said, but they rely more on acupressure applied to the affected areas for results than on the curative properties of herbs to alleviate their patient's ailments.[11] Jaramillo described *sobardoras* as specialists in muscle and bone manipulation as well—sisters to Western medicine's chiropractors and Chinese acupressurists.

Dr. Jaramillo believes *curanderas* inherit their power to heal, though some families with no heritage of healers will be given the "Don," translated as "gift" or, loosely, as the "heart."

"Legend has it that if a child cries in the womb," said Jaramillo, "she will be given the 'Don' and become a *curandera*."[12] So, it is truly a gift from God, either through heritage or as a result of a special designation from God, one that begins in utero with a fetus's tears. Both culminate in one of the most prestigious positions in traditional Hispanic society. The healers themselves naturally prefer the highest rung of the ladder and so they are all *curanderas*, regardless of their technical specialties.

Interestingly, if a *curandera total* needs advice in a particular area of treatment, she will call on a specialist. For example, she will consult the *yerbera* about certain herbs, or she will refer a pregnant woman to a *partera*. Jaramillo reported that in the network of Hispanic healers, most know each other and trust each other's judgment.

But, cautioned Jaramillo, there are also negative healers. These *brujas* (witches) have an extensive command of malevolent techniques of witchcraft and can cause great harm in the form of illness. They also analyze dreams, have premonitions, read cards, and indulge in other areas of the black arts. Dr. Jaramillo included *arbularias* in this group, putting himself at odds with Arthur L. Campa, a prominent researcher of traditional Hispanic societies. According to Campa, *arbularias* are the benevolent healers of the effects of witchcraft.[13] Marc Simmons, a prominent authority on witchcraft in the Southwest, supports Jaramillo's statement.[14] This type of confusion in nomenclature has been typical of this research experience.

Because *curanderas* are not as numerous as they once were, Jaramillo believes other specialists are moving quickly up the healing ladder. Traditional Hispanics now tend to utilize the services of the folk healer nearest their homes rather than undertaking a long journey to a renowned *curandera* in a village a hundred or so miles away. "The referral system depends nowadays on who's available," said Jaramillo with a shrug of his shoulders and some disappointment in his voice. "*Curanderas* are old, not as active as they once were . . . and not having the energy or time to put into their practice as they did before. The younger women are not moving into vacancies because of the lack of knowledge. . . . Many that are interested don't have the time to get involved and, being educated, they take off to New York or Los Angeles."

Because many contemporary Hispanics wish to acculturate, to seek the anonymity, acceptance, and achievements of the American melting pot, many traditional practices—including *curanderismo*—are fading. Many contemporary Hispanics see no need to bother with cultural healing. When they have sore throats, they go to a licensed physician and sit in the waiting room beside other patients of varying ethnic backgrounds, many of whom have either forsaken their own cultural healing methods or never knew them. By surrendering folk healing, today's Hispanic individual forsakes portions of the culture, family, and religion, and offers them as an initiation fee into American society. *Curanderismo* and *curanderas*, for generations one of the pillars of strength in the culture, are now the victims of acculturation. To many, sacrificing the emotional warmth and personal involvement of the *curandera* seems a high price to pay as an initiation fee. While there are some healers ready to replace the old *curanderas* once they are gone, the number of interested younger ones grows fewer as time passes. This is indeed a sad loss. *La curandera*, her traditional healing methods, and her cultural pharmacology, is truly becoming an endangered species.

Those who continue to practice must be willing to meet the many challenges. "We're always trying to maintain a positive, healthy image of traditional healing," says Jaramillo, "trying to neutralize the bad from the good, and that is why religion is really important, is *the* important factor in the treatment or part of the treatment of healing. It has to do with respect and the fear of the supernatural. And the equilibrium phase of the culture is that God fights against the devil. The Catholic religion is one of the positive influences on a patient, helping one recover. It's part of the integrated procedures, treatment, or techniques."[15]

All *curanderas* practice their art with a great deal of religious fervor. "En el nombre de Dios te voy a curar," many of them chant, or, "In the name of God, I will heal you." They are fully confident that Jesus, Mary, or the Holy Spirit is with them and, if it is willed, the sick patient before them will recover. Often the *curanderas* bring their own religious articles with them into the sickroom and arrange a small altar on the family's *mesita*, an end table. There, sometimes in the presence of the Angel of Death, they kneel and pray in front of their holy table with reverence and humility, asking the Blessed Virgin, the saints, or God for the ability to help the patient. Some of them stay until their knees hurt, rising only when the pain is too much to bear. The old ones get up slowly, leaning with one hand on the altar, before turning back toward the patient to continue a merciful vigil, their hearts filled with a new desire to help, their spirit refreshed from a religious communion.

Often in these homes a reproduction of a painting of the Last Supper is displayed prominently on a wall beside pictures of the saints or the Blessed Mother. Tucked into *nichos* in adobe walls are *santos*, plaster or wooden statues of saints who have special meaning to the family. In some northern New Mexico Hispanic homes, a statue of the Virgin, with fresh flowers at her feet, sits by itself on a dresser. Candles burn in various-sized glass containers. A Sacred-Heart-of-Jesus appliqué may be lighted from behind by a burning wick, casting a healing glow into the room. In a small corner, a makeshift altar will contain a wooden cross, palms from last year's Palm Sunday mass, rosary beads, more candles, and the Sunday Missal written in either Spanish or English. During the week, individual family members (usually women), kneel at the holy table and prepare themselves for Sunday morning, when the family and the community can all pray together at Mass.

But until then, if a loved one is ill and is being healed by a *curandera*, the family usually joins the healer at the patient's bedside to ask the Holy Ones for a miracle. Occasionally, they believe, *los milagros* occur, and the loved one recovers. When the lame walk again, it is the result, according to the *curanderas*, of the intercession of Saint Gudula, a woman revered for her ability to cure paralysis of all degrees and types.

Before she became a saint, Gudula, on leaving church, saw a poor mother carrying on her back a mute child who was crippled. The boy was bowed double and could not even feed himself. Gudula took the crippled child in her arms and prayed for God to have mercy on him. Immediately, his stubborn joints became supple, his back straightened, and he cried aloud, "See, Mother, see!" He leaped, ran, and skipped, rejoicing in his newfound strength. In her humility, Gudula begged the woman to tell no one, but the excited mother spread the news—and soon Gudula was widely known as the woman who performed the miracles.[16]

One popular Spanish saint, whose intercession is frequently requested by *curanderas*, is Teresa of Avila, the leader of the reforms within the Carmelite Order of nuns. Usually portrayed holding a crucifix and wearing a habit, this frail-looking, diminutive woman had the courage and stamina to establish sixteen convents despite censure, ridicule, and slander heaped against her by those within the church who were threatened by her piety and fearful of the impact the reforms would have on their comfortable ways of conducting affairs.

Religion is definitely a pillar of the Hispanic structure that reinforces family solidarity and reaffirms the family's commitment to Catholicism. Standing together in church on Sunday mornings, surrounded by relatives and friends, is proof to God that the family respects and reveres sacred teachings and welcomes holy blessings.

Generations of children have been reared in circumstances and traditions such as these, and the values have remained much the same through time: family, community, and church—constants in their world and as dependable as the accoutrements of Catholicism and the icons that have protected the family.

The intense, close contact within traditional Hispanic families gives rise to a fervid loyalty and stalwart allegiance to church and family that affects all aspects of the traditional culture, including healing.

Curanderas share these cultural values and emphasize one—great religious faith—as being the source of their talents and the fountainhead of their abilities. Their Hispanic heritage and the belief that they have been chosen by God to heal are the common threads in lives that are, in many respects, as different as their personalities. Regardless of what each is called on earth, however—*curandera, sobardora, partera*—their faith knows no such designations. They are healers.

But there is yet another aspect to the entire situation, a dimension not quite as obvious as the religious component in *curanderismo*, but a derivation of it. *Las curanderas* have challenged the normal female roles within their culture and have assumed the authority and leadership traditionally reserved for men. Even as youngsters, the healers never accepted the submissiveness and passivity that is the fate of nearly all traditional females in their societies. As a matter of fact, even in their earliest years, most *curanderas* knew they were different. They broke the rules in their own ways.

For example, among the *curanderas* we interviewed, Sabinita Herrera played hooky to pick herbs with her father despite her mother's wishes; Gregorita Rodriguez's forceful personality defied compliance; Jesusita Aragon "was never, never afraid to do anything."[17] These women represent the traditional ways, but they refused to be molded into stereotypes because they believed their destiny could not be determined by cultural standards that were designed on earth. Quite the contrary: *las curanderas* know their lives had been guided by God, and that reality is the only permission they need.

The *curanderas* utilize their strength, confidence, and courage to break out of traditional cultural roles reserved for women in Hispanic society. Ari Kiev, a prominent writer about the important traits of Hispanic folk culture, described an authoritarian family structure that, he said, perpetuated all the aspects of the comfortable status quo, including religion, male dominance, and social standing.[18] *Curanderas*, while seeming to be the exception to the documented patterns for women within their culture, do not really reject their heritage; they use its positive attributes, its structure—family and religion—as foundations on which to stand to call attention to themselves and their power to heal. Indeed, they are unique women. And they know it. While they share many characteristics, each of the *curanderas* we interviewed had her own style.

Sabinita Herrera's command of herself is apparent in the ease with which she welcomes strangers, and in her ability to be a friend. Gregorita Rodriguez is in immediate charge as she bustles around, chattering about the stomach and its problems and lambasting doctors who do not pay enough attention to loose organs. Jesusita Aragon is quiet and confident, sure of herself and her capabilities as a midwife.

It can be said that these *curanderas* are not sophisticated in terms of education or even in the modern ways of the world. It can be said that they have spent their years in the "back woods." It can also be said that they convey feeling of security and trust, an impression that they are well aware of everything and in total control of what they are doing. There is an ages-old glow about them that illuminates a visitor as well. Their spirituality was felt. Their power was sensed.

These are their stories.

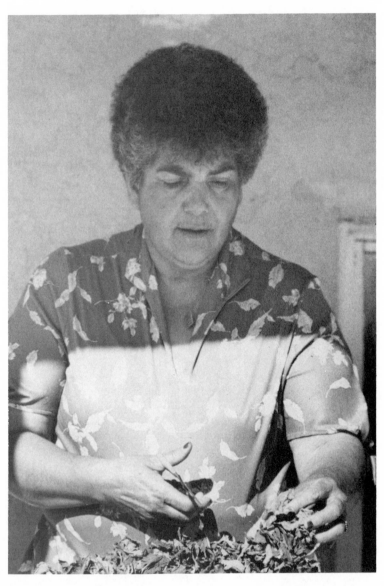

Sabinita Herrera: *la curandera y yerbera* (Photo by Bobette Perrone)

CHAPTER 7

SABINITA HERRERA
Curandera y Yerbera

We are learning from Sabinita Herrera, a *curandera* who lives in Truchas, New Mexico. Her physical presence alone is compelling, especially the vibrant quality she radiates that fills the rooms of her adobe home with a bubbling, lively spirit.[1] Sabinita seemed like an old friend to us when we first met her; her congeniality and warmth, the welcome in her eyes and her infectious grin made us feel that she was genuinely glad to see us, that we had been away too long.

Sabinita Herrera is a young-looking fifty-year-old Hispanic woman, born to and reared by traditions prevalent in northern New Mexico's mountain villages. She is solid and large, but not fleshy, as firm in her physique as she is in her mind. She knows what she wants, knows exactly what she says and does at any minute, even when she is distracted by a young granddaughter's demands for attention or by a pot boiling on her magnificent old wood stove. Standing beside this antique in the large, sunny kitchen is a more modern range, not always in use, but ready for service when all or some of her ten children and their own families appear at the same time. School pictures and snapshots of these children as young adults fill half a living room wall; twenty big eyes look across the room at a tapestrylike cloth, hanging behind a small-screened television set and portable stereo record player, depicting the Sacred Heart of Jesus. Between it and the door is a religious calendar advertising a mortuary. Plaster casts of saints and wax candles sit atop a room divider, the only separation the kitchen knows from the living room.

Sabinita is a happy woman and it shows—in her appearance, her joviality, her friendly style, and her obvious satisfaction with life in Truchas, a small, still-traditional Hispanic village. Although northern New Mexico's folk are not usually very mobile, Sabinita's family was an exception and set a pattern of individuality that she was to follow into adulthood. Sabinita was also very close to her father, another break with a traditional way of life that assigns girls to their mothers and boys to their fathers for socialization and cultural training. For two weeks at a time, father and daughter would take to the hills together with only a pack burro and horses for company. He was seventy-five years old and she was ten when he began to teach her the names of the roots and herbs growing amid the other splendors of Truchas Peak.

Mr. Trujillo also taught his little daughter how to respect the growing plants, saying, "When you dig for roots, you don't dig them all. You leave a few so the next time you come, you know where to find them."[2] Mrs. Trujillo protested these trips, preferring that her daughter attend school, but Sabinita "played hooky" and accompanied her father whenever she could, getting an education of a different sort, one that held her attention then and still does. Formal schooling was over at the seventh-grade level, but her education in *curanderismo* had just begun.

There was much to learn and a great deal of ground to cover. The land around Truchas is beautiful, high desert country, full of native vegetation, but a student of ethnobotany must know where to look. Learning the location of herbs is the first step and is in itself a glorious experience. The spirit feels free in these mountains, as blessed as the giant fir trees that stretch their tall arms to the clear blue heaven, even as their pine needles fall to the earth below. There is religion here in these hills, a way of God not confined to the brick and mortar of a church building, a feeling of healing loose in the earth, a perfect atmosphere to study the medicinal herbs in their natural settings. The clear mountain air, even thinner at this altitude than it is in town, seems crystalline, and in breathing deeply one can almost feel the sharp transparency of the oxygen. No foul air here, just purity, a beauty and chastity in idyllic surroundings made to order for a little girl and her father on an educational outing. On the ground, the rocks look up at teacher and pupil, forcing them to step aside, to jump over, to walk around. Filled with the warmth of the sun, boulders beckon tired bodies to lean on them, to rest a while and renew their strength. Ice-cold running streams invite the searchers to drink the same water the herbs do, the same snowmelt that refreshes the aspen trees along the secluded banks. Every so often, a cloud looks down on the vast classroom and blocks the hot sun for just a minute. Father and daughter relax, grateful for the interruption.

The old man's voice resounds on the mountain as he explains that dandelion is used for heart problems, *anil del muerto* is good for lung and liver problems, *altamisa de la sierra* lowers high blood pressure. The child stands, then crouches, her large eyes on the herbs, her ears attuned to her father's words. Day after day, they travel together until the child becomes familiar with the bountiful earth, with the private places special herbs grow and with the way to harvest them. Some are cut, some are clipped, some are pinched, some are pulled. But always, the teacher says, *always* leave some behind.

Occasionally the child was left behind, too, in her bed at home to recover from upper respiratory infections she caught in her outside classroom. "I was always out in the woods with my Dad and I used to come down with bad colds," she says as she points to a package of herbs. "*Inmortal*. We use it for heart problems, bronchitis, asthma, chest colds." When her head was clearer, when the fever was gone and the cough had stopped, she had other lessons to learn. Mr. Trujillo taught Sabinita how to prepare the herbs. He showed her how to clean them, then wash them, cut them, lay them in the shade to dry and explained that herbs lose their potency in the sun. Carefully selecting from among the native plants, he told her which ones go indoors to be placed on white-sheeted mattresses and which ones can remain outdoors. Roots dry in eight days whether indoors or not, he instructed, but most *remedios* (other than roots) take a day or so less to complete the process.

On other occasions, they ventured down the mountain to the land near Chimayo, a highly fertile region with excellent growing soil; an area, according to the folk, vested with religious mystique because of a special blessing from God. Legend has it that an old Spanish farmer saw a vision of Saint Esquipula in Chimayo and was cured of his rheumatic ailments. At the site of the vision a church has been built, and on the exact spot where the saint appeared, the earth is sacred. Pilgrims come from miles around to touch the earth, to step into the spot and absorb the energy and the power inside the small, dirt-filled well, to take a bit of it back with them to heal their afflictions, to petition God for relief from their many ills, and to offer prayers of thanksgiving for special favors.

On Good Fridays the pious of all ethnic backgrounds (Anglo, Hispanic, Indian) march for miles along the sides of roads from their northern villages toward the shrine at Chimayo. Some struggle under huge and heavy hand-hewn pine crosses, others travel in motorized wheelchairs, a veteran may double-time in Army fatigues, the elders walk slowly, the young race to fulfill promises. They come, hundreds of them, including the vigorous archbishop of Santa Fe, who usually treks a distance of twenty-four miles in the dirt from the nearest village, blessing the pilgrims with a wave of his hand and smiling his encouragement. Many who journey are Pueblo Indians who combine Catholic and non-Catholic tradition in their daily lives. But on Good Fridays, during the pilgrimage to Chimayo, the religion of the conquistadors prevails and dominates their lives. The folk believe that all of Chimayo has been blessed—and so it seems, to outside observers. Within a surrounding arid environment, everything grows abundantly in Chimayo—flowers, corn, chile, vegetables, fruit—especially *la flor de Santa Rita,* an herb used as a diuretic, one that Sabinita's father pointed out to her early in the lessons.

Sabinita learned her instructions and applied the *remedios* to ailments as she was growing up and after she was married and had started her own family. She treated her youngsters at home with the remedies she remembered from her classroom days in the hills and, like her father, passed on the information. "When I was bringing up the kids," she says, "I didn't have the time to work with my herbs. But if somebody came to ask for help, I'd tell them where to get it or I would go out and help them." Rearing ten children took all of her time until fate in 1967 swung her back on course, back to doing what she loved to do—working with herbs.

The Truchas Medical Clinic was in the planning stages in the late 1960s and, as is so common in a small village, word of mouth about Sabinita's skills reached the prospective director, David Trujillo (no relation). David convinced Sabinita, who was pregnant at the time with her last child, to work with the clinic, saying, "You are about the only one who knows the herbs, and the people are interested." After her little boy was born, Sabinita seriously considered the offer and was eventually selected as an herbalist associated with the Truchas Clinic. She easily passed the entrance exam, a plant identification test, and went back into the hills, this time alone, to gather herbs for the clinic's use with patients who demanded the natural *remedios*. In looking back over the decision to help the clinic, she said: "After I had my little boy, I really got interested in working with my herbs. I like to be free out in the mountains. I don't like to be locked up in a kitchen. So, I decided it was a way to make a living, and I do make a living with my herbs, just to keep us going— because it's expensive nowadays."

Says Sabinita, talking about the herbs growing wild in northern New Mexico, "God put them there so we can all share." But she objects to the secrecy some of her colleagues exhibit as part of their own healing ways. "There are people who won't give you advice at all. I ask them where to find a *remedio* and they won't tell me where to find it. They'll say, 'Well, I'll show you,' but when the time comes they say, 'I don't think I remember what it looks like,' even though they may know it. It's not good to keep it to yourself. I'll be here today and maybe I won't be here tomorrow. My Dad used to tell me, 'God gave us these *yerbas* [herbs] so that we could use them and whoever has it in their head gathers them for the rest of the people so that it will help them.' That's the best part of it."

Sabinita's sharing puts her in a class with most other *curanderas*, all of whom feel their special gift from God carries with it an obligation to help the sick, just as Jesus did. "Yes," she says, "I think my gift of healing was from the Lord, that the Lord reached down and said, 'Sabinita, this is what you're going to do.' It feels just like I've come out of Mass every day."[3]

Most *curanderas* believe their concepts are uncomplicated. God put the herbs on earth, they believe, and then selected certain people through whom to channel healing graces. Each chosen person knows at an early age that she has a special task on earth, one that is chosen for her by God and that she will follow with divine guidance.

In addition to believing that they personally have been selected by God to heal the sick, Sabinita Herrera and other *curanderas* fully accept the responsibilities this entails. Like medicine women and women doctors, *curanderas* put the art of healing first. If it is necessary to remain with a sick patient, the *curandera* is absent from her home and family, supper won't be ready, a celebration may be missed, the family's needs are attended to later, and so on. Yet, despite the demands on them, *curanderas* who were interviewed said they had learned at an early age how to juggle their time. Each of the women had ample forewarning of what was to come: the feeling, knowledge, and acceptance of the fact that they would be healers was always with them, bone-deep and spirit-high. "I always knew,"[4] they said again and again; they had been born to it. The pull toward the practice of healing is so strong that it is almost never ignored. After all, it is not she who chooses her path; she has been appointed by God.

Sabinita's deeply personal faith is an essential part of *curanderismo* and is a trait she shares with her *curandera* colleagues, ancient and modern. Although they have the power to call upon the saints for help, *curanderas* are still mortal, and every now and then they show concrete evidence of their own mortality by, of all things, getting sick themselves. Sabinita has high blood pressure, for which she takes raw garlic three times a day and says she is now doing well. And then there is *encerado*, Sabinita's name for an ointment she makes from a secret recipe she concocted to cure her severe case of acne. It healed her face and then worked so well on her son's pony's flesh injury that a veterinarian was astounded. A professor from the University of Arizona who met Sabinita at a folk festival offered her five hundred dollars for the recipe, but she politely refused.

She also refuses to take standard medications, including inhalers, for a serious case of asthma that she has had since childhood. "I used to get allergy shots because I was allergic to some of my *yerbas*," she said. "There's about three or four of them that I cannot work with. Everytime I work with them, I go to the clinic to have a shot, and the nurses gave me a mask to use when I pack them in sacks. But now, I take my own *remedios* and it works just as well."[5]

Many of the curative herbs work well, so well, in fact, that the medical and pharmaceutical professions use them as part of their own modern *materia medica*. "Most of my *remedios* have been used for pills," Sabinita proudly reports. "Like the *osha* roots for cough drops, the *inmortal* for high blood pressure pills. *Amole* is used for shampoo, and *estafiate* and *punchon cimmaron* are in asthma pills (sic)."[6]

Just as AMA physicians have regard for one another's expertise, so *curandero* José Ortiz y Pino has words of praise for Sabinita Herrera, saying, "Sabinita is a very significant and accomplished healer who is strong, powerful, sensitive, and dedicated. She is a woman who has given herself over to the art of healing in a very committed, deep, spiritual way."[7]

Gregorita Rodriguez: *la curandera y sobradora* (Photo courtesy Rodriguez collection)

CHAPTER 8

GREGORITA RODRIGUEZ
Curandera y Sobardora

Gregorita Rodriguez, a *curandera* currently practicing in Santa Fe, New Mexico, relies faithfully on her own combination of factors— religion, *remedios*, and rubbing—to help her heal. She calls frequently upon Saint Teresa of Avila as her strong hands massage the stiff muscles on a patient's neck. "Some patients say I have miracle hands," Gregorita says. "I just say God put me in his place to heal." [1]

We first met this spry, healthy-looking woman in her late eighties (in 1988) at a New Mexico political function in the early 1970s. She was surrounded by incumbents and candidates for local offices, all of whom sought her political support, not her medical advice. In Santa Fe, Gregorita Rodriguez is a political powerhouse, perhaps the only Hispanic woman left in a changing town whose ties into the large ethnic community can control and guarantee a block of votes any contender would be happy to have. And she loves politics almost as much as she loves *curanderismo*. Gregorita (no one calls her by her last name) has been a delegate to state political conventions, is active in senior citizens' lobbying efforts at the state legislature, works at the polls, and receives prominent politicians informally in her kitchen, where herbs may be boiling on the stove or a patient with a painful bellyache may be lying in Gregorita's own bed waiting to receive her ministrations while she tells the politician what it will take to get votes, votes, and more votes.

Our introduction to Gregorita, a *sobardora* who uses her hands to relieve abdominal symptoms more than she relies on herbs, came in the roundabout way that the folk culture in northern New Mexico still prefers. We knew a woman politico who had known Gregorita for years and was willing to call her and make an appointment for us over the phone. They chatted for about fifteen minutes in Spanish, each woman expressing her own worries about the sorry state of politics and the vanishing *patron* system, each lamenting the election defeat of a strong coalition of liberal legislative leaders. "Oh, by the way, Senora," our friend finally said as we sat beside her nervously, "I have some friends, *dos gringas*, who want to talk to you about *curanderismo*. When can you see them?"[2]

About a week later, as Gregorita opened her screen door and showed us through the sun room into the kitchen, our first impression was of sparkling cleanliness and total order. The linoleum floor was shiny-smooth with what appeared to be a freshly applied coat of wax; in one corner was an old washing machine, its wringer covered with clear plastic. We took care not to brush up against its tub as we made our way toward the kitchen table in the middle of the room. The stove was immaculate; the sink was scrubbed and had not one dish sitting in it. A representation of the Virgin of Guadalupe, wearing her blue cape with arms outstretched in welcome, overlooked the scene, framed in an ornate design pressed out of Mexican tin.

Gregorita gestured at us to sit down. "The doctors don't know anything about the stomach," she said, "and the *curanderas* know everything."[3] Gregorita produced a technicolor medical chart from a box beneath the table to show us the positions of organs in the abdominal cavity. Pointing to the pancreas, she explained, "The pancreas is the most dangerous sickness in the stomach. Sometimes you get weak, sometimes your appetite goes away and you can't eat or anything. So, the pancreas is loose. It is out of order and you can feel it jumping in your stomach. The *curanderas* put it in order and the doctors don't know nothing about it."

Gregorita traces her own career as a *curandera* back to her grandmother Juliana Montoya, who taught Gregorita's aunt, Valentina Romero, the art of *curanderismo*. When any of Gregorita's seventeen children became ill, she took them to her Aunt Valentina for treatment. *La curandera* taught Gregorita, encouraging her by asking, "Why don't you learn? Look, touch here." Using her children's bellies as a classroom, Gregorita felt the different abdominal disorders and learned how to manipulate the intestines to relieve the ailments. Another of her patients during this learning period was her husband. Responding to his complaints, Gregorita said, "Maybe I can do something for you." Mr. Rodriguez replied, "No, no no! You are not going to boss me!" So, off he went to see Aunt Valentina, who was elsewhere delivering a baby. Finally, Gregorita got her chance. Her husband was desperate and allowed her to learn, all the time howling about how much she was hurting him. "Cranky," she described him, "especially when I felt a big ball in his stomach and had to work very hard. Slow, slow, I fixed him and he got better. When he went to my aunt, she said he was okay now. After that I treated my husband and one of my sisters and then, her family. That's the way it started."

After that, the neighbors began to come for treatment of their various ailments and her reputation grew, but she was reluctant to continue her work while her aunt was still alive, not wanting to compete within the family. In 1950, Aunt Valentina died and Gregorita came into her own, her credibility already well established.

She began to practice *curanderismo* with the fiery, competitive aspect of her personality. The energy she emits through her words is akin to the power in her hands, and both factors are the by-products of her supreme self-confidence. She believes so strongly in her God-given ability to heal that she holds the medical profession and its scientific techniques in near contempt.

"A *curandera* is more than a doctor," Gregorita says firmly. "Doctors don't know the system of the stomach and they cure with pills. The *curanderas* cure with their minds, with their experience, and with herbs. With love to the people. That's what I feel. You have to know. Your intelligence and your experience tells you what the cure is. Sometimes the color will tell you. Sometimes they are very pale. I know that they are weak. And then I touch them."

In her touch, she feels, is the magic that she transmits from herself to her patients, a special feeling that flows from her hands to ailing bodies. "The first time I touched a person, I said, 'I'm gonna touch this person in the name of the Father and the Son and the Holy Spirit.' I don't separate my healing from my faith," she proclaims with a great deal of confidence.

More and more people came to her for treatment, some for herbal remedies, but most for massages. "I was always learning, learning, learning. I was not busy in going around with my friends and neighbors, but sometimes they came. I didn't like it because I was busy reading books," she complained.

Gregorita's formal education began in 1916 at the Loretto Academy, a Catholic girls' school in Santa Fe. Tuition was minimal, but her father died and the family could not afford to keep her in school. So she made a bargain with the nuns. She scrubbed floors and cleaned and, because they liked her, the sisters let her stay and even lightened her load the next year. She washed napkins and towels in return for her lessons and learned at a young age the effort it takes to achieve and to accomplish goals, whether they be educational, social, or religious. Dedication and perseverance are two of the lessons Gregorita learned at Loretto, characteristics that she still exhibits today, nearly seventy years later.

She tries to impart her experience to her students, nine in number, but only one of whom she considers promising, a possible competitor or eventual replacement if she decides to stop practicing. It is difficult for Gregorita to imagine retiring. She so deeply feels her obligation and ability to heal that any thought of surrender is a personal affront. Medical doctors, too, offend her; they don't impress her very much with their Western scientific methods and procedures. As a matter of fact, there is a continuing war going on, a battle between Gregorita and the medical profession, that keeps her at odds with certain local physicians. She does not hesitate to point out to doctors and other members of the health care industry exactly where they are in error.

When Gregorita was hospitalized as a result of an automobile accident, a chest x-ray revealed the possibility of pleural fluid or a possible blood clot in her lungs, something Gregorita did not believe, and a diagnosis that made her quite angry. "Don't give me any of your pills, your damned pills!" she loudly complained. "I don't want it. I know how they are." Eight x-rays later, the broken ribs appeared and blood tests were ordered. "I don't have nothing in my blood," she insisted, as a lab technician stood over her, poised to find a vein for the needle. "I'm not going to give you anything. I'm going home! You are selling my blood." The doctors canceled the tests.

That reaction was mild compared to the fight she puts up for friends or relatives, or relatives of friends, when they are being treated in the local hospital. Gregorita actually examines patients at their hospital bedsides and, on at least one occasion, she took a very ill woman home for treatment she considered more appropriate.

Gregorita diagnosed her patient as having a spleen that "jumped," and massaged her with strong hands, over and over again, all through the night. She poured eggnog with cinnamon into her patient's mouth and put thick towels soaked in cold water onto her abdomen. The next afternoon, the woman was singing and combing her hair, proof positive according to Gregorita that the patient had recovered from the ordeal because of *la curandera's* healing skills.

The showdown came when *la curandera* took the patient for a follow-up visit to the attending physician. He remarked how well his patient looked, and inadvertently opened up a hornet's nest. "Well, Doctor," Gregorita said, "I think that you must be ashamed of yourself. Doctor, you scare people first. Why did you spend so much money to get your degree and you don't know nothing?" At first he did not answer, then mumbled something that only served to spur her on. "Doctor, I hate to tell you," she said, "you are not a doctor because you don't know where the heart is and where the spleen is. This lady had the spleen loose and you said it was heart trouble. Now look. She is healthy. I heal her."

Needless to say, Gregorita's actions do not endear her to the medical profession, and she knows it—but she persists, believing in herself and in her cures, ready to lend her hands to those who have faith in her, her healing, and in her traditional ways. One concession Gregorita has made to modern science is to become licensed to massage. "I got it from the massage doctors in Albuquerque," she says, speaking of her diploma. "They introduced me to the board, you know, and then the board gave me the license. I paid $185.00 for it. I have to renew it every year."[4]

While the license gives Gregorita a legitimacy in the eyes of society and enables her to charge a fee for her services, it does not confer any type of status on her. She will search for the diploma and show it around when asked, but it does not hang on a wall and announce her credibility, as physicians' certificates do in their offices. Instead, pictures of Jesus and Mary, the saints, a wooden crucifix, all highly visible throughout her house, give Gregorita all the permission she needs to perform her healing rituals. When she is alone, she prays for strength to continue her important work, for her own well-being so she can heal others, and to offer special petitions for her sick patients. Convinced that the Holy Spirit flows through her hands into

ailing bodies, she prays for the ability and the right to continue healing, to go on putting her heart, her mind, her hands, her religion to
work for others—to be able to put her hands on their bellies and
make them well. It is no easy task, yet Gregorita is very good at it,
almost an expert in abdominal disorders, and capable of feeling with
her hands what physicians see on x-rays, others have said.

Gregorita Rodriguez likes Saint Catherine, a woman who, in her
mortal life, used her hands to restore life to a coachman. Overtaken
with sleep, the man fell from his coach box onto his head, and the
wheels of the carriage rolled over him. Catherine, then a Swedish
princess, went to the man, touched his hand, and he rose immediately—safe and sound. Another time, a workman toppled off of a
roof and was so mutilated by the fall that he could not be moved.
Catherine touched the body and the man was perfectly restored and
able to return to his work the same day.[5] Gregorita's hands, too,
work their "miracles," not exactly in the same way, but in ways that
relieve the modern ailments afflicting her patients.

One of the abdominal conditions causing Hispanic folk a great
deal of distress is *empacho*, an ailment Gregorita claims to cure practically with one hand behind her back. *Empacho* has been likened
to blocked intestines, constipation, indigestion, and various other
gastrointestinal disorders. Bloating accompanied by a bellyache is
the most common symptom in adults; in children, vomiting may
occur. Gregorita palpates the stomach and locates the hard spot
where the *empacho* has settled. Then, she goes to work. Through
careful but firm massage, kneading, pushing, and shoving, she ma-
nipulates the area of resistance and softens it. In effect, her hands
destroy the *empacho*, moving it along so that the natural processes of
elimination can take over.

Western scientific medicine would undoubtedly have a different
treatment for the same ailment and this cure would certainly arouse
Gregorita's ire. It may be difficult at first to understand her disdain-
ful attitude toward the medical profession, but it becomes clearer
when one discovers a hidden dimension to the matter. Gregorita is a
deeply religious woman who is quite humble when discussing her
faith. She sincerely believes she heals through God's will. Why,
then, should she honor those who use mere secular techniques to
achieve the same result? To Gregorita Rodriguez, physicians have no

religious legitimacy, whereas she does, and that is what matters. And each time Gregorita cures a patient she believes the doctors cannot, she reaffirms her own prowess and diminishes the medical profession in the eyes of her followers in the northern New Mexico Hispanic community. Because Gregorita's success at healing has been remarkable, she is, by reputation, quite a powerful *curandera*.

Jesusita Aragon: *la curandera y partera* (Photo by Bobette Perrone)

CHAPTER 9

JESUSITA ARAGON
Curandera y Partera

Jesusita Aragon, of Las Vegas, New Mexico, has spent all of her adult life as a *partera*, a midwife, and has delivered more than twenty thousand babies—including twenty-five sets of twins and two groups of triplets, according to her own records.[1]

Seventy-seven years old when last interviewed by us, in 1984, Jesusita got her training from her grandmother beginning in 1923, when she was only thirteen years old. Jesusita's classroom was the birthing bed, full of agonizing screams, wet with sweat, blood, and fluid—for a young girl quite an experience with life and with death, which sometimes brought its own force into the room. Jesusita stood beside her grandmother and saw the Biblical curse upon women made real time after time—babies born dead or alive amid torment and great suffering—a woman's reward for being female.

Born on a ranch, Jesusita began her experiences with birthing at a very young age, well before she was apprenticed to her grandmother. But, pulling a calf while a cow bellows is different from helping a woman give birth. Or is it? The promise of pain in childbirth to all women since Eve extends across the species into the animal kingdom, something Jesusita might have thought of as her small hand put a cold cloth on a laboring woman's forehead.

Headless babies, infants with deformed and bleeding spines, tiny rotting fingers being expelled separately, one at a time in some cases—Jesusita had seen it all before she was fifteen. Blood, blood, and more blood in the bed, on the floor, sometimes even soaking into the whitewashed adobe walls, was part of her young life—as were the shrieks, the grunts, the desperate pleas for God's mercy, unanswered until after the moment of birth.

But a girl of thirteen in those days was quite different from one of today's teenagers. At that age, she was just about ready for marriage; all it took was menstrual blood to announce her eligibility. A red stain on her underwear, and off she went into a prearranged marriage—one that would profit both families and would produce many children to help with the work. At thirteen, a ranch girl was already becoming tired. She had probably reared two or three younger siblings, could cook a meal for any number of ranch hands, and certainly knew what life was all about. Birthing was a breeze.

It was an especially happy event when all went well, when mother and infant came through the process easily with no apparent complications. The experience itself is a spiritual one; the "miracle of birth" is just that. Filled with wonder each time she participated in childbirth, young Jesusita must have felt again and again the absolute and overwhelming grace of the Lord fill the room each time a healthy baby was born. At the moment of birth, an observer senses what the witnesses to Christ's miracles claimed—awe, reverence, personal insignificance, and the presence of a power much greater than mortals could ever know. No wonder Jesusita chose midwifery as her life's work; no wonder she did not deny her desire, sent from above, to help mothers-to-be bring their newborns into the world.

"I wanted to be a midwife, that's all,"[2] Jesusita says modestly. Her grandmother recognized her abilities, and they talked, the old and the young, every day. The girl learned herbal remedies for each condition and how to examine a patient, first one way, and then another. Grandmother taught Jesusita other lessons, too—patience, how to take care of herself, and the fact that all people are different. Most important, she taught her granddaughter how to touch. "I touch the people as soft as I can, like my grandmother showed me," says Jesusita softly, paying tribute to instructions issued many, many years ago. Until she was forty years old, she worked beside her teacher and then, alone, she began her own career—one that has led her to many birthing beds and into cooperation and confrontation with the medical profession.

Women doctors have worked closely with Jesusita, training and teaching her the AMA aspects of obstetrics. Forty-five years ago, she attended a tuition-free class sponsored by a government entity whose name she no longer recalls. A Dr. Millikan, well known in the predominantly rural areas of northern New Mexico, was one of her mentors, a woman who took her time with the midwife, encouraged her, and supported her emotionally. True, Jesusita brought skills and experience in birthing techniques to the classroom, but Dr. Millikan refined them and taught her some of the AMA methods of delivery. Building Jesusita's confidence, Dr. Millikan saw more than a ranch woman/midwife with a limited formal education; she saw the potential and the dedication. Jesusita told us that Dr. Millikan said, "If I knew you when you were young, I'd take you to a good school and make you a doctor." Her faith in her student endured for many years. When Dr. Millikan retired from the profession, she gave Jesusita her medical instruments.

Jesusita Aragon has other tales to tell about her work, stories of situations all too familiar in traditional and contemporary obstetrical practices. Fearing a breech presentation in one of her laboring patients, Jesusita took the mother-to-be to a hospital after several efforts at manipulation had failed to change the fetal position. An obstetrician approached the midwife and her patient, a gloved hand ready to show Jesusita how it was done. During the examination, he turned to *la partera* and bluntly said, "This baby doesn't have a head." Over the frightened and anguished cries of the pregnant woman who had heard it all, Jesusita held her ground, insisting that the child was perfectly formed. "No, sir!" she protested. "That baby has a head." The doctor kept trying to turn the fetus, hurting Jesusita as much as the woman. At long last, he delivered the baby, head first. "So, I know better than you," she said, and continued to berate the doctor, telling him he did not have to scare the patient. "He didn't like it, but I told him anyway."

Those physicians who are able to deal with Jesusita on a more professional level find the association to be rewarding. Jesusita considers many doctors to be her personal friends, and they are. Doctor and midwife respect each other's judgments, do each other favors, and speak freely between themselves. Jesusita called one of her gynecologist friends on a patient's behalf and gave him a complete medical evaluation before referring her patient for surgery. The physician confirmed her findings and diagnosis postoperatively.

Another doctor, trying to be helpful, called Jesusita to his office for a lesson on how to hear a fetal heartbeat through a special stethoscope placed on the mother's belly. "I don't need that," she said, handing the instrument back to the doctor. Puzzled, he watched her move her hands across the woman's abdomen. "Put your instrument here and listen to the heart," she instructed the obstetrician, "the heartbeat is here." She was correct. Jesusita had listened to the pulse with her fingers, totally astounding the doctor.

An ability to perceive with all of the senses, some directly related to the immediate situation, some not, is what makes Jesusita the superb *partera* she has been for more than a half a century. "Intuition," she calls it, but added to that quality must be her training, experience, and deep faith in God. "It is a gift that God gave me," she says, speaking of her talents and telling a story about her favorite saint, Santo Niño de Atocha.

While traveling around the countryside, as she did in the years before she turned seventy-seven, Mrs. Aragon heard of a man who liked to slap his wife. One day, he became even more violent; he tried to stab his spouse, and the frightened woman called for help. "Santo Niño de Atocha, help me!" The man instantly stopped abusing her—and that, according to *la partera*, "was a miracle."[3]

Invoking the saints' names, calling upon the Holy Trinity or the Blessed Virgin, and making the sign of the cross are among the religious actions of the healers. It is believed that Saint Galla went into a house full of sick people, including a child who was deaf and dumb, where he blessed a glass of water with the sign of the cross and gave it to the child. Immediately the child's ears were opened and his tongue was loosed.[4] Saint Francis of Assisi sent a sick man to Saint Clara to be healed, and she did it by simply making the sign of the cross over him. After that, many who had infirmities went to the Convent of Saint Clara and were healed by her blessing. Saint Brigit healed a leper by making the sign of a cross over a basin of water and telling him to wash himself. His leprosy vanished, but when she instructed him to wash his companion, also a leper, the man refused. Instantly his disease returned, but his companion was cured.[5]

Faith, like every other plant in a spiritual garden, must be nurtured with love if it is to blossom—love of God and love of humankind. It is not difficult to tend one's garden, to "keep the faith," so to speak, when positive and reinforcing experiences happen consistently, when all of a *partera's* efforts are successful and all the babies are healthy. But to stand fast and firm, to still believe in the blessings of the Lord when infants are born dead or deformed, blind, imperfect, or hydrocephalic, and when young mothers die in childbirth from hemorrhages, from infections, and from exhaustion, requires a faith in the benevolence of the Almighty that few human beings can sustain over an indefinite period of time. Yet Jesusita's religion has been and is her mainstay. It keeps her going back for more and more birthing, to participate in yet another miracle from God. Her deep faith always sustains her regardless of whether she is alone, rendering prenatal care, or delivering a child.

Jesusita relies on her saints for endurance, too—for strength at her elderly age to continue her work. She trusts them all—San Antonio, San Martín de Poros, San Martín Caballero, San Lazaro, and her beloved Santo Niño de Atocha. They aid her in all ways, every day. When she is attending a birth, she prays for her patient, "Santo Niño de Atocha, help her . . . help everything come okay, the baby okay and everything."⁶ She says no one knows she is praying, but she prays fervently, trusting her heavenly helpers and putting her faith more in their powers than in her own. A nonbeliever, seeing pictures of saints in her home, told her once, "You don't need those things. You don't need those pictures." Quietly, she replied, "Well, I don't care. I believe in them." Another curious patient asked why she had a picture of John F. Kennedy beside her saints. "Because he was a good man," she said, "and I believe in him like I believe in my saints."⁷

PART THREE

WOMEN DOCTORS

CHAPTER 10

INTRODUCTION

That "the United States spends more each year on health care than it does on national defense"[1] is testimony to how highly the American culture values health and healing and the practice of medicine. Smallpox, tuberculosis, polio, and dozens of other deadly diseases have been nearly eradicated from civilization due to the availability of vaccines and antibiotics, the so-called "miracle" drugs of modern medicine. These drugs *would* have been seen as miracles as recently as fifty to one hundred years ago and, therefore, must be viewed in historical perspective: modern medicine is a very new 'science' in the scheme of history. Only in the last century have these drugs and other lifesaving medical techniques and treatments been part of our daily lives.

Anesthesia was not used until 1846; before then, patients were operated upon either while conscious or while unconscious with liquor. Antiseptic surgery ("wash your hands before operating") was not introduced until 1867. Sulfa and penicillin were discovered in the 1930s and not used widely until the 1940s. Not until the 1950s and the 1960s were vaccines against polio, measles, and other communicable diseases widely available and routinely disseminated. In the 1970s and 1980s, laser beams, dialysis machines, organ transplants, and CAT scans have become commonplace.

As a contemporary society, we tend to take these medical discoveries for granted, believing that they have always been with us, have always been an essential part of the medical regimen; they have not. Yet, though western scientific medicine is still in its historical infancy, futuristic technological weapons for fighting diseases, diagnostic proficiency resulting from computerized data bases, and treatment capabilities derived from a combination of sophisticated scientific sources are being developed on a scale heretofore unimagined in history; it is astounding.

Dr. Lewis Thomas, Chancellor of Memorial Sloan-Kettering Cancer Center, in New York, states in his book *The Youngest Science: Notes of a Medicine Watcher* that medicine went from "a profoundly ignorant profession to a technology based on science."[2] It is not surprising that there are growing pains: the focus on specialization and procedures instead of the total patient; on the physical rather than the psychological aspects of illness; on the individual, ignoring the social support system; on the selection process for medical students that emphasizes scientific and technical skills over the interpersonal.

An important aspect of contemporary health care is the American Medical Association. Its familiar acronym, AMA, will be used in part three to designate physicians trained in American medical schools and who have completed internships and residencies in hospitals accredited by the American Hospital Association. The American Medical Association is an organization of respected, licensed, and sanctioned medical practitioners who utilize healing techniques based on Western scientific principles. These doctors cut open bodies and heads, remove and transplant organs, and evacuate blood clots clinging to brain cells. They deliver babies, inoculate, regulate the body, inject radioactive tracers into bloodstreams, and chart the heart's electrical impulses. They probe, penetrate, and peer.

Very few Americans have not made use of the services of AMA physicians at some time in their lives—whether to be born, to be healed, or to die with less pain. Most Americans have gained, in one way or another, from the scientific aspects and advances of Western medical science. However, in the acquisition of such adroit technology, there have also been significant losses. Health care consumers are complaining that AMA-trained physicians lack warmth, are not interested in interacting with their patients, are inconsiderate, and prefer technical expertise to human compassion. Stories are swapped about physicians being overheard making statements such as, "I'm going to see the gallbladder in room 253" or "the liver in room 472." Such statements describe a "parts-versus-the-whole" concept of the human body and psyche, an idea that has become distasteful to many.

Perhaps the AMA form of medicine, which arose during the same historical period as the industrial revolution, borrowed from industry's parts-on-an-assembly-line concept. One could be a specialist in carburetors or spark plugs in an automobile factory, just as one might become a heart specialist or a brain surgeon. As a worker, one did not see the entire car assembled, only a part of the whole.

This approach leads to fine-tuning specialists in small technical areas but neglects the broader picture, be it of an automobile or of a patient. Older healing traditions, those practiced by Native American medicine women and Hispanic *curanderas*, treat an ailing person from a perspective that encompasses the total being, rather than a discrete segment or part. "Patients gripe that the products of this [current medical] regimen, the current crop of doctors, have no compassion, run their practices like assembly lines, and are more fascinated by tests and procedures than by the human beings they treat. Medical school deans and faculty members worry about turning out narrow-minded, unenthusiastic graduates who have little perspective on the facts they have swallowed. . . . [The] Dean of Johns Hopkins School of Medicine . . . says, 'We would like to reverse the trend toward early specialization and over-emphasis on science as preparation for medicine.'"[3] This quote, from a popular mass media magazine, is echoed in the *New England Journal of Medicine,* one of the most credible medical journals published. "For various reasons there seems to be an increasing dissatisfaction with certain aspects of conventional or orthodox medicine. . . . The view that there is a growing loss of faith by the public in a purely scientific approach to medicine."[4]

The age of specialization has been a significant factor in patient dissatisfaction. People are unhappy, not with the idea of specialization per se, but with the fact that when the concept is applied, an impersonal remoteness between doctor and patient results. This by-product is unacceptable in a profession whose hallmark was once a relationship of caring and trust.

Paradoxically, high technology processes are another factor contributing to health care consumers' discontent, even though these techniques may some day save their lives. By their very nature these treatment methods are procedure-oriented rather than patient-centered, and the close relationship between doctor and patient is once again sacrificed.

Economics have also dictated a "procedure" model of health care, in which monies from insurance companies and the government (the largest single purchaser of health care in America, through Medicare, Medicaid, etc.) have paid physicians for performing procedures but not for sitting down and talking with and understanding a patient.

One notable interview was with a woman chief of surgery at a well-known metropolitan hospital. The physician said she chose surgery as her specialty because "there are more procedures. Translated, that means money per procedure." Unfortunately, at the final hour, this doctor withdrew from our study, stating, "I am not a healer. I am a survivor of medical school." At least knowing that was to her credit.

The trend toward specialization and procedures, and away from personal interaction between doctor and patient, has been due to a mixture of causes: the legacy of the industrial revolution; the sheer volume of technical information available, needed, and required to complete the board certification exams in a given specialty (and almost all doctors specialize after taking the relevant examination); the training techniques and attitudes in medical schools, where, among other things, a forty-thousand-word vocabulary is added to the word-stock of each physician in training; of course, the financial system of rewards to physicians; and the selection process that has significantly, specifically, and especially excluded the selection of women. Historically, Western medicine has been a difficult field for women to enter because of the "For Men Only" sign on the door. But some went in anyway.

There was Mary Walker, M.D. Her situation was unique and so controversial that she is still being debated and analyzed in medical history documents today, nearly seventy years after her death. Born into a literate and educated family on November 26, 1832, in Oswego, New York, Mary Walker was educated at a private school just twelve miles from her home. At an early age, she became obsessed with the study of medicine and, encouraged by her physician father, continued her interest despite the fact that she knew medical schools accepted only male applicants. At her private school, she elected to take a course in anatomy, and on the first day of classes, the male students walked out, beginning a series of reactions against which she would consistently rebel during her long life.

Walker won admission to Syracuse Medical College, where she was the only woman in her class and one of only two students who survived the academic rigors to graduate in 1855. The other was her future husband, Albert E. Miller, M.D. Together they established a medical practice in Rome, New York, but Mary's participation was short. She became interested in a feminist movement and joined Amelia Bloomer and Elizabeth Cady Stanton in trying to achieve parity with men in dress code and admission to medical schools.

Then the Civil War erupted, and the Union Army, in 1864, commissioned Mary Walker as a surgeon despite the fact that many army medical officers were reluctant to entrust "the lives of sick and wounded men to such a medical monstrosity."[5] Alone on the battlefields, she worked among the wounded until she was captured by the Confederate forces and imprisoned in Virginia. Eventually the petite doctor was swapped for a Union prisoner, a tall medical officer from Tennessee. In June of 1865, Dr. Mary Walker was discharged and became the only woman in history to receive the Congressional Medal of Honor.

Her award was of no benefit to her, however. Her independence and persistence steered her in a direction of derision. The Medal of Honor was rescinded. Her reputation as a fighter was costly. She lobbied the New York legislature in an attempt to legalize what were then considered masculine clothes for women, and hounded Congress and the War Department for back pay allegedly never received during her military service. In every effort, she failed. While lecturing, she supported herself on a very small government pension. Nearly sixty years old at the end of the 1800s, she appeared in a circus, a freak in men's clothing giving lectures on dress reform.

In her heyday, Mary Walker kept her mind busy by making small contributions to the world around her. Some of her ideas remain in use today—the return notice for registered mail, the return address on envelopes, and the neckband inside shirt collars to protect one's neck from top buttons on shirts—gifts from Dr. Mary Walker to a society that discriminated against her, ridiculed her, and denied her the constitutional rights guaranteed to all people in a free nation.[6]

Mary Walker, M.D., just did not "fit in" as a woman doctor. She was shunned and ridiculed because she was a woman entering medicine, but she persevered and healed the sick whenever she could, despite the adversities imposed by male colleagues whose egos she threatened.

Among other courageous women who defied early prohibitions against females becoming physicians were Elizabeth Blackwell, awarded her M.D. degree from Geneva Medical College in 1849, and Linda Folger Fowler, who received a degree from New York's Rochester Eclectic Medical College in 1850. That same year, a woman who had been practicing medicine without a license for fifteen years, Harriet K. Hunt, tried and failed to be admitted to Harvard Medical School. Although she had been accepted as a student by Dean Oliver Wendell Holmes and the Harvard faculty, the all-male class reacted in uproar and submitted two petitions to the faculty that read:

> Resolved, that no woman of true delicacy would be willing in the presence of men to listen to the discussions of subjects that necessarily come under consideration of the student of medicine.
> Resolved, that we object to having the company of any female forced upon us who is disposed to unsex herself and to sacrifice her modesty by appearing with men in the medical lecture room.[7]

The faculty acquiesced and turned Harriet K. Hunt away, forcing her to illegitimately and illegally continue the practice of medicine without a diploma, while condemning her for doing so.

During the same era in American history, many women treated (as the frontier demanded) victims of accidents along the isolated trails west, and continued their ministrations once they were settled in the remote outposts they called their new homes. Elizabeth Perry, in 1845, at the age of seventeen, ventured from Iowa to Oregon and, having served as midwife to the pioneer caravan, collected herbs and roots for medicinal healing. She continued her work without a license for fifty years in Saint Helens, Oregon. Lillian Heath, of Rawlins, Wyoming, apprenticed herself to an accredited male physician, wore men's clothing to avoid detection, and carried two pistols. Calamity Jane treated victims of smallpox during an 1878 epidemic in Deadwood, South Dakota, because no one else would go near the patients. In the early days of the American West, women cared for the sick, women set broken bones, and women sewed wounds with cactus fiber. These women were unable to gain medical legitimacy through academic pursuits, but they did what was expected of them, got the job done without fanfare, without accolade, without public praise, and without recognition. By 1870, more than six hundred women were practicing their individual brand of medicine despite lack of certification in the United States.

Emily Blackwell, M.D., looking back over her career, commented, "We had held open the doors for women until broader gates had swung wide for their admission."[8] Maybe, maybe not. In 1949, fifty years after Dr. Blackwell's statement was published, a poll of one hundred hospital chiefs of staff recorded such remarks as: "Women doctors are emotionally unstable . . . they talk too much . . . they're always on the defensive . . . they get pregnant . . . if she is married and childless she is frustrated . . . or if she raises a family she is neglecting her practice."[9]

In 1875, Dr. A. E. Regensburger, of San Francisco, found it necessary to publicly denounce what he saw as a great threat to male physicians across the land. In an address to the state medical society, California's foremost dermatologist said, "Taken as a whole, they [the women practitioners] will never amount to much." Fortunately, many changes are now occurring with regard to women.

In recent years, medical schools have begun to pay attention to public opinion. They are beginning to teach subjects such as family practice medicine and bedside manners, and they are admitting more and more women to their institutions. In the late twentieth century, medical schools are acknowledging the need for necessary attitudinal changes by reducing their own institutionally sanctioned prejudices and by admitting more women. "As late as 1969, just 9% of students entering medical school were female. Today [January 1987], one-third are female."[10] The field now acknowledges that women doctors are an entity to be reckoned with.

Women in medicine have always had to be brave enough to do battle with the scientific community first and then with a society that accepted the male norm as the standard of excellence. "Women have never fared well in official institutions of science—past or present . . . Even now the vast majority of women scientists works only at the periphery. Women simply do not hold senior positions . . . from which they can guide the future course of science."[11]

Suppose they did. Would they direct tomorrow's medicine into the far reaches of the current scientific framework, thus enlarging the scope of male-oriented and paternalistically designed systems of providing health care? If the "task of making science less masculine is also the task of making it more completely human,"[12] then these women doctors are in the vanguard and are responsible for stimulating and causing these changes to begin.

One reason medical schools are selecting more women is that, as Professor Carol Gilligan states, "men in this culture tend to see the world in terms of their autonomy . . . and women tend to see the world in terms of connectedness."[13] Certain women doctors are today's representatives of the guiding principles for a new age— women who have fulfilled the total aspects of their personalities by harmoniously uniting the best of the masculine and feminine qualities that coexist in all of us. They integrate the best the historical cultures offer and the best modern technology offers with the best they themselves have to offer.

These women doctors have to be seen in the context of the medical profession and its own history. No woman becomes a doctor frivolously, half-heartedly, or for lack of anything better to do. Women are doctors first from a desire deep inside. A woman enters the field of medicine knowing certain things—she will have to be exceptional to compete, she will have to be certain of her ambitions, she will have to be in good health herself to endure the pace, and she will have to work hard to succeed. Most important, she must know she will be judged. Only strong women become doctors, and then only after painstaking testing by the system and by society.

Dr. Molly Radford Ward practiced medicine in the 1930s in a way that challenged society's usual perception of a physician. Dr. Ward had the fortitude to leave medicine several times, to walk away from her profession to take care of her family and be a wife to her husband, a happy priority for her. She was brave enough to go back to medical school after she was more than fifty years old to renew her knowledge before she reentered her profession.

Dr. Jane Patterson practices medicine with an acquired sensitivity and an acute awareness of feminist principles and theories that were never taught in medical school. Her forthrightness is important to her and enriches personal attributes that, in turn, help her to be the best physician that she can be. It takes immense courage to do that, a kind of valor different from that which helped her through medical school, but one that refines her even more completely as a human being and as a physician.

Dr. Stirling Puck practices genetic medicine softly and quietly and with dedication. She is unafraid to be a physician, wife, and mother simultaneously, and her ability successfully to combine motherhood and medicine is evidence of her intellectual and emotional ranges and of her strong wish to rear her children and treat her patients concurrently. She dared to say that discrimination in medical school did not affect her because she would not let it. Undaunted, she got through the height of the civil rights and women's movements as a sympathetic observer who, through the sheer force of her beliefs, refused to allow the biases she personally encountered to bother her, professionally or emotionally.

Dr. Josette Mondanaro, always socially conscious, has been a champion of the underdog, believing that doctors should serve the ills of humanity, including drug addiction, the victims of which are the pariahs of American society. While still in medical school, she had the courage to begin helping addicts, channeling her energies away from herself toward others who were less fortunate. Her idealism has remained, fed by her commitment and justified by her administration of a multimillion-dollar drug rehabilitation program. Her devotion to and treatment of patients whom society deliberately scorns clearly reflects an altruism that has defined the most gifted healers in the long, long history of international, cultural, and scientific medicine.

The successful women in medicine make up a self-selected group. Often from an early age they exhibited the attributes of strong dedication and persistence. When these women persevere in becoming physicians, they provide models and examples of what women can bring to the field of medicine. They can be viewed also as a specific population that makes a contribution by adding something different; they may modify Western medicine because they are women. Women physicians, like medicine women and *curanderas*, are different from each other and possibly from their male counterparts as well. Here are the stories of some who have succeeded.

Molly Radford Ward, M.D.: General Practitioner and Anesthesiologist
(Photo by Bobette Perrone)

CHAPTER 11

MOLLY RADFORD WARD, M.D.

She was seventy-eight years old when we were invited to her home, Los Piñones, on the Old Santa Fe Trail, and immediately she wanted to talk about the Olympic-sized swimming pool. It was the first of its kind in Santa Fe, she had designed it herself, and as a young woman she had mixed and set the mortar. She still does her laps. Daily. Wearing a bathing cap only. She still recalls the poolside parties, the good friends, and neighbors of the "swell" life in Santa Fe. She worries about her failing eyesight and is emphatically direct in her stance that there are no differences between female and male practitioners in her world of medicine. She started talking about her experiences as a doctor among other doctors. Then her own illnesses. And the tone changed. If the dedicated stance did not, the information seemed to. These are her words. This is her experience.

Molly Radford lived the idyllic childhood, learning to be herself while growing up on a private island purchased by her father in 1898, near Oshkosh, Wisconsin. In Dr. Ward's book, *Molly Radford, M.D.*, her mother writes: "As usual, I was looking for Molly. Even at age five she had a habit of suddenly not being where I thought she was. . . . I just happened to look high enough! There was my ragged, dirty tomboy perched on a limb . . . a good twelve feet above the ground. 'Molly, what are you doing up there?' The nonchalant child looked down at me and said, 'Oh, I always come up here when I want to be alone.'" [1]

During the summers Molly traveled in the old buggy, checking on the pups farmed out by her father, who developed the first all-white collies in the United States. She developed her swimming and boating skills in the lush lake surrounding her island, spending considerable time with Robert, her young playmate, climbing steep-roofed barns "to see what town looked like from there." Summer, too, was spent sliding down the wooden roof, and there were many "shrieks emitted . . . due to the sight of the needle"[2] used for removing splinters. While her sister played "lady doll," Molly was "usually being dragged out from under a pile of scrambled neighbor boys by the [neighbor's] cook who would say, 'Mrs. Radford, those bigger boys will be the death of your poor little girl yet!' Molly would reply only by pulling herself away to run back to the football or baseball game."[3] During winter, in town, the youngster took to ice ponds on skates of wood with double runners. During World War I, Molly and Robert dug six-foot-deep trenches and dugouts all summer long.

In 1923, Molly's mother discovered that her husband had taken a mortgage on the family home without her signature and had borrowed money from friends and relatives and townspeople without her knowledge. Mrs. Radford had been writing articles for the woman suffrage movement for many years, and now, with the family destitute, she placed her two daughters with relatives, located herself in a tiny New York apartment, and gave her husband one year to pay his debts. Instead, he went "East to live with his oldest spinster sister . . . who never ceased to adore him. He lived with her and on her from then on."[4] Mrs. Radford obtained a legal separation. In 1924! Molly earned her summer living by teaching swimming at Mrs. Gulick's (founder of the Camp Fire Girls) summer camp in Maine. The three women in the family worked. Two daughters went to college; the eldest was enrolled at Vassar. Mrs. Radford believed that the years of 1926–27 were important in their lives. In particular, Molly surprised her during that time by deciding that she wanted to go to medical school.

Molly Radford Ward's wish to enter medical school was a mixed blessing to her family. "When I entered medical school in 1927, many of my mother's friends as well as some of the family disapproved, saying that this was no field for a woman. . . . Her chief objection to my entering the field [of medicine] was that she didn't think I had the physical stamina to stand the rigorous courses, as I had had numerous illnesses while growing up."[5]

Molly Radford was one of three women in a class of one hundred medical students, and she claims she was never treated differently because of her gender "except possibly by a very few boys who showed rather romantic feelings toward me."[6] In a personal interview she elaborated on the topic, saying: "There wasn't even the slightest snarky remark or anything. They [the male students] just teased me as one of them. And it never occurred to me that they shouldn't or that they wouldn't. I grew up with a bunch of boys and I got along with them anyway."[7]

Numerous conversations, interviews, and years later, Dr. Radford acknowledged that because of her upbringing as a "tomboy," her male playmates had taught her to fit in as "one of the boys." She said that she had learned at a very early age to compete with men and it was a way of life for her that carried her into her professional years as a physician. She did, of course, acknowledge that many of her medical assignments were based on gender. In her book, she admitted that those who saw her as a woman, a possible romantic interest, also treated her differently. And so, one of the secrets of Dr. Molly Radford's comfortable feelings about her medical school career has its origin in her childhood, when she was treated like a boy within the carefree surroundings of a private island, sheltered and loved by a family who saw nothing wrong with their daughter's preference for outdoor life among trees, rocks, and water to playing with dolls.

Again, in her mother's words: "My only worry was Molly's determination to study medicine. I couldn't afford to send her through four more years of school . . . I hoped against hope that when she got her Bachelor's Degree she might change her mind—perhaps even stick to one beau and get married! My hopes were in vain. My grown-up Molly could be as single-tracked and stubborn as she often was as a child. When she returned from a summer in Maine in 1927, after she had acquired her B.S. degree, she plunked down her summer earnings for a small room . . . near the medical school and for her first quarter's tuition . . . got a job in the women's cafeteria . . . prepared breakfasts between 5 A.M. and 7 A.M. . . . in return . . . earned . . . three meals a day."[8] She also got a job teaching women's athletics and a third job making microscopic slides in the laboratory, earning tuition for future quarters. Asked about cost of clothing, she replied, "I'll just wear what I have and worry about new ones when present ones wear out."[9] Wanting to see and hear good plays and opera in those pre-Depression days, she also got jobs ushering at the theater and the Chicago Civic Opera.

In the spring of 1928, the mother's cousin Katie died, leaving her entire estate to Mrs. Radford and five thousand dollars to each of the daughters. Mrs. Radford "began to plot in Molly's behalf."[10] She found a "floating university," a round-the-world cruise of nearly a year, comprised of one hundred students and ten professors, and talked her daughter into putting down the cash for it. The next year was adventurous; Molly went everywhere the others did not; first class or baggage, toilets or no, she explored Panama, Hawaii, Japan, China, Singapore, Siam, Malaya, Burma, Calcutta, Bombay, Madras, Ceylon, Baroda, Cairo, Luxor, Jerusalem, Greece, Italy, Austria. Exhausted, she told her mother she could not visit one more thing—anywhere. But she was a world traveler for the rest of her life.

Her mother's stance: "After her remarkable trip around the world, I had, of course, hoped that Molly might change her mind about continuing medicine. . . . being her usual stubborn self, however, she refused to stay with me . . . but insisted in earning her living. She got a job in the admitting office of Billings Hospital."[11]

In 1930, Molly returned to her medical studies. In January, 1931, she developed a severe strep infection: "the virulent infection caused an acute glomerular nephritis, for which at that time there was no known control or cure."[12] It was six months of hospitalization and recovery before Molly was on her feet again. She developed allergies and "I was one big itch."[13] She was sent to New Mexico to recover, having two more years of medical school to complete. In the summer of 1932, she returned to Chicago and medical school for the fourth time, working as an apprentice obstetrician in the Chicago slums and delivering babies in the neighborhood tenements; these female physicians were called "hen medics" by their male colleagues.

Dr. Ward related one experience of working with a senior partner in obstetrics. Entering one apartment, Molly found the pregnant mother "had made no preparations for her delivery at home even though she had been given detailed instructions well ahead of time and it was her third child." The patient, according to Dr. Ward, "loudly proclaimed her suffering even when she was experiencing no contractions. She was wasting her energies, her breath, assaulting my eardrums and wearing my patience thin.

"'Shut up! You aren't having that much pain,' I said.

"The surprised woman looked up at the first woman doctor she had ever seen, stopped yelling, and said to me, 'Have you had a baby?'

"Lying stoutly, I said, 'Certainly. I have three children. Now get on with your job.'"

As she and her partner drove back to the hospital, he turned to her and said, "By damn, there is something to be said for female doctors, after all!"[14]

In 1934, Molly Radford received her four-year medical certificate. She then entered into research on tuberculosis. She received her M.D. degree in 1935 and, in 1936, presented her research paper to the National Tuberculosis Association. Alarmed by Molly's chest pains and acute pleurisy, her medical examiners told her: "Get as far away as you can. Leave any further work in this line to us old 'poops' who already have tuberculosis."[15]

Molly was thirty-one years old when she moved to New Mexico. She remodeled a chicken coop to live in, named it "Casa Gallina" (Chicken House), passed the state board medical exams, and met and married Bill Martin, the chief criminal investigator for the New Mexico State Police. She gave up her career after her marriage and settled down to build a house with Bill on the Old Santa Fe Trail in Santa Fe, New Mexico.

World War II intervened, and Bill went to war, leaving Molly alone with an unfinished house, no children, several animals, and a defunct career. But prior to his leaving, Bill had suffered a bad fall from a horse. His wife had to administer the anesthetic. "Not much fun," she said, "to work on your own husband but the ether put Bill to sleep. Al [a doctor friend] got the shoulder back in place, and instead of my patient awakening violently sick, he came to roaring drunk."[16]

The war effort took many Santa Fe doctors away from their practices. In the early years of that war, Dr. Radford conducted a well-baby clinic in the outlying small towns and villages of Santa Fe County. "One of my early patients was not 'sick,' he was simply starving. At six months of age he weighed six pounds." It seems the young mother was giving her baby two ounces of evaporated milk, filling the rest of the bottle with water. She told Dr. Radford, "there's not enough milk for the others. He's small, don't need so

much. Anyway, he no sick, no even cry now." Dr. Radford recalled
that moment. "Poor little scrap of humanity—he didn't have the
strength to cry."

"Another time we went into a home and found the grandfather in
bed in one tiny stuffy room. Even my unpracticed ears could diag-
nose a fulminating pneumonia in his chest. We left the house, leaving behind a few sulfa tablets we had, with instructions (there was no
penicillin in those days)."[17] The patient was later taken to Santa Fe,
twenty miles away, on a pile of straw in a horse-drawn wagon because
nobody in that village had a car. He died being carried across the
street to the hospital.

In 1943, Bill was shipped to the Pacific; Molly had applied to the
U.S. Navy Waves and had passed her physical when a delegation of
doctors arrived at her door, saying the general practitioner who gave
all the anesthetics at the only hospital in town had suffered a slight
heart attack. They asked her to work temporarily in the operating
room as an assistant anesthetist, his "understudy," which she did—
until the next heart attack killed him a couple of months later.

"When I started medical school," she told us, "there was no such
thing as an anesthesiologist. Any surgeon would just pour ether. It
really was World War II that made the whole specialty."[18]

While Bill remained in the Pacific, she continued her work as the
local anesthesiologist. "The science and practice of that branch of
medicine was nowhere nearly so complicated as it is today. . . . it was
a godsend to me that I not only had been 'put to sleep' myself . . .
but had suffered serious illnesses in my life. . . . I firmly believe [it]
is an enormous help in understanding the patient's frame of mind,
his fears of the unknown, as well as his apprehensions about many
little details. This, to me, is the 'art' of medicine, and I did my best
to be as concerned about my patients' state of mind as I was about
the technical side of anesthesizing a person. . . . there were no recovery rooms, no orderlies, and not enough nurses. . . . I always returned with my patients to their rooms and talked with members of
the family."[19] And then she added, "I had to buy all my own equipment as well as maintain it. . . . Often I would have some former
patients come up to me on the street and say, 'Oh, Dr. Molly, you
were good to me in the hospital. I got your $15 bill and can't pay it
all. Is it all right if I give you some of it now? I pay rest later.' Then

he or she would hand me a few dirty dollar bills and perhaps some nickels and dimes. I would scribble a receipt on whatever paper I had in my pocket and be sure to give the person credit in my books when I got home."[20]

Her nurturing nature was not shared by the male physicians she knew. "As far as I was concerned, most of the time I was the only one to do it," she told us, speaking of the special care she took of her patients. But, when we closely questioned her about the difference between male and female physicians, she demurred and retreated from this position saying: "I've never been struck by any big difference between male and female doctors. A person who really was determined to be a good doctor . . . would have that attitude toward the patient and somebody else wouldn't."[21]

Bill had gotten a medical discharge shortly after V-J Day and returned home to a house and windmill in need of repair. Santa Fe doctors returned, and Molly went home to Bill. Together, they built rock walls and terraces; by her cherished swimming pool they built a rock cabin fireplace with a twelve-foot opening overlooking the pool and enjoyed their life together. By 1948, Bill's health was rapidly deteriorating. Molly's mother was also ill and being cared for at home. With a physician friend, Dr. Molly "fashioned a homemade, portable oxygen machine which I could use at home. This was nothing like the compact 'Bennet' machines of present days which patients can operate themselves. . . . Fortunately, penicillin was then available and usually this marvelous medication cleared up infections quite rapidly. . . . I had now become a nurse rather than a doctor."[22]

Bill became so ill, he shot himself. Because of his barrel-shaped chest due to his violent emphysema, "the bullet missed his heart and he lived two and a half days. . . . To each of us . . . he said, 'I know I took the coward's way out.' But do you know something? It took a hell of a lot of guts to pull that trigger."[23]

Dr. Molly cannot remember the months that followed. "I weighed 106 pounds, had a hysterectomy, and then pneumonia, and was a mess." Trying to find herself, she considered going into forensic medicine, recalling an incident that took place prior to her marriage to Bill. He had telephoned her, inviting her to lunch at the La Fonda hotel, "but I need your help first." He gave her an address where they would meet. It turned out to be the morgue. Bill needed the evidence that was in a body. He told her: "I'll do the cutting if you'll only be good enough to supervise. All I need to do is get the bullets for ballistic examination and ascertain the cause of death."[24]

Instead, she decided to go into public health, was accepted by the University of California at Berkeley, rented out her home, drove her fully packed little car to California, found a two-room apartment across the street from the school of public health, sold the car and, at the age of 52, went back to school—again. She quickly became discouraged over the courses in organization, administration, and generalized health problems. Twenty years after she had first left medical school, she found these new subjects superficial, more full of talk than substance. The medical courses interested her more, but she had to work extremely hard to catch up on the advances that had been made. Finally, when all the academic learning was completed, the doctor returned to Santa Fe to head the state health department's division of gerontology.

The 1960 political season brought a new governor into office who was not very interested in gerontology. He abolished the department, and Dr. Molly Radford was out of a job. She later remarried, but she has never returned to the practice of medicine—at least not yet. And, as she told us, she has, indeed, "enough on her plate."[25] Dr. Molly Radford Ward, eighty years of age, has had a career that has been unusual and unique. From the beginning she did not fit the mold. She still does not.

Jane Patterson, M.D.: Gynecologist and Obstetrician (Photo courtesy
Patterson collection)

CHAPTER 12

JANE PATTERSON, M.D.

The office we sat in awaiting our interview with Dr. Jane Patterson was different from other waiting rooms. It was not sterile. It was not pretentious. There were large sea shells from all over the world. Pickupable. Large, overstuffed chairs and sofas of identifiable color protected our bodies. No, it was not like home. It was not supposed to be. We were not in the kitchen having coffee. But it was not like other doctors' offices, either. We were not sitting on cold, black Naugahyde chairs, waiting for hours to be called. What we were expecting, quite comfortably, was a physician of a different breed.

Dr. Patterson can get to the point rather quickly, and does. In her book, *Woman/Doctor: The Education of Jane Patterson, M.D.*, she recalled her feelings while at the University of Pittsburgh School of Medicine of being "swallowed up by a world so insular that I was only vaguely aware of the extent of my isolation."[1] Of the intensity of her internship, she said: "Having proved I could ovulate and think at the same time, an idea without a large following in those days, I was eligible for a prestigious internship, so I went off to Prestigious U for my internship year—the year of the walking dead, which is even worse than medical school."[2]

Speaking of her experience as a resident doctor in 1965, she said, "The head of the residency program there was widely quoted as having said that he supposed one day he'd be forced to take a woman or a black into the program and, if so, he'd take the black."[2] Stating further, she said, "We [women] doctors all came through the same brainwashing technique [i.e., discrimination] and it's as potent as anything I think a prisoner of war went through."[3]

Dr. Patterson related her own internal struggles in attaining her goal as a woman physician, stating, tongue in cheek: "As everyone in the medical profession knows, women are terribly emotional and not very good at controlling their emotions. I'd vowed to be as tough, as unemotional, as professional, as any of my male colleagues. And on the outside I was. No one ever saw me cry. But on the inside it was another story. . . . All though medical school I heard stories about women doctors who 'just weren't tough enough,' who 'just couldn't take it,' and 'broke down,' who 'fell apart.' (I envisioned a great slag heap where broken-down women doctors, their limbs all akimbo, were stacked in huge mounds that reached the sky.)"[4] Dr. Patterson added, "Very early on, my fantasies of being the great doctor, healing the sick and helping stamp out disease, which were what had gotten me into medicine in the first place, began to recede into a dim and unforeseeable future."[5]

Dr. Patterson's internship included a rotation on an atypical gynecology ward at a university hospital where most of the patients suffered from and were dying of gynecological cancers. She said: "I didn't know what to do or say or how to behave with a dying person. This wasn't included in medical school curriculums in my day. These women were dying, and I was terrified of their deaths. They were dying of gynecological cancers, and I was a woman, and maybe I would die like that. My terror of their deaths was all entwined with my terror of my own death. I kept my distance."[6]

"'Standard procedure' was for me an adequate explanation for anything."[7] Having selected obstetrics as her specialty, Dr. Patterson was faced with the Lamaze couples showing up in labor and delivery. Reflecting on that time, she writes: "I remained wary of it. I couldn't quite analyze why at the time, but I think what made me uncomfortable was the fact that the Lamaze parents were right there in the delivery room and the mother wasn't drugged out. Suddenly it was no longer a matter of our doing something *to* a patient but of our working *with* the patient and her partner—a much more personal and involving process. Having to relate to patients as people was not something most doctors were prepared to do."[8]

Dr. Patterson began to practice a different style of medicine, a more personal type, when she worked with women at a California feminist women's health center, an experience she described vividly. "That opened a door to alternatives. And I think once your mind is opened to alternatives, unless your own prejudices keep your mind closed, you can begin to see that there may be more than one way to do something and there may be better ways of doing something."[9]

Two major events at the clinic helped Dr. Patterson change her philosophy about herself and her profession. The women managing the clinic did not genuflect when the "Great White Doctor"[10] appeared, nor did they seem to have high regard for the "M.D. iety"[11] syndrome, as Dr. Patterson had expected they would. On the contrary, the clinic's staff felt the doctor needed further training and instructions on how to handle the women patients she was expected to treat.

The staff oriented Dr. Patterson in how to speak to women, how to be sensitive to their feelings, their personal situations, and their needs, how to view the patient as a whole person rather than as another woman who wants specific treatment. "I was utterly changed by what I heard," she related. "I began for the first time to see how abysmally arrogant the medical profession was and how women were victimized by it."[12]

Dr. Patterson had been trained not to tell the patient what the procedures of a pelvic examination were because silence was supposed to keep things impersonal and nonsexual. Also, she had learned to do the examination while a patient was unconscious in the operating room before undergoing gynecological procedures. Eventually, when she was adept enough, she worked with patients while they were conscious. As a result of her experiences in the clinic, her approach to patients has been drastically altered, as is her perception of the patients she now treats.

Now an obstetrician-gynecologist, Dr. Patterson has a flourishing private practice in Glendale, California, with two male physician partners. Her patients never feel rushed because she takes the time they need to sit and talk with them in quality conversational exchanges that benefit the healer and the healed, permitting each woman to get to know the other a little better, to develop a sense of one another that will aid the healing process.

It was not always this way for Dr. Patterson. She admits to being trained to address a disease rather than a patient, but now her female spirit is emerging after having been so successfully submerged by her medical training. She touches her patients confidently—a silent communication that speaks to the need of all people to be comforted.

"There are ways of touching patients," she told us, "that tell them 'I care about what's happening to you right now. I know you're suffering.'"[13] Male and female doctors touch patients differently, according to Dr. Patterson. She observes that a woman physician's touch communicates warmth and that men physicians frequently have a tendency to slap a patient on the back, as if to pass on their own strength to that patient.

In discussion with Dr. Patterson of the belief systems that cause people to be well or ill, we mentioned the American Indian healing ceremonies and the Hispanic *curanderismo*. Dr. Patterson thought the ritual itself sets the mood for what will be done, and for the healing that will take place. She agreed that rituals have power and set the psychological stage, citing the stethoscope and her white coat as being complementary to the Navajo Cedar Way Ceremony and the religious aspects of *curanderismo*. "If you're talking about, 'I am God the doctor coming in my white coat with my stethoscope and I'm going to heal you,' that sets the environment also. When I took off my white coat and the stethoscope and stopped behaving like that, I felt as if I had lost power, the power to heal. There was a decrease in my power to heal. The perception is gone. I don't feel that way anymore; it really was a naked feeling. I was literally divested of my trappings. But I didn't want to keep on doing that because I felt there was something basically dishonest about that. I don't do it anymore. I don't still have that loss of power feeling."

During the interviews with Dr. Patterson, she was asked about her views of some aspects of traditional Hispanic and Native American healing attitudes. For example, when asked if she thought illness could exist on a physical level without affecting a person's emotions and spirituality, she responded, "I think that would be totally impossible. Totally impossible." She said that the connections among the three entities—disease, emotions, and spirit—make her colleagues nervous, and so they tend to laugh about it. As a result, she prefers to discuss her beliefs with friends outside the profession.

On a different topic, miracles, Dr. Patterson is still probing, still testing and examining her personal beliefs about miracles, those documented spiritual events that have caused healing to occur inexplicably. The scientific side of Jane Patterson, M.D., has developed a hypothesis to explain instances of miraculous cures. "I always reassure myself that there's some complicated brain chemical feed-back mechanism going on and that's how it happens. There's a jolt needed [to effect the cure] and that's the place where it happens. The particular place. The example I can think of in a case like that is the woman who came running up to Jesus because she had a bleeding problem (we gynecologists like those kind of stories). She had un-explained dysfunctional uterine bleeding that had been going on for a long time. She touched Jesus' robe and she was healed. And so that was the jolt, rather than the fact that Jesus healed her. But," she added softly, "that's my explanation and I'm not really sure what I believe."

Recently, Dr. Patterson's attention turned from the sickness to the sick, a personal change in philosophy from the way she was trained in medical school to the way she now practices medicine. "The dif-ference between the North Pole and the South Pole" is what she calls it, adding, "the programming and the deprogramming and then the reprogramming." She said, "I think it wouldn't be too far afield to make the general statement that I think the woman physician is a little more likely to look at the whole person . . . with what the im-pact of that disease is going to be on her as a person, on her family, her friends, her culture." And then she referred to her training, say-ing: "I think American medicine has gone overboard with disease and has left prevention behind. I don't think 'disease-oriented' is quite right."

"It's more important to me that my patient be healed than that I be a participant in it,"[14] Dr. Patterson said, explaining her emphasis on the sick rather than the sickness.

It can be said about Dr. Jane Patterson that she understood and played by the rules made by men, for men. She played and she won. She won an M.D. degree and respect. Then, by her own description, her education in people began. And she has learned—and grown— and her patients have benefited from both her technical training and her personal understandings. She blended the best of both. She is a model worth studying in the AMA tradition. That is her story.

Stirling Puck, M.D.: Geneticist (Photo courtesy Puck collection)

CHAPTER 13

STIRLING PUCK, M.D.

Dr. Stirling Puck is a diminutive, redheaded firebrand. She is a geneticist. She works with the mind of a scientist and the heart of a loving woman. She is crisp yet compassionate, virtues that are apparent as she talks to parents of children who may be in genetic difficulty with Down's syndrome (mongolism), PKU (phenolketonuria), and others. One is impressed.

Parents of genetically damaged children are frightened. Scared for their children, scared for themselves. They feel guilty, angry, and do not know where to direct their emotions. Often, they deny their child has a serious problem. Dr. Stirling Puck understands all this, and when talking with parents, she is gentle but sure. She is sure that these parents have heavy responsibilities because of the child's special needs; she is gentle in reassuring the parents that they are not to blame, and her words try to absolve the adults of the guilt they impose upon themselves. She is firm and persistent in confronting parents' denial, in informing the parents that their youngster will need special care and attention, special diet, and special education. She brings parents, step by step, to the understanding of what their special child needs and requires. At the same time, she helps parents cope with the emotions that are flooding them upon the realization that "their" genes have given the child a set of lifelong problems. Dr. Puck compassionately explains how parents frequently could not have known their particular genetic biology would pass on such chronic ailments to their offspring.

She describes diseases such as Huntington's chorea, retinitis pigmentosa, phenolketonuria, and many other genetic disorders that have only recently been discovered and labeled. She says that the scientific community has just come to understand the causes of such afflictions and, as yet, has no cures to offer. But, the science of genetics is still in its infancy, and Dr. Puck works with children and parents to ameliorate and cope with the effects of these ailments until cures are found.

As one watches Dr. Puck, one observes her relating first to the child, taking blood and tissue samples, calming the youngster with a sweet voice and touch, creating security and lessening the child's fear of the doctor. She plays games, tells even an infant, "It's going to be okay; I need to do this to help you."[1] With honesty and reassurance, she warns a child, "This will hurt some, but it will be over soon."[2] Then she talks to the parents, describes the consequences—the child may not live beyond the age of thirty-five, or will be blind before age thirty—hard facts for parents to hear. Most often, parents are stunned, disbelieving, but Dr. Puck certainly knows the scientific facts and she conveys them with the heart of a loving woman.

When a mother broke into uncontrollable sobbing because she felt she had "poisoned" her two sons with retinitis pigmentosa (a genetic blindness that only women carry and that afflicts only men), Dr. Puck carefully explained to the mother that she could not have known back in 1942 what science and medicine did not know in those days, either. The logical explanation helped the mother feel less responsible for the disease and more able to provide the attention needed—because of Dr. Puck's blend of compassion and understanding with the cold, hard, hurtful truths.

Dr. Puck has opened a genetics laboratory in Santa Fe, New Mexico, called Vivigens. She takes skin, hair, and blood samples to analyze for genetic defects. Then she reports her decoded findings to the referring physician and to the parents. In the past, the nearest laboratories offering these services were five hundred to eight hundred miles away. For low-income families, many of whom have been referred to Dr. Puck, the distance has been prohibitive and so the analysis has not been done. It is different now, thanks to Dr. Puck. Dr. Puck's own role as mother makes her sympathetic to the heartaches (as well as the joys) of parenthood.

She and her husband, an ophthalmologist, are parents of three small children—two sons and a daughter—born in 1979, 1981, and 1983, whose pictures are taped to her office wall. When speaking of her husband and children, Dr. Puck said: "Frankly, this business of trying to do a career and a family, this isn't what society expects; this *is* what I expect. I expect that I can be as good as my father and as good as my mother. . . . I think I do give my children a lot, but it's hard."[3] Particularly difficult are the times when the children are ill. "When . . . they need me, I stay home. [My husband and I] have set it up that way. We're the ones who have taught our children,"[4] she said, contrasting her way of life with other professional couples whom she knows, families in which the husband shares equal responsibility for taking care of the youngsters. It is a hard task to balance profession and parenthood.

Dr. Stirling Puck is and is not the woman *Ms. Magazine* might write about. She is—because she is clearly a woman of the eighties, clearly a most successful physician, highly respected by her colleagues and her community. A true professional. She writes articles and a book about her beloved specialty, genetics, and she is thorough and knowledgeable.[5] She also loves what she does. She does not underestimate her accomplishments. Not at all. She simply seems to accept as one of the facts of life that she is who and what she is, lumps and accolades alike. She has been known to cry out of frustration for her patients' lives, and for the conflict she occasionally feels as a mother who has to leave her children to go to work. This, then, is how she got to the office—as a doctor.

The mold that Stirling Puck, M.D., was to fit as a woman/physician/mother was shaped early in her childhood by warm and loving parents who had three daughters, all of whom became doctors. Stirling's father was a renowned scientist and her mother a former social worker; both expected their children to achieve. "My father didn't really care what we did [as adults]," she said, "as long as we did something that made us happy and was productive for society. I think my real love for talking to people comes from my mother. She had been brought up to think that the family was most important and although she had a career, she didn't mind in the least giving it up in order to have three small children. She did go back to work part time when we were school age, but I don't think she liked it very much. Our breakfast table discussions had to do with physics or biology," she recalled, "not necessarily [my father's] work, but just an understanding of all kinds of natural phenomena. We were a very close family. I had friends in high school but I often preferred doing things with my family."[6]

Dr. Puck's academic and professional credentials are testimony to the early parental influences in her life. She received her undergraduate degree from Harvard in 1969, studied at Yale University's department of molecular biophysics and biochemistry and went on to Yale's School of Medicine. She was awarded a doctor of medicine degree in 1975, served her internship and residency at Yale–New Haven Hospital, was awarded a fellowship in human genetics at Yale in 1978, and was board-certified by the American Board of Human Genetics in 1981 and the American Board of Pediatrics in 1983.

As an undergraduate student, Stirling Puck was not sure she wanted to be a doctor. At the time, she was majoring in biochemical sciences, loved the research, and entered the graduate program, studying further for two years. "Even when I applied to medical school, I wasn't sure that I wanted to go," she admitted, "but when the letter of acceptance came, I never looked back. I just loved medical school."

No wonder. Dr. Puck's love of science had always been with her, introduced to her first by her father, later refined by a pediatrician whom she considers to be her role model, and then enhanced by her own undergraduate and graduate studies. Of the pediatrician, she said: "He was just wonderful . . . and it's probably because of him that I thought I was good enough . . . I thought people had to be really a kind of super person to go to medical school, not only intellectually but also emotionally." With a twinkle in her eye, she let us in on a delightful fact—her beloved pediatrician has now become a geneticist.

When Stirling Puck decided to attend medical school, she was pulled toward scientific research and found the call of genetics too loud to ignore. As a clinical genticist, she now combines the best of the two professional worlds that intrigued her—research and treating patients.

Although her years at Yale Medical School (1971–1975) were a time of increasing recognition for women, there were quite a few remnants left over from the days when women medical students were pariahs among their peers. "In 1972," she said, "Yale took all of the federal funds available to increase the number of minorities

and applied them to women. About a third of the class after me became filled with women. In my year there were a few—five or six—
in a class of one hundred. And the year after, there were thirty. But,
I had to change [clothes] in the nurses' locker room when male medical students could change in the doctors' part. They didn't call it
'men and women.' They called it 'doctors and nurses.'"[7] Because a
great deal of useful medical conversation went on among the men,
Dr. Puck felt particularly excluded as a result of her gender.

Just how important mutual access, and the discrimination that
prevents it, is has been addressed by feminist author Letty Cottin
Pogrebin. She states:

> White males perpetuate closed friendship circles and restrict key . . .
> information and strategies to members of those circles. Having friends
> who are like themselves reduces their uncertainty about what to expect
> from the other person's behavior. And they close ranks because of a
> desire to protect their economic power positions. Given an already high
> level of male job competition, the addition of female game players
> understandably makes men slightly hot under the collar, be it white
> or blue.

> The *impact:* Sticking to one's own kind may be an innocent impulse,
> but excluding people from workplace networks has serious conse-
> quences for those who are left out. Friendship networks in organiza-
> tions are not merely sets of linked friends. They are systems for making
> decisions, mobilizing resources, and concealing or transmitting infor-
> mation. When women are excluded from these vital systems, it costs
> them as surely as if they were left out of the company health plan. Al-
> though civil rights laws may temper the worst expressions of sexism on
> the job, women cannot fight discrimination in friendship. Only a clear
> conscience and raised consciousness can remedy that situation.[8]

Said Dr. Puck: "I think a lot of women have encountered prejudice . . . but I didn't seem to feel what they felt, or at least to the
same degree.

"I think that some women my age [thirty-seven years] with chips
on their shoulders have forgotten what it was like a generation ago.
We weren't there, but maybe they aren't as sensitive to what women
had to go through a generation ago . . . when women had to sit in the
back of classes . . . dissect their cadavers a little differently.[9]

"Premedical classes in colleges were extremely competitive. This was just when the Vietnam War was escalating and students in medical school had a deferment. So there was a lot of pressure, even in the premedical years, for men to excel so that one had a competitive chance to enter medical school.

"Yale, however, [became] a good place to be a pediatric intern, resident, and a good place to be in genetics and a woman."

In her own practice of medicine, Dr. Puck finds it an asset to be a woman. "In my particular field," she says, "it may be a plus to be a woman. First of all, as a geneticist, I don't in fact, undress people. I talk . . . and I have a lot of credibility with them because I think women tend to be more sociable in their interactions with patients . . . in establishing a person-to-person rapport. Maybe sooner than a man. Some physicians come on as doctor to patient, not person to person. But I think women find it more important [to act on a person-to-person level] . . . it's partly a natural reaction. I think a patient needs a person, a knowledgeable person and, in addition to medical knowledge, needs sympathy. Now, not all patients need that, of course, but more patients aren't putting up with [a chauvinistic, paternalistic attitude from their physicians]. They're changing doctors. But patients certainly want good medical care and that is probably their first priority. They will put up with paternalistic, chauvinistic attitudes if they feel that they are getting the best help."

Commenting on cultural healing, Dr. Puck said: "Certainly my prejudice is in favor of the scientific method and Western medicine's techniques. Much, maybe most of Western medicine, technological as it may be, is based on traditions . . . the things that work. Although there is more and more scientific understanding of disease processes and therefore more rational treatments of them, much of medicine is not scientific. Of the fields of medicine . . . [genetics] . . . is one of the more scientific. Many of the diseases are biochemical . . . discovered only after there was some kind of scientific method of studying them, and with those diseases, where there are treatments or cures, they are based on scientific thought. So, certainly my prejudice is all in favor of Western medicine. But, in fact, I believe that whatever works should be done, and there is so much of medicine that is not understood on a scientific basis that I am certainly not willing to say that Western medicine is all there is."

Dr. Puck practiced for a time at the Gallup, New Mexico, Indian Health Service Hospital. She worked in the Pediatric Outpatient Clinic and there learned another approach to healing, one that has stayed with her. She came to understand and respect traditional healing in and of itself and in combination with Western scientific methods of curing.

One of the children at the clinic, a little Navajo girl, needed antibiotics. The patient's family brought her to the hospital where an intravenous solution was infused. Then, they took her home for a Navajo curing ceremony—a sing—moving her very carefully. She came back six hours later, the bottle and tube still in place, for a new bottle of antibiotics; she went back and forth, between home and hospital, between the contemporary and the traditional, between Navajo sings and AMA-endorsed treatment. "The Indians don't feel whole or cured until they've done their ceremonies," Dr. Puck told us. "Although they've had white man's medicine, they still haven't been cured. And I am absolutely willing to believe that. My bias may be that I'm not going to get cured unless I have antibiotics, so even if I had something else, I might not feel cured."

Her words confirmed what we had learned from other healers—medicine women and *curanderas*. The belief system must work hand in hand with the ceremony, with the faith of the healers. If a patient believes in the cure, that patient will be cured.

In comparing parents' reactions to their heartbreak when a deformed child is born, Dr. Puck said: "I guess the only thing I find different in all three cultures, really . . . is the explanation for what happened. The emotions and willingness to listen are the same, I find. Nobody's ready to listen to that kind of thing right then. Parenthood is such a—I was always sympathetic, but until I had children I never realized quite the degree of responsibility and guilt that parents feel for what happened to their children when, of course, they couldn't have known. And, in a way, I find it's reassuring to tell them it's a genetic problem. Because that means it wasn't alcohol that they took, or a fall that they had, or going to a baseball game or staying up late. If they'll believe my Western medicine explanation, then I think that it can be quite reassuring."

Though she acknowledges having a high regard for traditional healing philosophies and techniques, Dr. Puck speaks very nicely of the remarkable accomplishments of Western scientific medicine, without which contagious diseases would still be among us, infant mortality rates would be so much higher, and surgical procedures would still be primitive. She speaks confidently when she says that all ways of healing are valid, and states her respect for all approaches to the practice of medicine.

Dr. Puck talked sincerely about society's empowerment of its physicians, saying, "There's a power that comes along with being an M.D., and in the beginning, in a way I resented that power." She told us that when she and her husband were purchasing car insurance and the salesman learned they were both physicians, he tried to convince them to take the company's maximum policy. The stereotype of a rich physician angers her, as does the belief that doctors want to make money and protect themselves from malpractice suits. "I think those are not the primary motivations, I hope, of doctors in general, and certainly not of me,"[10] she declared.

In analyzing the situation that leads to societal stereotyping of physicians, Dr. Stirling Puck has reached some interesting conclusions. She knows people hate being sick, hate giving up any part of themselves to anybody else and, when they do become sick, they have to surrender responsibility for themselves to their physicians.

She sees the situation changing. She believes that patients now are taking back some of the responsibility for their own bodies and are asking questions of physicians that they would never have asked in previous times. Also, state and federal laws are helping by giving patients access to medical information about themselves that, in the past, they were unable to obtain. This may be a harbinger of a more cooperative relationship between the healer and the healed in the arena of Western scientific medicine—a relationship that has existed for years in the Indian and Hispanic cultures.

Josette Mondanaro, M.D.: General Practitioner with emphasis on chemical dependency and women's health (Photo courtesy Mondanaro collection)

CHAPTER 14

JOSETTE MONDANARO, M.D.

"I really want to be a doctor," the twelve-year-old confided to her Girl Scout leader, "but I won't tell anybody. We don't have any money and I'm a girl, and there are all these boys in the family. It just seems so impossible."[1] The Girl Scout leader answered, simply and directly, "Where there's a will, there's a way." The girl had the will and found the way; she was a fighter and went the distance, so much so that the February, 1987, issue of *Ms. Magazine* quotes Josette Mondanaro, M.D., as a medical authority. She is that, and she is also a fighter.

Josette Mondanaro, M.D., former chief executive officer of the state of California's $46 million-budgeted drug programs, has always been life's sparring partner. Recalling her experiences as a candy striper, she said: "I was in the hospital corridor carrying a tray of urine samples, which I spilled. There was urine all over the floor, and the head nurse was very disturbed over that—upset, irate, nervous. Got very excited. Then a doctor came down the hall, saw the urine on the floor, shrugged, and said, matter of factly, 'Well, there's more where that came from,' and I was then and there cognizant of the power differential."

A reputation as a tough-minded, ambitious, achieving and hard-driving physician preceded her into the CEO position. She was known for her power and respected for it. Sometimes feared for it. Therefore, as our interviews began, we were ill-prepared for the softness of the doctor's spiritual underbelly. She had toughed it out all of her life in her efforts to become a physician, overcoming the "stigma" of being a girl with ambition while confronting the world as a woman who expected to achieve her goals. She pushed—and was often pushy in the eyes of many. Often, too, she was conflicted.

For, her truest desire was to become a healer even more than a physician. This is how she did it, for herself and for those whom she wished to serve.

Dr. Mondanaro came to her medical career following a long, long, informal experience of taking care of people. "I came from a kind of overdeveloped sense of needing to take care of everyone else," she told us. "Along about junior high school I started thinking about how I could stretch that to be more professionally rewarding. I had a sense of missionary zeal that I was going to cure the world and any disease that walked on the face of it." From the talk with her Girl Scout leader, she gained the courage she needed to tell her mother she wanted to be a doctor; her mother's reaction was mixed.

Her parents said they wanted her to be happy without having to work too hard the rest of her life. Being a doctor was hard work, they said, and they were not too sure the medical profession would make her happy. Instead, they had other plans for their daughter: nursing or teaching, or even becoming a nun. However, Mondanaro persevered and gained entrance to Syracuse University Medical School.

She took idealism into the anatomy room, but not for long. "I had read the classics and had been deeply touched by people like Michelangelo, Leonardo da Vinci, who spent hours and days and years going through the cadavers and learning anatomy and all the respect that I felt that they had, or at least believed . . . they had toward the cadavers, and what that means." During their first cadaver dissection in the anatomy lab, some medical students sang and joked. "This is the way we carve the cadavers to pass anatomy, to pass medical school, to become doctors, to buy our boats, to buy our. . . ." Mondanaro said, "It was so flagrant! It was just obnoxious. If it were a joke, it would have been funny. But it wasn't a joke and . . . that was just very hard."[2] Such attitudes and behaviors hit Mondanaro hard. She was shocked and offended. (It may also shock the reader, but other physicians reported similar experiences, requesting not to be quoted on this matter.) She became very discouraged, thought about quitting, because the attitude that pervaded the classrooms had nothing to do with healing people or stopping human suffering. Had it not been for some socially conscious people at Syracuse, she would not have finished her academic training.

It was Dr. Julius Richmond, later surgeon general for the Carter administration, developer of the Headstart program during the Johnson administration, and head of pediatrics at Syracuse University, who helped the most. "He was the first person to see all the work I was doing socially. I was running a drug treatment program . . . very active in human rights . . . involved in the anti-war stuff, you know, Vietnam . . . and he felt I would be able to contribute a lot to society. And he was somebody I felt had already contributed a lot . . . That kind of social consciousness . . . is really imbued in the entire training, and that really helped me. Because that made sense. Everything else in medical school didn't make sense to me. Medical school is a very cruel experience. Because we seem to . . . fragment people a lot in . . . a terrible way."[3]

She was surprised when, as a medical student, she made rounds with doctors who yelled at patients and made jokes about them. "When doctors can't take care of patients or they're confronted by a difficult case or a challenging case, then they get angry at the patient and make the patient wrong," she said. "The patient becomes bad, dirty, and ugly for bringing them a problem they can't solve. The patient isn't getting better quick enough. I wasn't prepared for it."

The way students were evaluated in medical school is also a sore spot with Dr. Mondanaro. As there were no grades, a student had no idea if he or she was doing well or not. The only clue came when a student did something wrong. Then when a group of students got together to address the issue with the faculty, the response was devastating. The faculty members said, "We expect you to do things right all the time and it's only when you do something wrong that we're going to tell you." Dr. Mondanaro believes that this attitude affected her so severely that later in her career she passed it on to the people who worked with her. "I was not a very good person to work with, just too perfectionistic. I worked very hard myself and could not understand why everyone didn't work that hard."[4]

Dr. Mondanaro told us about some other by-products of medical school, saying: "The process itself screens out the compassion. A good doctor is a good doctor because of what he was able to retain of himself while going through medical school, not what he was able to learn. It's a very dehumanizing process. By the time doctors get out of it, because it's such an effective process, they have very little insight into how dehumanizing it is. There are many, many things that go into it. One is the attempt to make medicine into a science, [trying to make] medicine and healing, the art of medicine and the art of healing, a very exact science like physics. The other part of it is the vast amount of information needed to practice Western medicine. It puts tremendous pressure on people. It's overwhelming. Western medicine is only a small part of what there is to learn about healing. But there's so much there."

During her internship, all the negatives, the problems a person faces in learning the practice of medicine, seemed to conspire against her. "How can a person have a personal life?" she asked. "I'd work these ridiculously long hours, night and day, 23 hours at a stretch. Then there would be an emergency and I'd get called. The patient would show up with a minor thing and I'd say to myself, 'You are going to see a bloody nose. Maybe it could be taken care of at home, but it's the only bloody nose they have.' I would try to talk myself into being a better doctor. I would talk myself into being much more understanding."

The distinction between a "bloody nose" and a "patient with a bloody nose" is crucial in that the former reflects an acquired attitude, a change in thinking that is learned behavior rather than a natural reaction to an acute condition. Outside the practice of medicine, people respond to a person's bloody nose; medical students react to the affliction, not to the patient who has it. "There's not enough appreciation of the connection," Dr. Mondanaro says. "Medicine is not set up for people who see the complexity of mind/body. My father was a very strong believer in the healing properties of body and mind. If there were something out of synchrony, it would create disease. And that's how I practice."

Now a general practitioner in Santa Cruz, California, Josette says: "Many, many times I thought I would have been more comfortable as a shaman. I'm so totally involved with the oneness of the mind and the body that there's no place for me, there's no comfortable niche already set out for me in Western medicine. I have to make it myself."

In that regard, Dr. Mondanaro respects the philosophy of traditional Indian and Hispanic people, a school of thought that is quite alien to Western scientific medicine's paradigm. Too, Dr. Mondanaro sees spirituality as very important to healing. "I think the flesh is just the outer manifestation of the spirit," she says, and adds that if one believes illness can be caused by witchcraft working on the spirit, it is a possibility for that believer. "If somebody's putting that much energy into somebody else, something's going to happen to both of them." In the opposite vein, she believes that miracle cures are the result of spiritual healing power rather than cures imposed from outside the body by a doctor.

She described two kinds of events in life in which diseases of the spirit can lead to physical ailments. First, primary life changes are daily events or alterations made according to immediate circumstances—stepping on the gas to beat an impending red light—which require only minor readjustments in one's life. Secondary changes are major events which require enormous readjustments, for example, death of a loved one, divorce, a new job, or any challenge greater than routine. If we are able to cope with the stress and adjust ourselves to the demands of the event, we will not become ill. If not, if we are "stuck," the body will feel the effects, the spirit will become ill at ease and we will become physically sick. But, that illness is a result of the *dis*-ease of the spirit. Traditional peoples take this into consideration when they heal; modern medicine does not. Often, Mondanaro says, she "feels like a left-handed person in a right-handed world" when she honors and respects the spiritual side of healing and the aspects of disease that the traditional cultures understand better than many doctors do. "It would be better if I were a shaman," she says, "because I have a sense their community helps them more, helps them relieve the energy—maybe even the negative energy—that they've taken onto their bodies. So, I feel almost like a stranger in a strange land. I end up taking a lot of showers because I know they [the traditional healers] have rituals to help cleanse them from all the things they take on."[6]

Dr. Mondanaro's affinity with Indian and Hispanic philosophies of disease and healing is quite unusual, as is her understanding of the traditional belief system. "I think their faith in the healer is what makes the healer heal," she says. "If they didn't believe in it, I don't think it would work. The condition [of traditional healing] is the belief that it will work. The power goes out from the sick person to the healer, opening a space to let the [healer's] healing energy in. If there isn't that belief, I don't think a space is created."

Dr. Mondanaro further believes that people who consult doctors are becoming more and more cynical and are expecting less and less from their physicians, challenging them to "cure me." She believes that pessimism closes off healing and then doctors fall victims to being unable to cure. She does feel that a new attitude between women and their physicians is developing, an attitude that bespeaks more of cooperation than of competition. She says that women are more knowledgeable about their bodies today than they have ever been, and that in itself causes women to seek out physicians with whom they have rapport. In many cases, women patients are consulting women physicians because the female doctors are more willing to share in a cooperative medical relationship than are male physicians.

Dr. Mondanaro discussed a new, different attitude in staffing, perhaps brought to the profession by women doctors and different from those held by male colleagues. "I look for people who have had similar experiences to the women who'll be coming through the door. They can be role models . . . I look for people who've been around the block and come out the right end of that. I've hired a very independent staff. . . . I wouldn't expect them to do all kinds of little favors . . . for me, . . . I don't demand that . . . I go buy them coffee some mornings, and some mornings they buy me coffee. Decaffeinated. I have no investment in keeping them [staff] subservient."

There is another side of the coin, however, for Dr. Mondanaro, probably because she is a woman physician: "Where I've missed the boat . . . because I don't think in the hierarchal sense, I have to understand that some people may still think that way, and that when I come in in a bad mood and I don't say hello to somebody, or I'm preoccupied, people really get hurt by these things. . . . they would never expect a man would do this and this, but they would expect me to be really compassionate and really understanding and to almost be a superwoman . . . it's a real double-edged sword."

Dr. Mondanaro has not missed much in what she has fought against and what she has fought for. She has fought social conditions and traditions. She has fought bias and prejudice. Her most recent victory is the receipt of a large grant, jointly with Sheila Namir,

Ph.D., for federally funded outreach, education, and counseling for women about AIDS. She has fought family barriers and expectations. Her early hunger to become a physician was "embarrassing; I guess that's not true in a lot of families—they'd be very proud, you know, but it was embarrassing because I felt like it was so out of sync with this family background." There have been other joustings as well. In another experience, Dr. Mondanaro said: "Here's a good story: When the Girl Scout leader was telling me I would be a doctor, we had this sodality, you know, the women's Catholic organization. We had a vocational retreat; we went to the convent, and we all prayed. We each had a separate meeting with the priest, and we were supposed to talk to the priest, tell him what our vocational goals were and all that. So I told him my vocational goal was to be a doctor. He said, 'Well, what stands in your way?' I said, 'Well, I have four brothers and we're poor and I'm a girl.' He said, 'That's God's way of telling you you shouldn't be a doctor. God put these obstacles there to turn you away from it.'"[7]

And from Girl Scout days to quotes in national publications, Josette Mondanaro, M.D., remains the strong knuckle-fighter as always, when she states, "No matter how far we've come, it's still true that the very nature of being a woman is *not* to fit in."[8]

PART FOUR

THE DARK SIDE OF HEALING

CHAPTER 15

WITCHCRAFT IN HISTORY

All cultures, ancient and modern, make reference to evil practices, such as bewitchment, sorcery, witchcraft, and other black arts, and their power to cause illness. Evil is still believed by many to have the power to cause illness. An understanding of the use of the dark powers by each tradition is useful and necessary to comprehend the scope of the dark side of healing.

The assumption is made by many, even as we enter the twenty-first century, that evil powers exist. The European history of witchcraft strongly influenced the Native American, Hispanic, and Anglo cultures of the Southwest by connecting witchcraft and healing. A brief synopsis of the history follows. God commanded Moses to tell his people, "Thou shalt not suffer a witch to live."[1] (The Hebrew word is *kasaph*, translated as "witch," meaning seer or diviner.) Later, Pope Innocent III issued a momentous papal bull that has come to be known as the "Witch Bull." The pope delegated priests to be inquisitors into heretical practices, as witchcraft was called in 1484. By doing so, he officially recognized witches and the "black art."

Next, priests Henry Kraemer and James Sprenger started the European witch craze by writing the *Malleus Malleficarum*, 1484 (nicknamed *The Witches' Hammer*). This 540-page tome is full of information about demons and witches as defined by the Catholic Church.[2] In the book, witches were described as "old hags who didn't weep, who were defective because of a bent rib that caused them to be imperfect and therefore deceptive."[3] This and other misinformation, such as the beliefs that witches make men impotent, devour newborn babies, turn their neighbors' milk sour, cause cattle to die, or cause children to fall ill, helped characterize a witch.

Protestants joined in and became outspoken about witchcraft as well. Most notably, King James of England succeeded in convincing Parliament to pass laws against witchcraft, thus beginning a serious witch hunt in Britain that resulted in the executions of fifty witches during his reign. Throughout all of Europe in the fifteenth, sixteenth, and seventeenth centuries, witchcraft was given attention by the best minds of the time, or at least by the most politically powerful.[4]

Women have been the primary group accused of practicing witchcraft. Throughout Europe approximately 85 percent of those put to death as witches were women. In one area of Germany during 1585, two villages were left with only one female inhabitant each.[5] In Salem, Massachusetts, of the twenty-one people executed as witches, nineteen were women. According to the Biblical mandate, the gender of witches was never specifically identified, but through the millennia the concept of women as witches has prevailed. The question is why.

To answer this, economic and political conditions and prevailing motivations must be examined. Politically, "up to the 15th century, . . . Europe's traditional doctors were women: clan mothers, priestesses of healing shrines, midwives, nurses (vilas). Women's 'charms and spells' were virtually the only repository of practical medicine."[6] As the Spanish Inquisition gained momentum, the very fact that such women could accomplish "miraculous" cures made them highly suspect of having powers also to harm. It was reasoned that they gained their power from being in league with the devil, or the dark forces. (It also made women highly suspect of having political and economic powers equal to those of men). The Catholic Church designated these healers as "witches," and the link between medicine, witchcraft, and women was forged in a lasting manner. Some believe the residual effects of this union remain in force today.

From the perspective of economics, most of the women accused were elderly and therefore unproductive in economic and childbearing capacities. It was almost impossible to evict them from their villages, so they were simply done away with by burning at the stake or some other equally brutal means. In Essex County, England, for example, 90 percent of those brought to trial and condemned in response to accusations of witchcraft were women who were poor, old, and powerless. They were often quarrelsome and difficult for their neighbors to tolerate, especially when they went from door to door begging for food and clothing.[7] Ridding the community of these economic burdens served to assuage the consciences of the enthusiastic participants in witch hunts.

Another economic consideration regarding women was the formation of the guild system. Under this system, one had to be a member of a guild to practice one's craft or profession. In an era of male domination in all matters of life except healing, men in power began systematically persecuting women and designating them witches to maintain a male monopoly over the profitable enterprise of healing. "Witches" also became convenient scapegoats for doctors who failed to cure their patients, because it was the common belief that witch-caused illnesses were incurable.

Male doctors frequently learned their healing trade from the village wise woman, who was the peasants' family doctor. Then, "the men who learned doctoring from witches were allowed to practice, but their female teachers were persecuted. . . . Officially, women were often forbidden to do any kind of healing. In 1322 a woman named Jacoba Felicie was arrested and prosecuted by the medical faculty of the University of Paris for practicing medicine, although, the record said, 'she was the wiser in the art of surgery and medicine than the greatest master or doctor in Paris.'"[8]

Later, witchcraft was economically important in another way. Estates of wealthy witches, especially women without a man to protect them, were confiscated by the authorities. Even individuals could make money on witches. A man by the name of Hopkins, a resident of Manningtree, in Essex County, England, claimed to know how to identify these women. In 1644 he charged twenty shillings per town for services that he guaranteed would rid the area of these evildoers. When an epidemic of witchcraft actually arose in his hometown, the witchfinder general (as he called himself) stripped the accused women, stuck pins into various parts of their bodies, wrapped them in sheets, and dragged them through a pond or a river. If a woman sank, she was considered not guilty of the charge, but if she floated, she was condemned.[9] Hopkins got rich.

In the context of the politics of the Middle Ages, the primary task of rulers was to coalesce the exceedingly fragmentary populations into what we now call nations. To do so, any powerful group needed to be brought under control. Since only the richest could afford physicians, women healers held power in the eyes of the peasants and the less wealthy royalty. Therefore, they had to be brought under political domination. For example, in 1631, a woman called Frau Peller (the wife of a German court officer) was on trial for witchcraft because her sister had refused to have sexual relations with the witch judge, Franz Buirmann. Before the trial, she was stripped to determine whether or not she was a witch and then was raped by the court employees.[10]

Women healers were especially dangerous to those in power because they, the women, were among the community leaders. However, their abilities were not confined solely to the practice of healing. Women healers were also religious guides in a system of informal worship that was incompatible with the established political position of the Catholic church in society. Consequently, the women were extremely vulnerable to punitive measures instituted not only by the political rulers but by the religious guardians as well. These women healers came to the attention of the authorities because of their popularity. Uneasy, the church ordered investigations, quickly concluding that the women/witches were a direct threat to its exalted position of supremacy.

The church accused these women of challenging the will of God, of defying religious doctrine, and of undermining the rigid, established, social structures and patterns that comfortably ranked priest over penitent, lord over peasant, and man over woman. Furthermore, the church declared that the healing techniques used by the women were an affront to the Almighty, interfering with the fate of bodies and souls that belonged to the Lord and to his representatives on earth, the Catholic clergy.[11]

Dominicans Kraemer and Sprenger, authors of the *Malleus Maleficarum*, developed and expounded upon the theme that women were witches. In inflammatory, sensational chapter headings, such as "Jesus Preserved the Superiority of Men," "Beware of Old Women," "Midwives Are Wicked Witches," "Evil Began With Eve," and "Never Allow Women to Exercise Power," they insisted that women predominated within the witch colony. From descriptions included in the book, thousands of women were identified as witches and executed, and thousands more were tortured; they all were accused of having committed heresy of one sort or another, and all were found guilty of being practitioners of the black arts.

This incredible book, brought into being through an edict of the pope, served as a guide for more than two hundred years, a "how-to" book on identifying, convicting, and executing witches. There was almost no recourse against accusations. Ironically, the accused women who somehow escaped torment did so by proving themselves beyond a doubt to be witches, because one of the stated characteristics of a true evildoer was that she could bewitch her inquisitors and thus escape punishment.

Reprinted as an introduction to the *Malleus Malleficarum* was a pope's edict. Positioning the church's official document beside this volume of accusations led readers to believe that the Catholic church endorsed the book and ratified its inflammatory language. Thus the full power of the Roman Catholic church was brought to bear against the offending women, and the practice of witch hunting was established. These women served as convenient focal points upon which to vent the anxieties and frustrations of a simple, feudal people, victims of a serious religious contest for their souls and their money; the price tag for penance was high—and collected by the church. Blaming witches and witchcraft for the ills that befell villagers served to reduce tensions only temporarily, but that was enough for a while.

Records show that witch burnings became something of an industry, spawning many different types of actions and businesses. Money was collected from confiscation of estates and possessions of accused witches. Doctors formed guilds and unions to protect their jobs and safeguard their income. One author estimates that in 250 years (from the fifteenth through the early seventeenth centuries) 100,000 to 9 million women were incinerated for allegedly having had "social and sexual intercourse with the devil."[12]

Given the history of witchcraft and its devastating effect on women, one would hardly imagine that such beliefs could endure. Yet, they have endured. Why?

One possible reason for the survival of witchcraft in any form in any society may be found in C. G. Jung's psychological concepts of the collective unconscious and the archetypal images. Jung postulates that all humankind shares common ideas, stored in the unconscious areas of our minds, but available to the conscious mind at will. "Among the most important of such ideas," said Jung, are "the idea of creation and of absolute evil . . . and the image of a great mother of all men."[13] For example, the Hindu image of Kali, the female creator/destroyer, has a sword in one hand and a baby in the other. If Jung is correct, there has always been and will be in all cultures an archetypal image of woman as having the power to create (give birth) and destroy (cause illness and death). Perceiving women as "witches" who do evil may be one cultural expression of this archetype.

There are several other explanations of why concepts of witchcraft continue. One is the weight of tradition and history. If one's parents, grandparents, and great-grandparents believed or believe, then one has the feeling that "there must be something to it."

Moreover, the concepts of evil and witchcraft also have societal functions, such as controlling the behavior of children and adults. For example, most southwestern Pueblos socialize children through fear of *koshare*, ceremonial characters in black-and-white striped body paint who appear at ceremonial rites to harass, tease, threaten, and punish children who are either misbehaving or who have misbehaved throughout the previous year. Many Christian groups also promulgate a theology that describes punishment and retribution (hellfire and damnation) for adult members who veer from prescribed behaviors. When this theology is joined to the ubiquitous twins of economics and politics, it can be used to enforce adult behavior. Many churches and religions retain their members, who are also the sources of their economic survival, by threatening that evil forces will take command of individuals if they do not stay within the group and the belief system. Thus, the threat of evil maintains the organization, its politics, and its economics.

The concepts of evil and witchcraft may also persist because they explain the inexplicable and serve various societal functions: they relieve individuals of responsibility for illness and grant them permission to be comforted by relatives; they create the belief that something can be done about mysterious afflictions; and they offer legitimacy to doubters.

An extensive legacy of belief in witchcraft still permeates the entire mainstream culture in the form of superstitions. Most people say "God bless you" or "*Gesundheit*" when someone sneezes. The source of this belief is that sneezing is a breeze from Satan's wings, and at the moment of sneezing one is as close to death as one can be. When yawning, do you think you are being polite by covering your mouth? People of the Middle Ages believed the devil entered the mouth through a yawn. Those of other cultures thought they would lose their breath and die, so they covered their yawns. The tradition of wearing black at funerals stems from a belief that evil spirits were plentiful around a dead body, and so the mourners, wanting not to attract them, wore black. Mistletoe at Christmas originated as a sign of welcome to priests and a protection against witches. Is eye shadow exotic and modern? Judge for yourself: "Eyeshadow was used in ancient Egypt to draw a circle around the eyes (as lipstick was used to draw a circle around the mouth) so that the evil eye couldn't enter through them. The Devil has no powers against the strengths of a circle."[14]

These are but a few of the hundreds, perhaps thousands, of common daily activities and beliefs that have as their source concepts from, and connections to, witchcraft. They have the power to evoke feelings, even if in a watered-down form. Without knowing the source of their vague discomfort, most people will acknowledge a slight squeamishness or hesitation, or at least a second thought, over Friday the thirteenth, a black cat running in front of them, walking under a ladder, or breaking a mirror. In this way, witchcraft and notions of the dark forces are covertly embedded in mainstream culture.

CHAPTER 16

INSIDE THE DARKNESS
Three Cultural Views of Witchcraft

In 1628, while the Spanish Inquisition was in full force in Europe, Spain extended its farthest landholdings into the New World. Hispanic pioneers settled an area known as New Spain and came in direct contact with indigenous peoples. Familiar with the concepts and techniques of European witchcraft, the settlers learned that in New Spain the Pueblo Indians believed that revenge, spite, or jealousy stirs a certain type of individual into action, and, because witches are not easily identifiable, it is very important to be polite and hospitable to everyone. The term and concept of a "witch" may have been strictly a European designation, and it may be a mistake to conclude that indigenous peoples of New Mexico used the same frame of reference when describing malevolence and malevolent people. Nonetheless, if the two cultures' terms were different, the difference seems to have been lost to history. The concept of evil beings, including witches, was culturally shared.

An example of a collaborative effort between Hispanic pioneers and the Pueblo people to deal with the effects of witchcraft occurred when one of Spain's agents, Señor Sotelo Osorio, was governor of New Mexico. According to reports, Governor Osorio was charged by the Spanish Inquisition for the infraction of bringing an Indian woman from Santa Clara Pueblo to Santa Fe to "try to save the life of a soldier who had been bewitched."[1] The man, Juan Diego Bellido, had quarreled with and beaten his lover, Beatriz, who had cast a spell on him by burying idols in her hearth. She also hung a clay figurine resembling Bedillo from a tree, a sure sign that he was marked for death. Try as she might, the Pueblo Indian woman was unable to reverse the spell, and the soldier died. These events contributed to the governor's eventual removal from office; there is no record of what happened to the Santa Clara woman.

In 1848, American jurisprudence entered the field of Native American and Hispanic witchcraft in the Southwest by imposing laws against bewitchment, laws that were confusing and difficult to understand, much less obey, for the two cultures already in residence.

Under American laws, crimes committed by witches were no longer legal matters, because lawmakers, still well aware of the earlier atrocities at Salem, took great pains in Washington to ensure that innocent people would no longer be prosecuted or killed for crimes they did not commit. To the Native Americans and Hispanics, this political philosophy was interpreted to mean that witches could perform their black arts and escape punishment. When *brujas* (witches) learned that the old laws prescribing punishment had been replaced by the American laws that granted them "immunity" from prosecution, witchcraft ran rampant in the hills of remote northern New Mexico. Vigilante squads were formed among the Hispanic communities, because the people felt compelled to take circumstances into their own hands and stop the evil acts in any way they could. Occasionally the vigilantes caught their witch, and newspapers of the day reported the event, some in large headlines, some on back pages.

One 1882 newspaper report is particularly revealing of what was considered an inequity between the way witches were treated and the punishment by law of those who attempted to protect themselves against the effects of witchcraft. The story was written about Felipe Madrid and a woman with whom he was intimate. Madrid had broken off relations with his friend and later, years later, suffered a loathsome disease. He believed he could free himself from the spell put on him by his former acquaintance if she could be found and persuaded to withdraw her poison. Three acquaintances brought her to him, but she refused to cooperate; subsequently, he whipped her until she was near death. She finally escaped and eventually brought the matter to the attention of the American authorities, all the while proclaiming her innocence. Madrid was indicted for assault and battery, fined $150, and remained, in his opinion, bewitched, while the witch went free.[2]

General beliefs attributing ailments to bewitchment were constantly reinforced by specific incidents that occurred quite frequently in villages and communities wherever the Hispanic folk congregated. For example, the story is told about Juan Reyes, a man who lived in Santa Cruz, thirty miles north of Santa Fe. Juan's elderly mother fell ill, was unable to speak and lying on her deathbed. Juan asked her for his inheritance and she pointed a finger toward her husband. Juan's father denied there was any money, but Juan didn't believe him and threatened the old man by waving a dagger in his face. Juan's father cursed him, shouting: "May the earth swallow you. Not money, but a deformed and twisted body shall be your inheritance."[3] The ground opened and Juan sank down. When he pulled himself out, his lower limbs were completely deformed and his right arm was useless. Juan was destined to roam the high country begging for scraps of food.

Then there was Pedro Chavetas, who beat his mother and dragged her on the floor. She eventually lost her mind but before she was taken away to an asylum, she placed a curse on her son. "You will crawl on the ground forever like a horned toad," she said.[4] Pedro's legs shriveled until they were no thicker than broomsticks. He was forced to drag himself about for the rest of his life, just as he had dragged his poor mother across the floor.

Another story describes a Hispanic man whose right arm suddenly began to wither and become weakened. He traveled from doctor to doctor, but no one was able to restore the arm to its normal functioning. Finally, he faced facts: he was bewitched for a wrong he had committed as a younger man. When he visited an *arbularia*, a healer who specializes in curing and/or alleviating the effects of *brujeria*, she diagnosed the condition immediately and went to work rubbing his arm with a salve she specifically concocted for his problem. She massaged for hours, and eventually salt crystals began to fall through the skin onto a white sheet spread on the floor. The patient began to complain of increasing pain, but the *arbularia* could not stop. The more she rubbed, the louder the victim hollered. At long last, they both stopped. On the sheet was a frog that had fallen out of the patient's biceps. He was healed, and time proved it: within a few months, his arm had returned to its normal strength and functioning. Such stories keep the traditions alive.

In the Hispanic tradition of curing, bewitchment was the only reason a patient did not improve after a *curandera's* treatment. In such cases the patient would consult an *arbularia*, a village healer/specialist who removed the effects of witchcraft. Centuries ago, *arbularias* innocently dispensed herbs in the small hamlets of Spain, side by side with their sisters, *las curanderas*, *las parteras*, and *las sobardoras*. Somewhere in history, lost now to knowledge, the *arbularia* turned away from healing the general ailments of her people toward undoing the work the devil had done through his friends, *las brujas* (witches).

Arbularias are still very popular within Hispanic communities, highly visible (if you know where to look), always available for consultation, and always ready to use their own special, secret techniques to cure bewitchment. The point at which an individual seeks the services of an *arbularia* varies, but it is virtually certain that she is not a first choice. Usually, all the acceptable cultural healing methods are exhausted before the patient believes he or she is *embrujada*—bewitched—a horrifying admission. By consulting the *arbularia*, the patient comes face to face with the mysteries of the devil and stands before a healer who has had firsthand experience in overcoming evil. From the *arbularia*, the sufferer seeks to recover self-esteem, confidence, and, most of all, health. Unlike *brujas*, who work their craft shrouded in blackness, the *arbularias* have a positive outlook, are optimistic, are not censured by the community, and are accepted within the full circle of the healing arts, albeit with a little more caution than are other Hispanic healers.

A patient expects the *arbularia* to know a great deal about witchcraft, and she certainly does. She can recognize the symptoms of bewitchment and can recommend treatments that result in a relief or, better yet, in a cure. She will tell patients how to prevent future episodes. How does she know? She understands the culture, the assumptions patients make before calling on her, their physical condition, emotional state, and the disequilibrium they feel that brought them to her in the first place. Most of all, she knows they believe they are bewitched, and this belief is her starting point.

Through a carefully conducted examination and discussion, the *arbularia* discovers the patient's malady and confidently attributes the ailment to a witch. At this point, the individual feels greatly assured that the illness can be treated and that recovery is possible. After close questioning, the *arbularia* will offer remedies. The patient can put a ring of salt around the suspected witch's house, and throw salt into the air at an owl, but must make the sign of the cross at the same time. If the patient suffers from *susto*, a common result of bewitchment that appears as shock or fright, a pinch of dust will help. But the dust must be taken from the four corners of a grave-yard, placed on a piece of red flannel, and boiled with the victim's mother's wedding ring. The healer will make the sign of the cross over the water and give it to the sick one to drink. The patient takes three swallows and repeats a one-line prayer between each sip before being cured.[5]

In the Hispanic tradition, there are as many ways of treating the effects of bewitchment as there are ways to bewitch. Religion is part of all of the healing methods. One of the determinations made by an *arbularia* is whether or not the victims have lost their souls to the devil. If she believes so, she urges her patients to confess their deeds to a priest, to wear special amulets and, through prayer, to seek God's help. The healer helps the patient with her own prayers, her unfailing support, and her own religious sacrifices.

Reliance on prayer is essential in curing cases of bewitchment, be-cause it guides the patient from a bewitched state toward a better place—standing in the glow of God. Through the prayers of patient and healer, the Lord will know that the patient is sincere, truly wants to restore equilibrium into her or his life, and has honestly sought the help of a healer, a believer, to make her or him well. By all of these efforts, the bewitched individual renounces the devil and all the devil's ways and is convinced that through these actions the Lord will help.

According to traditional Hispanic beliefs, most *brujas* voluntarily take up *brujeria* (witchcraft) after entering into a Faustian pact with the devil. Cultural tales reveal that Hispanic witches allegedly meet as a group to discuss their techniques and conduct secret rites. They are said to dance with the devil, who is disguised as a man wearing a coat (but the devil's identity is given away by hooved feet and a tail, which protrudes from a trouser leg). Usually a billy goat enters the room during the meeting, followed by a snake who kisses the *brujas* with his forked tongue. At the conclusion, several skeletons carrying a coffin parade before the group. After an orgy of cannibalism, the meeting adjourns and the witches go forth, refreshed and renewed in their evil ways, more than ready for their next victim.

Tools and Symbols of *brujeria* (Photo by Bobette Perrone)

It is at these sessions that new recruits learn how to put a spell on someone, especially on Tuesdays or Fridays, witches' special days.[6] Directions on how to make rag dolls and wax figures, called *monos y muñecos*, are discussed and include specifics such as where to stick the pins for maximum result. Newcomers are told that magic charms and amulets sometimes work alone, without accompanying incantations for the victim's illness; insanity is often the result of this type of slow, deliberate bewitchment. Recipes are exchanged, because eating food contaminated by a *bruja* always creates a live animal in the victim's stomach, usually a frog, snake, toad, worm, or rat, which causes excruciating pain by constant gnawing. Frogs have entered rooms and tried to attack sick people. Beginners also learn how to transform themselves into animals or birds so they can attack their victims without revealing their identities.[7]

If an individual exhibits any symptoms of bewitchment, such as outspoken sexual, aggressive, or jealous behavior, a mysterious ailment that does not respond to conventional methods of treatment, or any form of mental illness, it is obvious that the *bruja* has done a good job.

Many Southwest Hispanic people have enduring beliefs in witchcraft because of tradition. For centuries, concepts about bewitchment persisted in Europe and were then carried across the ocean to the New World. The concepts were so ingrained in the folk culture that it was natural, not unusual, to conclude a neighbor was under a spell when a bad stomach got progressively worse despite being treated with available remedies. Interestingly, Eileen Lujan, M.D., a physician of Hispanic descent practicing in Las Vegas, New Mexico, said: "When I first opened up the office . . . I had about three calls . . . asking me, 'Would you take care of *brujaderas*,' or bewitchments. I just told them I didn't take care of it, and I thought they should get checked out medically before they did anything else. If they were medically okay, then they could probably look for somebody that took care of that. . . . If people believe in it, it can happen and I think you [as a physician] have to be aware of that."[8]

Regarding bewitchment in the American Indian cultures, Alex Hŕdlicka, a major observer of southwestern Indian life, writes that the type of illness in Indian patients reveals whether or not they have been bewitched. Hȓdlicka learned that a person may become ill because of ailments of an ordinary character (old age, accidents) or through ailments of a more mysterious nature, "sustained by some material agent introduced secretly into the body."[9]

Each tribe has its own rules about bewitchment. For example, in the 1880s, a white man named Frederick Schwatka visited several Apache tribes and reported that Apache witches were usually women, but accusations against them could come only when one particular band had more than its share of calamity.[10] The accused witch was prosecuted by the highest-ranked chief in the vicinity, sometimes the leader of another band sharing the same general location. The entire group participated in the proceedings, which usually resulted in an execution. As punishment, the witch was stripped, tied up by her thumbs, and left hanging just a few inches above the ground. Unless she confessed, she was flayed with mesquite or willow switches until the villagers were exhausted and abandoned her to die. If at any time during the flogging she confessed, she was then beaten to death. Afterward, all of her property was burned, including her house and utensils. Proper mourning procedures were denied the dead witch, but her family was able to bury her, provided they did not insult the dignity of the tribe in the process. By 1886, the Apaches may have learned from the Spanish colonists these traditions of dealing with witches, or they may have been practicing an ancient tradition of their own.

Apaches believe there is good or evil power in everything—people, lightning, rocks, animals, plants. Good power presents itself to an individual after meditation and prayer, making its wishes known to that particular person. Evil power can be obtained by (1) a person allowing evil powers to enter himself or herself and accepting the full knowledge of what such powers mean; or (2) a person having the power to do good and twisting it to wicked ends.[11] When a specific power enters an individual, that individual owns it and may do anything with it. For example, if an Apache claims to have power from lightning, considered to be one of the most powerful elements in the universe, that person is indeed respected and even feared. The owner may use lightning's tremendous force against enemies in the form of bewitchment. The degree of havoc that can be wrought is commensurate with the force of the power brandished. While having great power does not necessarily mean its owner is evil, every Apache can twist power around. Consequently, Apache witches of both genders keep their power and its source a secret in an effort to protect themselves, believing that if an enemy is unsure of the force of retaliation, chances are the enemy will not do anything foolish.

The element of time is an important factor in Apache witchcraft. The retaliatory power of evil enters an offender but does not have to manifest itself immediately. Thus, a man can reach middle age having committed an offense as a younger person, and still be waiting for the reaction, knowing it has to come. Apaches never know at what point they will be affected by their actions, what form the revenge will take, or how long it will last. As they live with these fears, they must be very cautious and constantly aware of their actions.

One of the major differences between Apache witches and Apache healers is the place each goes after death. Witches are relegated to a place where very little air or light penetrates. The healers are rewarded by an afterlife where little or no work is necessary, where corn and wild crops are always available, and where game is plentiful.[12]

Apaches, male and female, answer allegations of witchcraft in front of a council. If they respond to the charges satisfactorily, they will not be harmed. If not, the worst punishment they can suffer, short of death, is banishment from the tribe. The physical torture Apaches used to inflict on their witches, including hanging them upside down over a fire, was preferable to being evicted from the group.[13] Outcasts are rootless, forbidden to take refuge with another tribe, and forced to survive on their own without help from family and friends—a terrible fate for an Apache.[14]

Caution about bewitchment still prevails among the Apache people. We attempted to interview a modern-day Apache medicine man, but he refused to discuss the subject of witchcraft with us, believing that even talking about it, even thinking about it, would bring negativity all around him.

Apaches protect themselves against witchcraft by wearing turquoise beads or carrying eagle feathers and cattail pollen. Should these fail, Apache curing ceremonies (particularly the lightning, bear, and snake rituals) are performed. During the ceremony the medicine person pits individual power against that of the witch. If the healer is successful, the witch will die, and the patient will recover. If the ceremony fails, which can be determined only after waiting a reasonable time, the witch's power is seen to have been greater than the medicine person's power, and the patient continues to ail. Too many defeats can certainly end a healer's career.[15]

In witchcraft among the Pueblo Indians, a favorite weapon is a magical injection that inserts a foreign object into a victim's body. To do this, Pueblo witches use clay figurines and symbolically implant thorns, sticks, splinters, glass, or even small animals. Dolls made from the earth on which the unfortunate person has urinated are more effective, and work faster, than those made of hide, cloth, or wool, especially if they contain hair and nail clippings from the intended victim.

The Cochiti Pueblo people believe witches appear in human, animal, or bird forms—particularly as owls or crows—or objects such as fireballs. Six to twelve inches in diameter, the fireballs have a black center in the middle of red flames and bounce around, especially at night. Cochiti witches, regardless of the form they take, speak in the victim's own language, seducing or inciting him or her to perform evil deeds. By going through a magic hoop, witches can also change themselves into snakes, toads, or frogs to make access easier to the victim.[16]

In Pueblo societies the specific identity of witches is generally not clear and is left to the imagination. Anyone can be a witch and use actions provoked by revenge, envy, spite, or jealousy to get even with an offender. The Pueblo people, therefore, guard themselves very carefully in their behavior within their families and their communities, never knowing who is able to retaliate against a wrong. Should a Pueblo person become ill with an ailment whose cause is not obvious, witchcraft is considered to be at fault. Symptoms are caused by two definite actions: penetration of the body by a foreign object or loss of the heart through theft. Members of Pueblo curing societies are specifically empowered to treat both of these illnesses through elaborate rituals that utilize symbolism and ancient rites of healing.

At Cochiti Pueblo, medicine men with painted faces, wearing breechclouts, start curing witchcraft maladies by rubbing their hands with ashes and a secret, sacred solution before massaging a patient's body to locate the injected foreign object. They sing and pray over the victim as smoke from a fire fills the room. Once the affected area of the body is palpated, they suck the object out and spit it into a clay bowl. Loss of the heart, however, requires more complex curing measures. After diagnosis is made by the healers, they announce their intention to find the missing witch and the stolen heart. They leave the sickroom armed with flint knives and bear amulets (for their own protection) and disappear into the darkness. They may fly through the air if the witch is far away. When found, witches can overpower the healers by blowing bad breath in their faces while the forces of good and evil confront each other. Usually, however, the healers are triumphant and return home with the witch and the patient's heart, symbolized by a bundle of rags containing a kernel of corn in the center. Covered with blood and soot from their fight against evil, the medicine people give the patient the corn to swallow, and as he or she does, health is recovered. At the conclusion of the ceremony, the medicine people are given chili stew, bread, coffee, and baskets or cornmeal by the patient's relatives as payment for their services.[17]

At Santa Clara Pueblo, two groups called the Bear Societies are responsible for healing the effects of bewitchment through curing rites. The leader of the ceremony gazes into a bowl of water drawn from one of the sacred lakes in the area. In the bowl all things may be seen, including the identity of the witch, who is usually an unimportant villager or an unpopular Mexican.

Cures are usually made with food or cornmeal in the least complex ailments, but in more complicated afflictions, hot coals and bear or mountain lion hairs are put into a bowl. The patient is required to kneel before the bowl and inhale as the Bear Society member prays aloud. The ash is eventually removed from the bottom of the bowl, and water is added. The bewitched individual is then bathed with this solution and drinks the remaining liquid. Lastly, the patient is given a fetish to wear at the waist. The ceremony is then considered to be concluded.[18]

Most Pueblo people believe that because one can never know for certain, people of either gender who have unusual traits are quite possibly the evildoers: the senile elderly, the physically deformed, dishonest or rich persons in the village, those who make enemies easily, and those who wander around at night. Twins are definitely witches, but if the mother urinates on them at the time of their birth, they will grow up to be ordinary children.[19] Added to this list are members of other tribes, and even some people who appear to be perfectly "normal" within a given pueblo. As an aside, it is interesting to speculate on who may *not* be a witch according to Pueblo tradition.

To the north and west of the Pueblo villages live the Navajos, who have had frequent and not always pleasant contact and interaction with the Pueblos. But, shared beliefs exist. Navajo and Pueblo "witches" have certain similar characteristics: senile men are suspect. Great care is taken not to offend them, and they are urged by their families to leave the reservation and visit other family members—permanently.

Navajos believe that many persons become witches because of a greedy desire for wealth, and so rich people are suspect. To obtain power and wealth in the form of material goods, witches cause someone's death and then rob a grave of all the possessions.

However, some Navajos believe that becoming a witch is desirable as protection against spells from other witches because one witch can counteract the power of another. Resistance to bewitchment is possible but requires a strong counter-effort, reactions that demand combativeness and other assertive responses that are out of character for Navajo people. Individual action against the effects of witchcraft has been, in general, a lonely endeavor within the Navajo culture, as William Morgan reported in 1936: "Keeping out of trouble . . . might even be called a preoccupation. It is understandable why a man who sees another practicing witchcraft against him will not go about working up hostility towards this man. Public opinion will be strongly on his side, but he cannot count on physical help."[20]

One study of Navajo life has found that "Beliefs and practices related to witchcraft are thus refuges for those persons who are more under stress of misfortune than others, or for those who by reason of constitutional or other factors are less able to endure misfortunes, real or imagined."[21] The concept of blamelessness is extremely important in the Navajo culture, where maintaining a good position in the society is essential. If an individual violates a taboo and becomes ill because of it, the individual is strongly disapproved of by the culture.

Breaking a cultural taboo may cause illness, and in that case, the illness is the individual's fault. For example, the Navajos (and Apaches) know that if people practice incest, they openly declare themselves to be witches, because only evil persons are capable of such dastardly deeds, and their actions travel with them throughout eternity. But, if witchcraft can be blamed, the victim is blameless and not responsible for what has occurred. The victim then receives support and reassurance from peers and continues to hold a benign stance in the eyes of family, friends, and neighbors. The victim is free to seek sympathy and understanding and receives, in return, the maximum amount of support from family, friends, and neighbors. This allows an individual to release anxiety and complain openly in terms that, under more optimal and normal conditions, would be unacceptable in Navajo society.

In Navajo witchcraft practices, as stories have it, witches use images of their victims; they draw pictures of the enemy on the sandy floor of a cave. First, the men gather together and develop their plots to do harm, have sex with the dead, and indulge in cannibalism. They shoot a symbolic arrow from an imaginary magic bow, and after it hits its mark, the arrow and the spell it carries conceptually enter the body of the victim, and bewitchment occurs. While the missile is looking for its target, the witches chant to bring forth evil intentions, and they spit and urinate on the picture.[22] Occasionally, corpse powder is used in the ceremony. This special preparation, made from decomposing bodies, is quite potent because it requires a great deal of effort to obtain, including grave robbing. How the witch prepares it is a well-kept secret, one that perhaps will never be revealed because of the very strong Navajo taboos prohibiting contact with dead bodies.[23]

One particularly graphic example of a Navajo bewitching technique is "skinwalkers," human wolves who live among the people. Skinwalkers don the skins of wolves and, through a variety of methods, successfully practice witchcraft. Usually men, these witches climb on top of hogans at night and peer down through the open smoke hole, making sure their intended victim is present before dropping a magic preparation, usually corpse powder, into the dwelling. These human wolves use sharpened sticks as long as pencils to stab their prey once they enter the hogan. Stories tell of their aggressiveness, of how they seek out their victims and take definite steps to harm them.

Among the Navajos, cures of bewitchment begin with friends and relatives discussing their loved one's plight. Navajo culture patterns intervene while the victim relates the story to the assembled group. Only indirectly, if at all, will the patient accuse a specific person of witchery, and the listeners are equally reluctant to give the victim any definitive guidance. The group will, however, recommend the name of a diagnostician, who, after an initial examination, tells the victim which of the many curing ceremonies will help.[24] Navajo medicine people perform the ceremonies, charging the victim or the family for their services according to the type and length of the ritual performed. Because of the economics involved, one Navajo claimed: "It's only the rich people the witches go after. The poor people don't have so many witches. But they don't have money for a medicine man. Lots of those people have to go to the hospital. If you are rich, you can have sings and then if they don't help you, you can go to the hospital."[25]

By the time ceremonies become necessary, it is clear that the early measures used for protection from bewitchment have failed. In each home are various ceremonial objects, such as talking prayer sticks and medicines, imbued with the power to protect their owners. Gall medicine, made from the gall of eagles, bears, mountain lions, and skunks, is usually an extremely effective preventive, and is carried by Navajos whenever they enter a crowd. Ground corn goes along when Navajos travel. Certain plants and rock scrapings provide daily protection, as do specific songs sung in sweathouses. If, despite these measures, an individual becomes bewitched, three specific prayer ceremonials serve as antidotes, all of which are designed to "pray the evil back to the witch: the Shield Prayer, the Bringing Up Prayer, and the Bringing Out Prayer."[26] Of course, if the affected person is unable to afford a curing ceremony or unwilling to go to the hospital, family or friends might retaliate against the witch, but that also requires identifying him or her, something Navajos do quite reluctantly.

In the old days, extreme measures were taken against witches, but the Navajos could not or would not give any information on the then-current (1936) practices except to state that because of white man's laws, the Navajo people did not kill their witches anymore. Kluckhohn, however, learned from his informants that witches were killed by shooting or hanging, but mostly by clubs wielded by a group of relatives and friends of the victim.[27]

Witchcraft beliefs provide cultural explanations of why people have ailments that are unnatural and not able to be explained in the usual manner. Witchcraft is an approved way of "explaining why one's life was not all that one desired it to be,"[28] a culturally sanctioned method of shifting responsibility, when it becomes too great to carry, from oneself onto something everyone is vulnerable to— bewitchment. The victim releases emotional tension in a safe, acceptable way—transferring anxiety to a witch. "Belief in witchcraft provided a channel for the expression of hostile feelings; it was a form of hating that was socially approved and justified."[29]

In modern, mainstream Anglo-American society, beliefs about witchcraft do not appear as overtly as they did centuries ago. References to bewitchment have been replaced by scientific words—words that explain what is wrong, words that never speak of witches, words that never hint at the dark, mysterious reasons why some people become ill. Doctors' prescriptions are reassuring, and shed the light of reason on ancient fears, so old ideas about witchcraft are usually not mentioned anymore. Many fears about connections between bewitchment and ailments have also disappeared, defeated by penicillin, insulin, heparin, psychotherapy, radioactive tracers, and x-rays. Now, supposedly, there are no effects of witchcraft. The U.S. Congress has passed no laws punishing witches during the last two hundred years. As medicine entered a world of transplants, dialysis, and chemotherapy, all fears about harm that witches may do have been left behind. Really? Is Anglo society free at last from witchcraft? Yes and no.

Witches still convey the power of evil in children's movies such as *The Wizard of Oz, Sleeping Beauty,* and *Snow White and the Seven Dwarfs.* The concept of an evil force is taught through popular movies such as *Star Wars,* where Darth Vader embodies an evil force threatening the entire universe; *Rosemary's Baby,* which involves impregnation by the devil; *Poltergeist I, II,* and *III;* and other movies that earn literally millions of dollars of profit on people's fascination with evil entities and forces.

Modern interest in evil and dark forces also often may be less obvious, disguised because of Anglo society's skill in using the psychological defense mechanism of denial—denial of death, denial of sexuality, denial of many of the "basics" of human life. Is denying the existence of evil part of America's cultural pattern? Perhaps. Stated differently, just because a large percentage of contemporary society does not believe in evil or witchcraft does not necessarily mean that it does not exist and that people cannot be bewitched. To draw a parallel: because a majority of the populace of the middle ages believed the world was flat did not mean that it was.

A corollary argument regarding the role of belief is commonly offered. "To be effective, witchcraft must be generally believed to be effective."[30] The fear and anxiety generated internally if a person believes witchcraft is aimed at him or her can indeed cause illness, even death. In other words, if faith can heal, fear can kill. The concept is that witchcraft can work if one *believes* it can. Supporting this idea, author Sybil Leek, in her book, *The Complete Art of Witchcraft*, recounts her experience with a woman who contacted her in great fear, having been sent a voodoo doll. "Her health was affected through her fear, and doctors were puzzled by her sicknesses, including great loss of weight and appetite and general malaise. Her relatives were sure she would die and medical opinion was that she could not continue to live with such a constant loss of weight. That was in 1964. Today [1973] the woman is still alive and healthy. The curse was taken off her by Sybil Leek."[31]

Yet another argument put forth is that we experience evil all the time but give it different names.

Evil breaks in upon people in sneaky ways. There are natural catastrophes which engulf us—earthquakes, fires, tidal waves, plagues, famines. There are the social evils of war and battle, of oppression by powerful and ruthless leaders; there is poverty, social condemnation and betrayal. And then there are the more personal and intimate evils which may or may not be associated with these others. Here we find physical sickness, mental illness, and also the less dramatic and perhaps even more agonizing evils of loneliness, meaninglessness, depression, guilt and anxiety. From the point of experience these all seem to be of one piece.[32]

If evil is a doctor cutting off the wrong leg, or accidently sewing up a sponge into a patient (called iatrogenic illnesses, meaning doctor-caused), then medical inattention and lack of caring could be classified as evil.

This way of thinking may raise the response that such evils are not what is meant by "evil," implying that only conscious, malicious intent counts truly evil. "It is a reflection of the enormous mystery of the subject that we do not have a generally accepted definition of evil."[33] So states M. Scott Peck, one of the few modern theorists who defines evil, saying: "Evil is 'live' spelled backwards. Evil is in opposition to life. It is that which opposes the life force. It has, in short, to do with killing. Specifically, it has to do with murder—namely, unnecessary killing, killing that is not required for biological survival . . . Evil, then, for the moment, is that force, residing either inside or outside of human beings, that seeks to kill life or liveliness."[34] Concommitantly, Christina Larner defines witchcraft as "harming through release of power activated by hatred."[35] This author's definition is probably closer to most people's ideas of evil and witchcraft.

If one's definition is similar to the above, then a broad array of modern examples of both group and individual evil spring to mind and are in the literature on evil: Nazism, Adolf Hitler, Karl Adolf Eichmann; Charles Manson; the Mylai massacre; the National Guard at Kent State; and the possibility of nuclear holocaust, to name a few. Peck writes: "Mylai Massacre is an example of group evil. Approximately 500 men participated in the massacre."[36] Morton Kelsey states that "there is the evil to which some people dedicate themselves. From this kind of dedication the Black Mass and most of black witchcraft spring. One suspects something of this sort in the Manson family."[37]

While these examples are commonly accepted as evidence of evil, how is evil described from the point of view of science? The predominant explanation is mental illness. "To a greater or lesser degree, all mentally healthy individuals submit themselves to the demands of their own conscience. Not so the evil, however. In the conflict between their guilt and their will, it is the guilt that must go and the will that must win. . . . This willful failure of submission that characterizes malignant narcissism is depicted in both the stories of Satan and of Cain and Abel."[38]

Historically, one of the forms witchcraft has been believed to take is madness. In a recent popular news magazine, a story depicted this type of manifestation.

> Most never act on the dark impulses, but a few new mothers—less than 1%—become psychotic. These may suffer extreme agitation, feel persecuted and begin hallucinating. Angela Thompson of Sacramento drowned her nine-month-old son in the bathtub after hearing the voice of God tell her the child was the devil. It has been five years since her son's death, but her recollection of her mental state is still vivid. "I thought if I killed the baby that my husband would raise him to life again in three days and that the world would know that my husband was Jesus Christ," she explains. "When he was dead, I thought his face was contorted like the devil's." Postpartum mental disorders are so far poorly understood.[39]

One reason for the lack of more complete knowledge regarding mental disorders is that psychology and psychiatry are, relatively speaking, in their infancy. Yet some interesting speculation is occurring with regard to the role of evil as it might be related to mental illness. For example, Peck speculates, "I very much doubt that somebody can go walking down the street one day and have a demon jump out from behind a bush and penetrate him. Possession appears to be a gradual process in which the possessed person repeatedly sells out for one reason or another."[40]

Peck further theorizes regarding treatment of such disorders, stating that "there is no way to penetrate the disguise of evil except in the role of a healer, one who, in the interest of healing is willing, as a psychotherapist, to wrestle with the demonic behind the pretense . . . there is always the risk of contamination."[41] This language reveals that at least some modern, sophisticated, AMA physicians, not laypersons only, may think of mental illness in terms of possession and demonic forces.

For many groups in Anglo-American culture, evil and witchcraft are alive, thriving, totally, and unequivocally, and unabashedly real. Most notably, a vociferous number of Protestant fundamentalists strongly believe that Satan exists, has power, and affects human lives. "New Age" spiritual seekers, odd bedfellows with the fundamentalists, also frequently subscribe to the idea that "dark forces" oppose the forces of light and that a person can be "psychically attacked." Some American rock music *afficionados* idolize rock stars who sing of Satanic cults, and there are suggestions that many of these devotees experiment with Satanism in various forms. Many Anglo Catholics also believe in the literal existence of the devil, e.g., "the Evil One is more deeply rooted and entwined in our lives than we ordinarily realize. This one still is hard at work."[42] Certainly one should not assume that witchcraft is dead in all of Anglo-American culture. It is not.

Why not? A variety of answers are possible. First, it is possible that evil and evil ones actually do exist and can affect one's life and health. A second hypothesis is from the psychological point of view. One author writes that "the practice of witchcraft appears, in fact, to spring from the very sources which produce accusations of witchcraft: unfulfilled desire, frustration, envy, and need for 'power.'"[43] Another author writes, "The rise of witchcraft belief may be an attempt by various people to regain a sense of control over their environment and their lives."[44] A third author states that "one of the most profound aspects of evil is that he who does the evil is typically convinced that evil is about to be done to him. He regards the world or at least part of it as dangerous or bent on destruction and therefore something justifiably to be destroyed."[45]

Regrettably, witchcraft and women continue to be linked in the popular mind. The connection is renewed annually at Halloween when the rubber mask face of a witch is always female. A nationally syndicated cartoon, *The Wizard of Id,* ran a cartoon in June, 1988, that contained the following dialogue:

King: "What do you want to be when you grow up, little girl?"

Girl: "I want to go into a field where women excel."

King: "Why don't you become a witch?"[46]

More complex are modern reminders within current religious instititions. As this is written [1988], there are no women Catholic priests, no Orthodox Jewish women rabbis, only four Conservative Jewish women rabbis, and only a handful of Protestant women ministers. Even among religious groups that permit women in the pulpit, with few exceptions, women are denied access to certain positions within the hierarchal structure of western religions. For example, the Episcopal church has no women serving as bishops, cardinals, or archbishops; the Methodist church has only one woman bishop. The most progressive action taken to acknowledge the spiritual legitimacy of women has been the Presbyterian church, which elected a woman as moderator of the general assembly, the highest position possible. This reluctance to include women in spiritual sanctuaries has been "explained" in a variety of ways, e.g., woman's place is below man (the Adam's rib argument); spiritual precedent; lack of congregational (cultural) acceptance; and, yes, that women are inherently evil due to that "sin of Eve," and other "explanations." No matter what the rationale, however, excluding women from positions of religious prominence and authority is a "sin of omission" that allows a continuation of the fallacy that women are either spiritually weak, dangerous, or wicked. This is a disastrous legacy of the link between women and evil from past centuries.

Regardless of gender, "Satan cannot do evil except through a human body . . . it cannot murder except with human hands. It does not have the power to kill or even harm by itself. It must use human beings to do its deviltry."[47] Humans must participate if evil and witchcraft and bewitchment are to occur.

Today, it is quite difficult for most modern Americans to regard bewitchment as a legitimate cause of illness. Many have been convinced that such a condition does not exist, but others definitely do believe in the concept. The debate expands and continues, with no resolution currently in sight, but with plenty of ideas to fascinate the scholar. Of special note, and giving one pause, is Erich Fromm's succinct statement, "Hence, as long as one believes that the evil man wears horns, one will not discover an evil man."[48]

PART FIVE

THE AUTHORS SPEAK

In the course of researching and writing this book, we all learned. New ideas were generated; old ones validated—or invalidated; and experiences were lived. Some ideas profoundly affected our lives. Each of us is as diverse from the others as are the healing practitioners presented: different backgrounds, careers, interests. Each of us has previous experience with various forms of writing and publication (both fiction and nonfiction): poetry, short stories, novels, technical and professional journal articles, journalism, and magazine articles. We can speak in many voices. Each of us chose a voice to use here. We have learned respect for the form of presentation.

Each of us will describe what we experienced or felt; what ideas were generated. The focuses and styles vary. Yet there is a connectedness of themes, just as with all of the women we interviewed. The themes are about women, cultures, values, assumptions, and the necessity and advisability of integrating values and methods, to name a few.

In keeping with the established format of each healer speaking in her own voice as much as possible, each writer will now speak in her own voice.

CHAPTER 17

TALKING AND LISTENING
Bobette Perrone

I have gained new vision in writing this book: I have learned in my eyeballs. There has been a strain, an ache of learning, focusing, paying attention, in trying to see correctly, without my own blinders. I have strained to see more and more clearly. I have learned the meticulousness of the process of honorable respect. I have learned how truly wrenching it sometimes is to learn, and to accept other perceptions, and to learn without hubris.

The integrity of respect came while eating mutton, fat-floating-globules-in-the-juice mutton, and hating it, while almost crying in the realization that the delicacy was given to me at the expense of a family member's supper the next night. Respect came on the muddy mountain road where a woman carried the food for her animals on her shoulders, with her boots, hair, and jeans caked with hardening adobe mud-mucous and her rough, frozen hands unprotected but remembering how to weave exquisite fibers into baskets of deep medicine healing. I know that I cannot easily live in a world where the concept of dirt roads is not understood and innately appreciated.

The respect came at odd, darkening moments. At midnight on the hard ground of a Navajo hogan, the youngest girl of a nearby family knocked fearfully, telling of being afraid and alone in the night, when skinwalkers might appear. As a white woman, I made proper (or improper) assurances that all was well, because nothing could get through the door, all the time dismissing the girl's jerked thumb gesture toward the large, round hole in the hogan roof. The respect came following her departure. I, in my sleeping bag laid on the cold, clay floor beneath a hot, summer sky, spent my night watching the smoke hole, falling asleep only as Grandfather Dawn lighted my heavens, *and* the smoke hole.

Respect entered my consciousness in unexpected places. In the waiting-for-the-baby room of Jesusita Aragon's home, three women, bellies exposed, awaited the touch upon their stomach by *la curandera's* hands. Instead *la curandera* instructed me to "smooth out between their stretch marks" with my thumb, in long, even strokes. The soothing mood was interrupted by Jesusita's outcry. "*Agua. Agua. Desvencijado.*"[1] "Water! It's broken," I thought she said. I was focused on my job. So I carefully studied the laboring woman. But no evidence. Jesusita was referring to the house's plumbing. (I later learned that a different verb would have been used—*se rentavo agua*—to mean the bursting of a woman's water while birthing.) But there I stood without my Spanish dictionary, without proper knowledge, a common problem in cross-cultural matters, if one admits honestly.

But Jesusita's faith in her God-who-would-provide was adamant and unswerving. Privately, I wondered. Jesusita bent her head in prayer as the plumber presented her the bill in the exact amount of the check in my purse, which I had picked up from the mailbox that morning. She needed it; I had it. So I gave it to her. But it did occur to me that it was a fine coincidence. In Jesusita's mind it was no coincidence at all. The water works got mended. Three healthy children were born, two girls and a boy. Somebody's belief system was working. Maybe everybody's.

I learned about respect from Sabinita Herrera's ancient wood stove, with all of those burners and all of those short lengths of kindling, each one having to be cut to size to fuel the stove so Sabinita could feed all of those people within the family. I learned respect for generosity as I hungered for the brewing coffee and then ate one after another of the *biscochitos* Sabinita baked for us. I learned respect for this teacher as she spread out hundreds of herbs on the oilcloth-covered table, repeating the Spanish names until we truly "got it right."

I learned respect when my hubris was confronted by Dhyani Ywahoo, who would not accept my "authentic" writing on Cherokee history. Would not accept? Refused is more accurate. It was refused on the basis of its American educational system origins. But I had sent for all those university books from Cherokeeland. Still it was refused on the basis of "brainwashing." "Not I," said I. There was not a quaver or falter in Dhyani's response. It was simply not negotiable. I had to live with that for a long time before I understood how correct she was. And I am chagrined and delighted and embarrassed and more knowledgeable. I am also aware that in believing what I believe, I do not always see clearly.

From Molly Radford Ward, my respect for living a good life, based on the premise of enjoying it, was reaffirmed. From Josette Mondanaro, Stirling Puck, and Jane Patterson I learned it is not necessary to hide my own blue lace geode of sweet-being from the outside world. These women do not. Yes, the external crust of the doctors is, indeed, protective. But, ah, the gentle sweetness of that inner core. Each one allowed me in. The gift they gave me was more of myself.

Annie Kahn? I love that woman. She is sometimes so damned blunt. And I am a direct woman myself. While I lived there, in a hogan separate from hers, she would not let me use her outhouse. I was steamed. I started desperately digging my own, which I was supposed to do in the first place. Then she sent help for the digging.

She taught me the most wondrous rituals of respect. We had worked all day. Hard. Annie announced, "Time for a sweat bath," so we spent the next four hours in a mission of respect. We went to the road and collected a rock as representative of the "place people pass." We went to the streambed for the representative of smoothing the hard ways; she sliced a branch, one branch of representative willow with one swoop of the axe; a shovel blade in the desert earth to remove one representative of the yucca root to wash our hair in preparation; taking only what we needed then, not storing for later. And each of the representative spirits was thanked by Annie's Navajo prayers. Then she said prayers to the Collective All. Meanwhile, I stumbled with the concept of thanking, actually thanking a stone or a plant—and meaning it.

I gained what I had sought. Healing and learning. I learned that there are actually assumptions about medicine and healing. Assumptions. Mostly overlooked. I learned to think about underpinnings, learned how to find them, and how to utilize them. I learned about the dark side of healing and the power in the dynamic of believing darkly. The undeniable relationship between the politics and the economics of witchcraft was gently hammered into my consciousness by Professor Sue-Ellen Jacobs, who insisted we look "at" before looking away.

I learned to view the universe through the doorway of Annie Kahn's hogan. Horses straggled by, one by one in single file, framed by that doorway each morning. The highlight of my afternoon was waiting for their return. I became one with the All-That-Is, the Universe, through Annie Kahn's hogan door beneath the vermillion cliffs. I learned. Not in a microscope. Not in a telescope. Not in an hourglass.

"I want to be healed." Somewhere along the way, I articulated that deep realization. I clarified. "I don't want to be mended. I want to be healed." Somewhere I discovered the difference.

The difference? On a recent television segment entitled "Talk Back To Doctors," the physician panel members had a dialogue regarding attitudes some physicians have toward their patients. It went as follows:

"In public, doctors call them hypochondriacs, malingerers, and hysterics. In private, physicians have been known to describe some of them as turkeys, hospital hobos, and GOMERS, an acronym for Get Out Of My Emergency Room. . . . As a result, a doctor may reject a patient outright."[2]

As the dialogue went on, Dr. Robert Mendelsohn stated: "Doctors . . . get taught a different set of ethics, and they get taught a different set of responses. . . . If you ask a doctor a question, he is taught to respond with 'just trust me, dear.' If you come to the doctor with information that is at variance with the information that he gave you, he says to you, 'What medical school did you go to?' If you're an older person . . . he says, 'What do you expect at your age?' Doctors are taught a different set of ethics."

Dr. Nancy Dickey: "There has been a time when technology was growing and changing so fast that we became inundated with the amount of knowledge we had to teach, and perhaps lost sight of how much you have to teach the ability to interact with sick patients."

Oprah Winfrey: "You say that doctors are taught to be omnipotent."

Dr. Peter Gott: "Absolutely."[3]

Further, according to Dr. Susan Block, a psychiatrist at Harvard Medical School, "doctors miss up to 70 percent of symptoms that reveal anxiety and depression. Typically overlooked or misdiagnosed: headaches, fatigue, and restlessness. By focusing solely on physical ills, a doctor may fail to treat the real problems."[4]

What is wrong with an approach to healing that can produce a plethora of such statements and attitudes? It would appear that both sins of commission and sins of omission produce such a system. What is "too much with us?" What is overly present? Too much power, too much ego; too much money; and too much of a belief system based on a legacy of male values. Frequently, doctors make the assumption that they have power over life and death and are ego-threatened if a patient dies or a disease is incurable. Too much money is involved. The one common denominator of AMA medicine is that it is all very expensive; the average income of physicians is $113,000 per year, and each neophyte physician leaves medical school owing upwards of $30,000.

On the list of attitudes that are too much with us, and which negatively influence health care, is the male mindset that has firmly established a system excluding both women and their values. "Aristotle argued that women were colder and weaker than men and that women did not have sufficient heat to boil the blood and thus purify the soul. The medical and scientific assumptions of these ancients were incorporated into medieval thinking with few revisions and came to dominate much of Western medical literature."[5]

Medieval thinking denied women healers access to their own skills by branding them as witches. Any ability perceived by men to be "unusual" was frequently deadly for women. For example:

> The so-called Witch of Newbury was murdered by a group of soldiers because she knew how to go "surfing" on the river. Soldiers of the Earl of Essex saw her doing it, and were "as much astonished as they could be," that "to and fro she fleeted on the board standing firm bolt upright . . . turning and winding it which way she pleased, making it pastime to her, as little thinking who perceived her tricks, or that she did imagine that they were the last she ever should show." Most of the soldiers were afraid to touch her, but a few brave souls ambushed the

board-rider as she came to shore, slashed her head, beat her, and shot her, leaving her "detested carcass to the worms."[6]

And that was for surfboarding!

The legendary frailty of women was also employed to demonstrate the "failure" of women in comparison with the male. Biologically, women have been undervalued. Another male norm. The possibility that such 'frailty' could be due to socially sanctioned expectations of "being a lady" was dismissed.

It has been well documented that access to the institutions of medical authority has been vigilantly guarded against the inclusion of women and women's values. C. Christ says, "During my years there, Yale's president was to make the infamous statement that Yale would never admit women as undergraduates because its mission was to educate 1,000 male leaders each year."[7] She continues:

> Doctors used their authority as scientists to discourage women's attempts to gain access to higher education. Women's intellectual development, it was argued, would proceed only at great cost to reproductive development. As the brain develops, so the logic went, the ovaries shrivel. In the twentieth century, scientists have given modern dress to these prejudices. Arguments for women's different [and inferior] nature have been based on hormonal research, brain lateralization, and sociobiology. Science and the authority of science have often been turned against women.[8]

Has it ever been postulated that as the male brain develops, the testes might also shrivel? One wonders. Or does one?

Women contribute characteristics and values that are missing from, and are, in fact, shocking in their absence from, the current health care delivery and provision system. The canons of health care omit connectedness, interpersonal sensitivity, empathy, and touching, to name a few. Not all women demonstrate these qualities, and some men do. However, Carol Gilligan, associate professor at the Harvard School of Education, summarizes a large body of developmental theory and research, saying that "since masculinity is defined through separation while femininity is defined through attachment, male gender identity is threatened by intimacy while female gender identity is threatened by separation. Thus males tend to have difficulty with relationships."[9] Gilligan believes "that men in this culture tend to see the world in terms of their autonomy (and are over-threatened by intimacy), whereas women tend to see the world in terms of connectedness (and are overthreatened by isolation)." [10]

Nancy Chodorow, respected developmental theorist and researcher, states, "The fact that women, universally, are largely responsible for early child care . . . results in any given society, that feminine personality comes to define itself in relation and connection to other people more than masculine personality does." [11] Chodorow also states that "girls emerge . . . with a basis for 'empathy' built into their primary definition of self in a way that boys do not. Girls emerge with a stronger basis for experiencing another's needs or feelings as one's own." [12]

Yet, again and again, studies and attitudes and definition of developmental "norms" and societal "norms" erroneously exclude the feminine and adopt the masculine as the norm against which all else is measured. For example, the charge made against women is that their "failure to separate then becomes by definition a failure to develop . . . since masculinity is defined through separation while femininity is defined through attachment." [13] Therefore, attachment, or involvement, the relationship so badly needed in medicine, is viewed as a "developmental liability." [14]

Theorists and practitioners alike are saying an infusion of women's values such as connectedness, empathy, and nurturing into current medical practices would be desirable. The question before the medical profession is which style to adopt in patient treatment—physician-oriented, disease-oriented, or patient-oriented. Which values do each of us want to select as we go to a doctor, a healer?

Lily Tomlin and Jane Wagner make the choice amusingly clear in the following piece:

At the Doctor's

You're sure, Doctor?
Premenstrual syndrome?
I mean, I'm getting divorced.
My mother's getting divorced.
I'm raising twin boys.
I have a lot of job pressure—
I've got to find one.

The ERA didn't pass,
not long ago I lost a very dear friend, and . . . and
my husband is involved . . .
not just involved, but in love, I'm afraid . . . with
this woman . . .
who's quite a bit younger than I am.
and you think it's my period
and not my life?[15]

A "revolution of values" is bubbling up to the top. When Gilligan speaks of this "revolution of values,"[16] she entreats the earnest to thoughtful contemplation. As a nation, as part of the earth's people, as components of the larger universe, we are all threatened by isolation and disconnectedness. Disease and healing take place at the national, societal, and world levels as well as at the individual physical level. For example, the brave, now middle-aged men maimed by Vietnam detest themselves for their buried hurts, and their country for ignoring this hurt. They are in need of healing. The dying who are detested because their disease is AIDS are in need of healing. All of the bent old men, the broken old women, hated for their age, their "uselessness," are in need of healing, as are all of the beaten, burnt, lacerated, tortured, mutilated, murdered children, children whose disease is in having no power at all. Letty Cottin Pogrebin has asked a question in her article, "Do Americans Hate Children?" Her answer: "The society that kneels before the commercial altar of childhood in the adorable forms of Strawberry Shortcake, Peter Pan . . . Charlie Brown . . . is the same society that murders its children, rapes them, starves them, whips them, shuns them, burns them, stunts them, poisons them and hates them to death. And we who do not do it ourselves let it be done."[17] Surely, children are in need of healing. And is not the nation whose values allow such atrocities in need of healing? All women and men and all of the children whose lives are being ruptured by disconnectedness need the healing values of empathy, attachment, harmony, and connectedness.

How can healing occur for these conditions? Incorporate female values. "The failure to 'build women in' to conceptual models has impaired our understanding."[18] In one attempt to remedy the omission, Gilligan has extensively researched and documented that boys are taught to compete for what they want, whereas girls are taught to cooperate to reach the same goal. Girls have turn-taking games like jump rope and hopscotch "where competition is indirect since one person's success does not necessarily signify another's failure. Consequently, disputes requiring adjudication are less likely to occur."[19] Van Gelder, quoting Gilligan, also states:

> Then we have this group here—women—who seem less warlike, and we say that "they're having a problem with aggression . . . what is it about the way women deal with conflict that makes it less likely to erupt in violence?" And what if you said, "Our notions of winning and losing have been rendered obsolete by nuclear technology, so we need a new set of rules, and you in fact have this microcosm of little girls who've been saying all along that they don't like to play games where people win and lose and get their feelings hurt and feel bad—I mean, instead of ignoring them or thinking that there's something wrong with them, why aren't we out there *studying* them?"[20]

Susan T. Fiske, in "People's Reactions to Nuclear War," states, "When asked directly what emotions come to mind regarding a nuclear war, the typical person does report fear, terror, and worry . . . or fear and sadness . . . some studies indicate that women report more anxiety than men do."[21] That women report more anxiety than men do over nuclear holocaust can be interpreted two ways: women are just nervous or cowardly, i.e., "What's wrong with them?"; or, women love the world enough and are connected enough to have anxiety over nuclear holocaust and are saddened by it. A different emphasis. Different values. Women's values. Healing values.

What is "too much with us" in the current model used in medicine, then, has been the preponderance of male values. What has been lacking has been enough women's values of connectedness, empathy, harmony, cooperation, and more. These attributes can be added and integrated. But they must be acknowledged, studied, seen clearly, valued, and then described to others. Storytelling is a way of describing. Storytelling is an excellent way to get values known, and stories present values in the least-threatening way, which increases the likelihood of their acceptance and inclusion. Carol P. Christ in her book, *Diving Deep and Surfacing*, states:

208 THE AUTHORS SPEAK

> Women's stories have not been told. And without stories there is no
> articulation of experience. Without stories a woman is lost when she
> comes to make the important decisions of her life. She does not learn to
> value her struggles, to celebrate her strengths, to comprehend her
> pain. Without stories she cannot understand herself. . . . She is closed
> in silence. . . . If women's stories are not told, the depth of women's
> souls will not be known. . . . Stories give shape to lives. As people
> grow up, reach plateaus, or face crises, they often turn to stories to
> show them how to take the next step. Women often live out inauthentic
> stories provided by a culture they did not create. The story most com-
> monly told to young girls is the romantic story of falling in love and
> living happily ever after. As they grow older, some women seek to re-
> place that story with one of free and independent womanhood.[22]

That is what this book is about: Storytelling. It is an answer to
Gilligan's question, "Why aren't we studying women?" We are! And
we are telling their stories.

Carol Christ says: "Women have lived in the interstices between
their own vaguely understood experience and the shapings given to
experience by the stories of men. The dialectic between experience
and shaping experience through storytelling has not been in women's
hands. Instead of recognizing their own experiences, giving names to
their feelings and celebrating their perceptions of the world, women
have often suppressed and denied them." She proclaims that "in a
very real sense, there is no experience without stories."[23] For millennia the male norm was accepted, and male stories were told. Now,
new stories must be told and new myths must be created for the culture to live by and to learn from. Stories must be told of women's
values and ways to prepare both women and the world for including
more of women's values in medicine. That is why the format of this
book is predominantly in story form.

Leslie Silko, a fine Native American writer, addresses the healing
aspect of stories when she says: "There's sort of a continuity. In
other words, this telling is a creating of a kind of identity for you so
that whatever kind of situation you find yourself in, you know where
you are and you know who you are. It's that whatever you do, you
never feel that you're alone, or you never feel at a loss for. . . . You're
never lost, you're never lost."[24] Paula Gunn Allen, another noted author, states: "The tribes seek, through song, ceremony, legend, sa-

cred stories (myths), and tales to embody, articulate, and share reality, to bring the isolated private self into harmony and balance with
this reality, to verbalize the sense of the majesty and reverent mystery of all things, and to actualize, in language, those truths of being
and experience that give to humanity its greatest significance and
dignity. The artistry of the tribes is married to the essence of language itself, for in language we seek to shape our being with that of
the community, and thus to share in the communal awareness of the
tribe."[25] Starhawk states, "We challenge the emptiness of estrange-
ment whenever we make a deep connection with another, whenever
we love, whenever we create community."[26] In other words, stories
connect people to each other and to their community—which is
healing.

Stories connect people across time as well. Stories transcend time.
Stories bring the then to the now. Stories bring the possibilities for
the future to the now. Stories connect us with each other; they connect us with the concepts by which we operate. They even connect
us with the archetype. What does occur, in actuality, is that stories
give one a historical and spiritual home through creating a sense of
well-being.

Stories also teach values. For example, Phyllis Chesler's words in
Women & Madness take on broad meaning when she says, "her
mother has not taught her to be a warrior, i.e., to take difficult roads
to unknown and unique destinations—gladly."[27] "Gladly" is the
crucial word, the crucial concept or value. For men, in their stories, the "difficult roads" *are* taken gladly; they are called "adventures." Women have not had their own stories of difficulties taken—
gladly. They have been "protected" against such excursions and
denied access, by virtue of not having stories that teach the glad-
ness of obstacles to overcome—with joy. The value of the stories presented in this book is that they are stories of women who have acted
"gladly." Unusual roads have been traveled—gladly—by the women
we have met.

Each story has value in contributing identity to each reader; in
linking creative community; in demonstrating connectedness. In
doing so, the stories heal. Plato said it well: "As you ought not attempt to cure the eyes without treating the head, or the head without
treating the body as a whole, so you should not treat the body with-

out treating the soul . . . and the treatment of the soul, my good friend, is by means of certain charms, and these charms are words of the right sort. By the use of such words is temperance engendered in the soul, and as soon as it is engendered and present, one may easily secure health to the head, and to the rest of the body also."[28] He speaks of "words of the right sort," words by which "one may easily secure health . . . in the soul, . . . to the head . . . and the rest of the body also." Plato knew that words and stories heal.

I have lived my way through this book. I will not repeat all that has been said by the medicine women, the *curanderas*, and the women doctors. But, to their stories I have added my own.

In my girlhood, the only stories and images to emulate as a female were those of nurses or grammar school teachers or perfect wives and mothers. Having accepted the societal brainwashing that I, a girl, could not excel in higher mathematics or science, I found the story of Madam Curie an exception and an aberration. To be a woman judge or a woman doctor was not a story presented. The newspaper accounts of Amelia Earhart and her adventures had marvelous appeal. They hinted at the mysteriousness of possibilities.

The stories that held passion for me were the ones I lived and saw and heard. They were of the land and hardships. I lived in the high desert, homesteading 160 acres of raw and wild canyon with my mother. The stories I lived I heard around the campfires with the women who fought for their piece of earth during the Depression. Where gender was not the issue, survival was. As a kid, with my wired-together, single-shot .22 caliber rifle (each bullet having to count because of the cost), I killed the game for the night's meal: each day, survival. Hauling my bucket of water: survival. Collecting rattlesnakes to sell for their venom: survival.

And afterward, I spent my time on Rocky Mountain. The climb to the summit was exhausting for little legs yet exhilarating for a growing intellect. At the apex of my mountain were two huge, flat boulders, a deep, dark, wide and fearful chasm between them. To reach the outer boulder, I had to jump over that abyss, past the terror of it, stopping abruptly on the second rock giant, balancing to keep from going over the far edge. I sat with my legs dangling over the sides of boulders for many of the growing years of my life. It was in that position on Rocky Mountain, as I viewed our tiny cabin on the canyon floor below, that I realized, in the grand scheme of it all, how very insignificant I was. In comprehending this, I also knew of my importance. And I had acted gladly.

My story of this book is that I have learned the meticulousness of the process of respect. I have truly gained healing. I have learned that there must be love in the healing process. In fact, love is the healer. Before, I might have said of love, "I have found that, too." But I am now more comfortable in saying, "Perhaps it was given to me." Maybe that is the difference between being mended and being healed—some enriching harmony to whom I can say, "Thank you." To the healers, to each of them, to all of them, and to those in close proximity to my once-torn heart, I thank you for loving. In this generous clanship that we share, thank you for knowing that I, too, am a representative. Thank you for teaching me the respect to know that you are. Thank you for your stories. Thank you for your healing.

CHAPTER 18

A PHILOSOPHY OF COMPREHENSIVE HEALING
H. Henrietta Stockel

In most Native American and Hispanic American societies, it is the authority of tradition that confers lasting credibility on medicine women and *curanderas,* healers who gain legitimacy within their communities through skill, spirituality, religion, and reputation. These healers have the courage to disregard the stereotypical roles reserved for women; they are the trailblazers, the pathfinders, the restorers of integrity, harmony, balance, and health to those who are ailing. Medicine women and *curanderas* are the feminists in their universes.

Women doctors, on the other hand, receive their authority to practice medicine by being graduated from medical schools. In the past the numbers of women attending these institutions was seriously disproportionate to the numbers of men (and still is), but the current trend is toward numerical balance. In the days before antidiscrimination laws forced medical schools to admit more females, many graduate women doctors specialized in the extensions of women's natural roles: pediatrics, anesthesia, family practice, obstetrics/gynecology. Now female physicians are widening their areas of specialization to include those previously "off limits" (for example, neurosurgery and orthopedics). These healers too have the courage to disregard the stereotypes reserved for women in their culture. Like medicine women and *curanderas,* women doctors are feminists in their universes.

It is well known that many of the present conditions in contemporary society contribute to illnesses. What is not agreed upon, however, is the means to heal, to make whole, the fabric of private and

public well-being that has been torn asunder in a society characterized by patriarchal values and male dominance, in a culture that has
been accused of rejecting humanistic values in favor of attitudes and
conventions that foster isolation and independence.[1]

Recognizing that the patriarchy, through its imposition of the
male values (aggressiveness and control, among others) at the expense of female qualities, has caused these circumstances, many
have begun to take an objective look at the alternative—women in
power—and have suddenly realized what most women have known
for centuries: there is another way to be in this world, and it is a
woman's way that relies on cooperation rather than competition to
succeed.

The process women undergo that instills the restorative and nurturing female philosophy begins at birth with gender-specific socialization techniques that determine the way a child will view and
act in the world as an adult. Carol Gilligan believes that women are
socialized from the cradle to be cooperative and caring,[2] while men
have been socialized to be competitive and autonomous.[3] This analysis has generated disagreement, but if one subscribes to this thesis, it
becomes clear that one reason why women healers have been such an
accepted part of the Native American and Hispanic cultures is that
these societies recognize the need for cooperation in healing, i.e.,
with the Great Spirit or with the saints. However, although women
healers' characteristics personify that ethic, medicine men and curanderos also collaborate with their cultures' belief systems and integrate their skills with the basic infrastructure of cultural healing—
cooperation. On the other hand, Western scientific medicine relies
on competition, domination, and combat in healing (i.e., the medication fights and defeats/conquers the disease); male physicians represent that philosophy.

But there is yet another difference, one that ties women much
closer to healing. When women of all cultural backgrounds exercise
the female qualities in curing, the actions reflect and pay tribute to
the cycles of nature in a manner that tells of women's embodiment of
these precepts through their communion with all of creation. Women
ministering to the ill, comforting the ailing, soothing the sick, con-
firms an ages-old association with nature and with the body.[4] Women
are webbed to the moon, to the tides, to the earth, to children, to

pain, to emotion, to wholeness, and to each other. To subjectively understand these intimacies and influences in women's lives, one must intuit the meaning; to objectively understand, one must dismantle the patriarchal structure and build a new perspective based on women's experiences in women's words. Fortunately, it is apparent in the growing volume of writings and theories about women's spirituality that construction has begun, but until unanimous agreement is achieved and the dream of a common language becomes a reality,[5] I prefer to think of women's spirituality as being comprised of courage, communion, and connectedness.

These words convey only an essence; they are meant to imply that women have the courage to experience their power fully, that women are able to consciously and unconsciously commune with the powers of all creation, and that women are universally connected to the powers of all living things. For these reasons, women are natural healers.

Women themselves have, for the most part, been unable to utilize their spirituality to become healers of a stature equal to men in contemporary patriarchal society. The omnipresence of a male God, some say, has convinced men that they have divine permission to dominate, and they have done so, chiefly in the fields of medicine and religion.[6] This exclusionary situation has not been as blatant in some traditional societies where spiritual/religious credos have been assumed to be integral to healing, and where the cultural consensus that bestows an authority to heal disregards gender. In Native American healing, spirituality is such a basic element woven into the entire process that it cannot be captured and separated out. In Hispanic healing, Catholicism unites the healer and the sick in a plea for health so intense that it attracts the attention of the saints.

Spirituality and religion were never deemed necessary in applying the principles of Western scientific medicine. Although individual physicians may have been privately worshipful, all that was required to make the entire contemporary process of healing legitimate was a diploma from an accredited medical school and a belief in the mechanistic world of science. Using scientific processes, medicine concentrated first on understanding the function of entire organs and organ systems, then on mapping the physiology of cells, and finally narrowed its vision to the examination of molecules.

The concepts are outdated and no longer explain the reality of ill-

ness, according to at least one male physician-author who calls for a
new perspective about healing, one that women (with their connections to the physical and mystical cyclic rituals in the natural world)
have always instinctively known; healing should encompass all the
dimensions of being because illness disrupts every aspect of wellness.[7] Women know also that rituals are an important part of recovery and utilize them easily, naturally, in healing. One respected
theorist of female spirituality believes it is possible that, because
womanhood manifests the rituals in nature, "scholars of religion
suggest that the myth of female power may have led to the celebration of religious rituals and to the existence of religion as such. They
interpret initiation ceremonies, at which one of the elders of the tribe
confers adult status on the boys, as efforts by men to act out the rite
of birth which nature denies them."[8]

No doubt there is disagreement on the role of female power, but I
believe the actions associated with rituals reinforce a woman's courage, reestablish her communion with nature, and in the case of illness, reconnect an ailing individual with the energies inherent in nature. Balance and harmony are restored easier by women healers
than by men because of women's unique spirituality, regardless of
whether the ceremony is conducted in a hogan, in a home, or in a
hospital. In a hogan, the medicine woman utilizes her courage to
commune with ancient ceremonial rituals that connect herself and
her patient with the healing power of the spirit world. In a home, the
curandera utilizes her courage to commune with a ritual liturgy that
connects herself and her patient with the saints who may intercede to
help the healing. In a hospital the woman doctor utilizes her courage
to intuitively commune with the body's ritual reaction that names its
own disease; then she connects herself and her patient to the scientific knowledge available regarding that ailment and its treatment.

There is more: ritual is response, ritual is rejuvenation, ritual is
reassurance. Ritual repeats "the crucial values of the believing community" according to one researcher.[9] Rituals have at their core a
system of beliefs rooted in faith. Everyone in a culture subscribes to
a collective ideology and reinforces its credence implicitly as long as
the promises made by the system are realized. "Beliefs are formed
and held because they satisfy . . . equally significant is the sharing of

such beliefs with others which is their indispensable social reinforcement," states one specialist on systems.[10]

Rituals honor beliefs each time healing ceremonies are conducted, and the rites, regardless of cultural affiliation, validate the belief system over and over again when an ailing individual is healed. As an illustration, just one segment within a particular ritual related to healing (e.g., lighting the match that starts a smoky fire, making the sign of the cross before praying for saints' intervention, picking up a pen to write a prescription) is sufficient to activate an entire system of belief insofar as healing power is concerned. The end point of this process is reached when members of a Native American culture believe that a medicine woman or a medicine man has the power to heal by reading smoke from a fire, when members of an Hispanic American culture believe that a *curandera* or a *curandero* has the power to heal by summoning the saints, when members of contemporary society believe that a female or male physician has the power to heal by writing a few words on a prescription pad.

A belief system, however, is vulnerable. It may lose its credibility through being challenged and found wanting. Then, the network of beliefs shifts into another arena and subsequently gains legitimacy, after many trials, through the consent of the culture.

The widespread adoption of Western scientific medicine's theories and methods is an example of a major shift in cultural consensus about traditional healing. Although in many cases the dominant culture has imposed itself on Native Americans, physicians render modern medical care in Indian Health Service hospitals to ailing patients who opt for these methods of healing. Occasionally, both the traditional and contemporary aspects of healing are combined, and the patient recovers through the benefits of both philosophies. Usually, however, contemporary medical techniques of healing are requested on and off the reservation.

As well, few Hispanics visit *curanderas* in the 1980s, perhaps for at least two reasons: Western scientific methods have been accepted, and a decreasing number of *curanderas* actively practice traditional Hispanic healing. In the predominant view, the benefits of traditional healing have been superseded by the benefits of contemporary medicine, and because of today's sophisticated technology, the shift in cultural consensus regarding healing seems reasonable. And most ailing individuals, when given the options of being treated in the traditional or modern ways, would select the latter. However, there are certain philosophies and cultural healing properties that must be acknowledged.

Natural healing herbs and plants are not isolated cultural curatives. On the contrary, what may be considered "primitive" healing elements when compared to modern pharmaceuticals often may be the parent preparation without which a sophisticated drug would be impossible to produce. It is fair to assume that there are dozens of medications currently being dispensed whose trail leads right back into cultural *materia medica* rather than to a sterile laboratory test tube. Too few "folk remedies" are respected as having successfully crossed the cultures and transcended time.

The factor of spirituality/religion, included in popular alternative healing practices, is rapidly gaining credence in medicine practiced the AMA way. When one enters Annie Kahn's hogan, the extension of Annie's own spirituality can actually be felt. It is an expression so strong that it fills the lifespace around Annie and remains when she leaves the hogan. Tu Moonwalker's spirituality can be felt in each twist and coil of her baskets carrying the centuries-old knowledge of craftsmanship given to the Apache people by the spirit world. Each depiction of an animal or a symbol woven into a basket conveys a message that joins the past to the future in a single reed produced by the earth. Dhyani Ywahoo's spirituality flows across the nation in her words of peace and healing, now twenty-six generations old, brought to public seminars by ministers she has personally taught. These "peacekeepers" instruct their audiences on personal and planetary transformation—a healing of the universe and all creatures in it through will, wisdom, and intellect.

The *curanderas'* relationship to a higher power is obvious in a different way. Their religion occupies the space around them in the form of replicas of saints in wood and plaster, in reproductions of Christ with thorns and the Virgin Mary hanging on the walls of their homes, in holy candles burning on private altars, in the steaming pan of water on a stove in which *yerbas* are cooking to be used perhaps by Sabinita Herrera in making an ointment, or by Gregorita Rodriguez to rub into a sore body, or by Jesusita Aragon to calm a laboring woman. The spirit of God is everywhere in their lives and the *curanderas* breathe it in, transform it into their own powers to heal, and speak it out. *"En el nombre de Dios, te voy a curar,"* they say. "In the name of God I will heal you."

The women doctors' spirituality is expressed in individual strength and courage that each needed to surmount personal and professional obstacles. Cultural conditioning still defines women's work in terms of "child rearing and nurturance; men's in terms of protection and occupation. . . The main work of adult women revolves around . . . pleasing, serving, and assisting men and children—tasks which eventuate in a state of dependency, passivity, and powerlessness."[11] Women doctors ignored these values when they chose the field of medicine as a career. As young women, they were bold enough to disregard the expected sex-role behavior in favor of a position that was out of favor for women. Nevertheless, the women doctors— Mary Walker, Molly Radford Ward, Jane Patterson, Stirling Puck, and Josette Mondanaro—relied on the courage (such an essential part of their spirituality) to fulfill their professional goals with awareness and clearsightedness. In so doing, they ventured into a new way to be, one that joined them to an entirely different system—the medical patriarchy.

This is the same network whose delivery of health care is now being faulted and forced into change: but it is folly to advocate a medical matriarchy to replace the medical patriarchy. Such substitution would leave the established system intact. Instead, women doctors should be the vehicle by which the two gender-specific socialization patterns identified by Gilligan are merged in the practice of Western scientific medicine. Then the system itself becomes altered and produces a medical prototype that integrates the female values of cooperation and caring and the existing male standards of competition and autonomy. Combining these behavior forms brings healing to the system and creates a concept of curing individuals that imitates the winding and weaving molecular structure of the double helix—the fundamental structure of life. With the use of this premise, balance and harmony are restored to the system and to the ailing patient as an essential component of the spiraling architecture of the DNA-like design of the proposed model of medical care.

The next step is expanding the newly imagined prototype so that it includes the female characteristics present in cultural healing, especially the traditional women healers' contact with religion and spirituality. After that, the variety of cultural procedures and philosophies are connected throughout the model, wherever they most appropriately fit. When these are placed, the evolving configuration of the thesis resembles the actual DNA structure even more closely because of its increasing complexity. All of the cultural contributions have enhanced the model's appeal and facilitated its ability to function as an applied theory of comprehensive health care—one that is truly limitless in its diagnostic ability and in the full spectrum of remedies it provides for recovery. On reflection, it seems so natural for a theory of healing to reconstruct the very basis of life, which has been disrupted through illness.

Like DNA, this model is dynamic. It is constantly flowing from the present to the future and back into the past to review and select patterns of medical treatment that may be prescribed successfully today. Unlike the current linear form of healing that propels itself directly into the future, this proposed formation connects traditional and contemporary healers and ancient and modern processes of healing by making whole the disrupted DNA of illness and health care. Importantly, the strand that will begin the entire system is the spirituality of women healers who have the courage, the communion, and the connectedness to bring life to this hypothesis by applying these natural female attributes to healing.

Understanding this concept requires basic knowledge and acceptance of the assumptions and myths underlying each culture's therapies and a recognition of the intrinsic worth of each philosophy of healing. Often, tolerance of another culture's ways is difficult to adopt wholeheartedly. The customs and conventions that swirl throughout a space-age society do not give much credence to values that appear to be "less advanced," nor do they support health-seekers' explorations of alternative methods of healing. However, there are at least two crucial confirmations of the validity of this syncretic approach in curing ailments: the current political economy of health care and the connections among women healers in traditional and modern cultures.

In the late 1970s, it became strikingly apparent that equal participation in Western scientific medicine's technological achievements

had been denied those whose financial resources or medical, surgical, and hospitalization plan benefits were inadequate. Simultaneously, as the costs of sophisticated health care rose, the size of this
group increased dramatically so that, in a relatively short time, the
numbers of individuals who were unable to afford appropriate medical care became alarming. Other extraneous circumstances contributed to the situation as well: a burgeoning birth rate among adolescents, greater longevity among the elderly, escalating enrollment in
the Medicaid program, a resentment against physicians who seemed
abrupt and remote, and a growing belief that health care was a right,
not a privilege. As a partial solution, Health Maintenance Organizations (HMOs) were created by Congress to address the need for
medical, surgical, and hospital care at lower monthly premium payments; regular health plans required second opinions before hospitalization could occur; urgent-care centers provided immediate
attention on an out-patient rather than an in-patient basis; many hospitals changed their policies to encourage shorter stays, and so on.
The list of changes is lengthy and well documented,[12] still one of the
major benefits of the original situation remains less well explored:
the increasing prevalence of and preference for alternative healing
methods.

As one result of the high cost of medical care, a serious interest in
some of the previously peripheral medical theories and procedures
developed. Acupuncture, chiropractic, crystals, vibrations and har-
monics, bioenergetics, massage and hydrotherapy, Native American
healing, Hispanic healing, and spirituality, as examples, became acceptable modes of treatment and gained legitimacy among the broad
populace. Inadvertently, the high cost of standard medical care had
given birth to an embryonic, synthesized approach to health-seeking
behavior—a justifiable and socially permissible admixture of all
available methods of treatment to increase the likelihood of healing.

A belief system that validated these paths to health was created
when the variety of treatments actually caused healing to occur.
Coupled with a shift in public values, the repertoire of remedies ex-
panded into an arena where women healers are almost on a par with
male healers. It is the latest stage within the evolution of centuries-
old practices conducted by cultural healers.

It is unfortunate that this particular syncretic approach to health care has long been ignored, and it is naive to believe that the medical establishment will cooperatively coexist. Politically and economically, it is not in the best interests of the business of medicine to permit serious competition,[13] but if Western science is developing an antidote to neutralize the challenge, it remains a mystery.

What is clear, however, is that women healers, by being quite diverse in their lives, practices, and cultures, are living examples of an approach to health care that symbolizes a more unified spectrum than the status quo affords. The viability and eventual survival of integrating traditional and modern treatments to cure illnesses depends upon a system of beliefs held in common and enforced by a society slowly relearning its options in the area of healing. It is essential that this public education process include a more widespread acceptance of women healers than is currently held. The belief system that is able to completely validate women as healers is in place. What remains to be infused is a massive shift in values that will eliminate the stubborn, patriarchal obstacles and justify a new medical infrastructure through all of society, one that combines male and female and traditional and modern patterns in its total scope of healing.

Opponents of this approach to healing will cite their convictions about retaining the medical status quo. No matter. It is time now to challenge the rigor mortis that has caused the current system of health care delivery to stagnate. It is time to realize that diversity in the gender of healers and in ancient and modern healing practices is a source of strength, not a danger to the existing technology. It is time to refocus one of the hallmarks of humanity—the care of the sick—so that it encompasses all of the available healers and healing knowledge to cure.

Initially, the new infrastructure will recognize and respect the fact that women, regardless of their cultural backgrounds, are communally connected to what socializes them to be powerful and skillful healers: combining the gender-distinctive processes of learning that are conducive to curing and vary only slightly from society to society; the apprenticeships that all women healers serve to refine their natural and acquired skills and that differ only according to established cultural practices; the esteemed positions they hold within their communities that enhance their reputations as able healers; and the courage to make social choices, including the decision to connect the practice of traditional and contemporary medicine with motherhood, with nationwide learning seminars, with independence, with solitude, with feminism, with an extended family, with leadership, with unpopular causes, even with building a house or performing in a circus or with a barnyard full of birds and animals, and with all of the other facets of living that are a woman's experience of power in her culture and beyond.

To anticipate the enormous potential for improvement in the entire spectrum of healing, should this syncretic model of health care become a reality, the traits women healers hold in common may be combined with their natural empowerment to heal and to utilize spirituality in the forms of courage, communion, and connectedness in their healing ways. The total scope of what may then become possible is monumental.

CHAPTER 19

REFLECTIONS
Victoria Krueger

Bright people have always existed. In every age, there have been inventive, creative, imaginative, and productive thinkers and doers who made the discoveries of the past on which our current technological science and civilization is built. The living general populace, as well as the scientific community, tend to dismiss the brightness and creativity of the earlier generations because their *products* seem simple in contrast to, or in comparison with, our technological-age products. But to dismiss the people and the *process* of their discoveries because their products seem "simple" is an error in assumption-making.

In a process-oriented model (as opposed to an outcome-oriented model), how one gets from a to b is at least, if not more, important than the specific outcome. Science puts great emphasis on correct experimental procedures; processes, not just outcome. The intellectual process of inventing the wheel, or developing metal tools, was no less sophisticated than is the process used now in our high-tech sciences. The generation of an idea often starts with, "There's got to be a better way" or "I wonder if it's possible," or an "ah ha—that's a nifty new thought. I'll try it this way." In the past, determining edible plants, for example, had to have been a very careful procedure since one's very survival depended on correct choices, surely motivation for precise, controlled experiments. Consider the rhubarb: the leaves are green and are poisonous to humans; yet the stalks, which are red—and frequently red vegetation is poisonous to humans—are delicious.

How did someone figure out that it is safe to eat the stalks but not the leaves? A little taste of this; a little nibble of that? Annie Kahn educated our taste buds and our minds this way as we walked in the

225

desert. She would point to plants and say, "Chew on that for several minutes and tell me about it." Some were bitter, some sweet, some dry, some moist. There were "families" of taste. Just as chemists now group various elements into groups that function or are structured similarly, so, too, earlier "scientists" grouped plants into families and used them according to their functions, e.g., to eat and to heal, among other functions.

Another example of scientific principles at work in the past was the task of locating a home or a tent for shelter, comfort, and utility in the desert. Water and breeze for cooling were important. First, one had to learn the concepts of water and breeze as they apply to comfortable housing; this was done by using the observations made over a long period by many independent observers—a scientific process. Then one looked for trees or plants that were bigger and greener than the others nearby. And one looked for moist or darker ground, indicating a water spring, seep, or stream that surfaced part of the year. One watched locations near water for which way the trees grow, since prevailing winds force growth toward one side more than the other. Then one formed a hypothesis: the wind comes this way. Testing the hypothesis was then in order: standing in the pathways where the wind may blow at various times of the day, verifying whether the hypothesis really worked. If all was right, a home was built—right there—with good weather and breezes attending. Is that process not science? It uses the methods of careful independent observations, generation of a hypothesis, repeated testing of the hypothesis by independent observers, and so on. How many of our modern houses are placed so carefully and with such pleasant results? People have always used the principles of science. For us "moderns" to think we invented them is arrogant. The ancients just did not do science in laboratories; they did it in caves and kitchens, in forests and fields.

If one accepts the premise that there have always been bright people discovering things, then it is a shame and a loss not to incorporate all that they learned, both in content and process. The traditions of the past are the foundation for our current civilization, in which such pride is taken. Does it not make sense to learn from these traditions, since they obviously worked well? Frank Waters states that "the change in American society's attitudes toward American

Indians came when the word 'ecology' came into vogue. Indian life has always been based on ecology."[1]

The processes used in the past are preserved for us in the form of rituals; there are casual rituals in every culture and subculture. As rural women gather in someone's kitchen at canning time, they swap insights they have harvested during that year's growing season. A ritual. As physicians meet at an AMA convention, they swap insights they have gained in the past healing season. A ritual. Boys squat or hang around the men discussing what is wrong with the car or lawnmower, determining how to fix it, or planning hunting strategies: these casual rituals inculcate values, world views, and processes. Meeting at the mall or going to the Saturday matinees each week is a childhood ritual for some subcultures, a ritual that teaches a common view of the world, a common set of assumptions, a common language, common images, and common goals.

Comfort comes with such rituals and commonality; comfort and faith and security due to predictability and the knowledge that other people share similar views and rituals. It makes one feel known and knowing. Both bring comfort and faith. Some rituals of healing have been stripped out of modern medicine, and people miss them and miss the comfort, and so are complaining, and suing, in record numbers.

A key variable in comfort-producing rituals that I observed in the course of researching this book is the attitude toward time. A healer taking the time to sit and talk, even about topics not directly related to the illness, makes the patient feel known, and the healer is known to some degree also. There is a connection between two people. Since fear of strangers has historically had survival value (strangers may indeed be up to no good), it is unlikely to go away readily. Such fear produces mistrust. Perceiving the healer as a stranger, being fearful and mistrusting, is not productive. "Most medical-judgment errors are caused by overbooking. The doctor is so anxious to move on to his next patient and start the next billing, he doesn't spend enough time on the patient he is with."[2] Any measures that reduce fear and mistrust are desirable. But many of them take time.

Not the kind of time that can readily be billed by the minute or the quarter-hour. People comment on "Indian time" or "the land of mañana," which means there is a tomorrow because there is a differ-

ent time consciousness. You may make an "appointment" with a
medicine woman for 2 o'clock and she may arrive, ambling, at 5
o'clock. If one is geared to tightly scheduled, fast-paced time consciousness, this can be irritating. But as one delves deeper into the
reality of another time consciousness, one realizes that the medicine
woman is late because she took the time with the last person she was
healing. Time was required to emotionally calm the patient; it took
time to make real human contact, to make the patient comfortable;
the person had to be given time to adjust, assimilate, learn, heal.
What is more, the medicine woman spends this kind of time with
you, too—with everyone. In the relief and pleasure of really being
taken seriously as a human being, it is also easy to forget that at the
very moment one is being helped to feel at ease, the healer may simultaneously be putting off someone else for whom she will then be
"late." That kind of time consciousness includes time to be compassionate and human. Taking time and tuning in. Values.

The process of integrating a value such as time will be difficult. It
is difficult. There are benefits to the highly structured time frame:
predictability (which makes people feel safe, too); an order and harmony of its own; it can fit and function well in an eight-to-five world.
But it does not create "knowing" and comfort. The more fluid time
consciousness has its own benefits: making real human contact,
creating ease, creating comfort through knowing an "other," and
faith. This kind of time does not fit as readily into an eight-to-five
structured world. Integrating the differing time perspectives is a thesis within itself. But there are real gains from each kind of time,
which makes the struggle worth the effort. At least an issue such as
time will be looked at as relevant, debated, and discussed, until some
creative integration occurs. Time is just one value of many that are
needed in modern medicine. Only one of many. The road ahead is
difficult—and necessary. It requires toughness and openness.

I have reflected that to be a healer one has to be tough; because
when people are ill, they flounder. It is rather like lifeguard training.
One of the primary principles taught in lifeguard training is that a
drowning person will grab onto anything, including the lifesaver,
with such a panic grip that it can drown the rescuer as well. People
do that when they are afraid of dying. So too, the healer learns how
to appropriately, powerfully grasp the sufferer in such a way that that

person can be saved. To do so, one must sometimes take temporary command of the situation in order that the sufferer can later take back command. It is this part of healing that requires a certain kind of toughness.

On the other hand, gentleness brings comfort. Comfort and ease. Diseases can be cured with tough gentleness. I am well aware that all women do not and many men do bring comfort. But women have a certain brand of tough gentleness that can be learned. It is the value of tough gentleness and the style of tough gentleness that need to be incorporated, not only the gender, specifically. Rather the principles and values and styles from the cultures and from women need to be integrated. To incorporate them, the politically and economically dominant culture must examine its values and assumptions and alter some of them. Women have been a voice crying in the wilderness for a long time; other cultures within the larger culture have been voices crying in the wilderness for a long time. Perhaps now, with consumers adding their voice, the time is auspicious to reexamine all assumptions, values, and methods. The difficulties are worth the end result. And if one can put aside some of the fear of the "strange" and the "stranger," the unknown and the "other" (on which prejudice is based), the process of learning new ways can become an adventure that is both fascinating and fun. It has been for me.

NOTES

Chapter 1
Bridges: An Introduction

1. Swartz, "Development of Self," 8.
2. Tarvis and Offir, *The Longest War*, 47.
3. Rosenthal et al., "Body Talk and Tone," 68.
4. Hoffman, "Sex Differences," 720.
5. Rosenthal et al., "Body Talk and Tone," 68.
6. Swartz, "Development of Self," 8.
7. Christ, *Diving Deep and Surfacing*, 4.
8. Hager, "The Myth of Objectivity," 576.
9. Schiebinger, "The History and Philosophy of Women in Science," 315.
10. van Gelder, "Carol Gilligan," 37.
11. "Talk Back to the Doctors," The Oprah Winfrey Show, 2.
12. Fairchild, interview with the authors, January 1983.
13. Cherry, "The Power of the Pill," 67.
14. Wallis, "Medical School, Heal Thyself," 56.
15. Lister, "Occasional Notes," 1,524.

Chapter 2
Introduction

1. Gray, "Rediscovering Native American Medicine."
2. Ibid.
3. Dea, *The Instructional Module*.
4. *Santa Fe Reporter*, December 3, 1986.
5. Ibid.
6. *Santa Fe Reporter*, February 4, 1987.
7. Ibid.
8. Ibid.
9. Ibid.
10. Gray, "Making the Spirit Whole."

Chapter 3
Annie Kahn: The Flower That Speaks in a Pollen Way

1. Kahn, telephone conversation with authors, December 18, 1982.
2. Ibid.
3. Kahn, interview with authors, January 8, 1983.
4. Kahn, interviews with authors, February 1983–September 1986.
5. Ibid.

Chapter 4
Tu Moonwalker: Apache Weaver of Healing

1. Moonwalker, interviews with authors, August 1982–August 1984.
2. Ibid.
3. *Albuquerque Journal Impact Magazine*, April 30, 1985.
4. Moonwalker, interviews, August 1982–August 1984.
5. Ibid.
6. *The Santa Fe New Mexican*, June 17, 1982.
7. Moonwalker, interviews, August 1982–August 1984.
8. Ibid.

Chapter 5
Dhyani Ywahoo: Priestcraft Holder of the
Ani Gadoah Clan, Tsalagi (Cherokee) Nation

1. *The Dallas Times Herald* and *The Dallas Morning News*, October 10–13, 1982.
2. Ywahoo, interviews with authors, December 1982–December 1983.
3. *The Movement Newspaper*, November 1980, 6.
4. McNamara, "Ancient Wisdom," 2.

Chapter 6
Introduction

1. Grahn, *Another Mother Tongue*, 76.
2. Pineda, interview with authors, January 2, 1987.
3. Cobos, *A Dictionary of New Mexico and Southern Colorado Spanish*, 83.
4. Arenas, Cross, and Willard, "*Curanderos* and Mental Health Professionals," 407–20.
5. Jaramillo, interview with authors, September 28, 1983.
6. Skallman and Herrera, "A Conversation with Juanita Sedillo."
7. Ibid.
8. Jaramillo, interview with authors, September 28, 1983.

9. Ortiz y Pino, interview with authors, October 7, 1982.
10. Ibid.
11. Jaramillo, interview with authors, September 28, 1983.
12. Ibid.
13. Campa, *Hispanic Culture in the Southwest*, 40.
14. Simmons, *Witchcraft in the Southwest*, 40.
15. Jaramillo, interview with authors, September 28, 1983.
16. Luce, *Saints for Now*, 250.
17. Aragon, interviews with authors, September 1982–December 1985.
18. Kiev, *Curanderismo*, 149.

Chapter 7
Sabinita Herrera: *Curandera y Yerbera*

1. *Albuquerque Journal Impact Magazine*, August 21, 1984, 4.
2. Herrera, interviews with authors, September 1982–May 1986.
3. Ibid.
4. Herrera, Rodriguez, and Aragon, interviews with authors, September 1982–May 1986, September 1982–September 1984, September 1982–December 1985.
5. Herrera, interviews with authors, September 1982–May 1986.
6. Ibid.
7. Ortiz y Pino, interview with authors, October 7, 1982.

Chapter 8
Gregorita Rodriguez: *Curandera y Sobardora*

1. *Albuquerque Journal Impact Magazine*, August 21, 1984, 4.
2. Martinez, conversation with authors, August 1982.
3. Rodriguez, interviews with authors, September 1982–September 1984.
4. Ibid.
5. Brewer, *A Dictionary of Miracles*, 135.

Chapter 9
Jesusita Aragon: *Curandera y Partera*

1. *Albuquerque Journal Impact Magazine*, August 21, 1984, 4.
2. Aragon, interviews with authors, September 1982–December 1985.
3. Ibid.
4. Brewer, *A Dictionary of Miracles*, 123.
5. Ibid., 106.
6. Aragon, interviews with authors, September 1982–December 1985.
7. Ibid.

Chapter 10
Introduction

1. Easterbrook, "The Revolution in Medicine," 40.
2. Wallis, "Medical School, Heal Thyself," 56.
3. Ibid., 55.
4. Lister, "Occasional Notes," 1,524–25.
5. Brussel, "Pants, Politics, Postage and Psychic," 335.
6. *Women & Health*, 87.
7. Karolevitz, *Doctors of the Old West*, 157.
8. WMJ 6, *Transactions*, 80.
9. Walsh, *Doctors Wanted*, 245.
10. Easterbrook, "The Revolution in Medicine," 59.
11. Schiebinger, "The History and Philosophy," 315–16.
12. Ibid., 332.
13. van Gelder, "Carol Gilligan," 37.

Chapter 11
Molly Radford Ward, M.D.

1. Ward, *Molly Radford, M.D.*, 1.
2. Ibid., 19.
3. Ibid., 20.
4. Ibid., 39.
5. Ibid., 91.
6. Ibid., 92.
7. Ward, interview with authors, July 29, 1982.
8. Ward, *Molly Radford, M.D.*, 44.
9. Ibid., 45.
10. Ibid., 46.
11. Ibid., 92.
12. Ibid., 94.
13. Ibid., 100.
14. Ibid., 104.
15. Ibid., 113.
16. Ibid., 129.
17. Ibid., 145.
18. Ward, interview with authors, July 29, 1982.
19. Ward, *Molly Radford, M.D.*, 148.
20. Ibid., 152–53.
21. Ward, interview with authors, July 29, 1982.
22. Ward, *Molly Radford, M.D.*, 158.
23. Ibid., 161.
24. Ibid., 173.
25. Ward, interview with authors, July 29, 1982.

Chapter 12
Jane Patterson, M.D.

1. Patterson, *Woman/Doctor*, 1–2.
2. Ibid., 3.
3. Patterson, interview with authors, August 23, 1983.
4. Patterson, *Woman/Doctor*, 14.
5. Ibid., 3.
6. Ibid., 31.
7. Ibid., 36.
8. Ibid., 39.
9. Patterson, interview with authors, August 23, 1983.
10. Patterson, *Woman/Doctor*, 176.
11. Ibid., 178.
12. Ibid., 186.
13. Patterson, interview with authors, August 23, 1983.
14. Ibid.

Chapter 13
Stirling Puck, M.D.

1. Observations by Krueger.
2. Ibid.
3. Puck, interviews with authors, November 30, 1983 and December 3, 1983.
4. Ibid.
5. Puck, "Absence of H-Y antigen," 23–27; "Trisomy 22 mosaicism," in preparation; Review of *Penetrance and Variability*, 571–72; Review of *Diagnostic Approaches*, 572–73; and Puleston, "Genetics, Environment, and Your Baby."
6. Puck, interviews with authors, November 30, 1983 and December 3, 1983.
7. Ibid.
8. Pogrebin, "Work Friendships Are Very Difficult," 50.
9. Puck, interviews with authors, November 30, 1983 and December 3, 1983.
10. Ibid.

Chapter 14
Josette Mondanaro, M.D.

1. Mondanaro, interview with authors, August 4, 1983.
2. Ibid.
3. Mondanaro, telephone conversation with authors, September 6, 1983.
4. Ibid.

5. Mondanaro, telephone conversation with authors, September 16, 1983.
6. Ibid.
7. Mondanaro, interview with authors, August 4, 1983.
8. Ibid.

Chapter 15
Witchcraft in History

1. *Holy Bible*, Exodus 22 : 18.
2. Weigle, *Spiders and Spinsters*, 186.
3. Major, *Faiths That Healed*, 234–39.
4. Ibid., 38–44.
5. French, *Beyond Power*, 167–70.
6. Walker, *The Woman's Encyclopedia*, 1,082.
7. Garrett, "Women and Witches," 461–70.
8. Walker, *The Woman's Encyclopedia*, 1,082–83.
9. Scott, *Letters on Demonology and Witchcraft*, 218–19.
10. Daly, *Gyn/Ecology*, 201–2.
11. Szaz, *The Manufacture of Madness*, 86–87.
12. Starhawk, *Dreaming In The Dark*, 183–219.
13. Cox, *Modern Psychology*, 83.
14. Potter, *Knock On Wood*, 75.

Chapter 16
Inside the Darkness: Three Cultural Views of Witchcraft

1. Scholes, "First Decade of the Inquisition," 208–22.
2. *Santa Fe Daily New Mexican*, October 2, 1882.
3. *Santa Fe Reporter*, April 24, 1985.
4. Ibid.
5. Campa, *Hispanic Culture in the Southwest*, 200.
6. Hurt, "Witchcraft in New Mexico," 78–79.
7. Campa, *Hispanic Culture in the Southwest*, 199.
8. Lujan, interview with authors, September 27, 1982.
9. Hŕdlicka, "Psychological and Medical Observations," 221.
10. Schwatka, "Among the Apaches," 10.
11. Kluckholn and Leighton, *The Navajo*, 244.
12. Ball, *In The Days of Victorio*, 56.
13. Debo, *Geronimo*, 120.
14. Ball, *In The Days of Victorio*, 56.
15. Haley, *Apaches*, 66.
16. Lange, *Cochiti*, 253.
17. Simmons, *Witchcraft in the Southwest*, 75.
18. Hill, *An Ethnography of Santa Clara Pueblo*, 323.
19. Ibid., 125.

20. Morgan, "Human Wolves Among the Navajo," 20.
21. Kluckholn and Leighton, *The Navajo*, 242.
22. Simmons, *Witchcraft in the Southwest*, 138–40.
23. Kluckholn, *Navajo Witchcraft*, 50.
24. Morgan, "Human Wolves Among the Navajo," 22.
25. Ibid., 30.
26. Kluckholn, *Navajo Witchcraft*, 50.
27. Ibid., 46–52.
28. Niethammer, *Daughters of the Earth*, 163.
29. Ibid., 163.
30. Larner, *Witchcraft and Religion*, 83.
31. Leek, *The Complete Art of Witchcraft*, photo 120–21.
32. Kelsey, *Discernment*, 87.
33. Peck, *People of the Lie*, 42.
34. Ibid., 33.
35. Larner, *Witchcraft and Religion*, 80.
36. Peck, *People of the Lie*, 212.
37. Kelsey, *Discernment*, 99.
38. Peck, *People of the Lie*, 77–78.
39. Toufexis, "Why Mothers Kill Their Babies," 81.
40. Peck, *People of the Lie*, 190.
41. Ibid., 261.
42. Kelsey, *Discernment*, 97.
43. Moody, "Magical Therapy," 356.
44. Ibid., 381.
45. Sanford and Comstock, *Sanctions for Evil*, 17.
46. *The Santa Fe New Mexican*, June 27, 1988.
47. Peck, *People of the Lie*, 206.
48. Fromm, *The Anatomy of Human Destructiveness*, 432.

Chapter 17
Talking and Listening

1. Aragon, interviews with author, September 1982–December 1985.
2. "Talk Back to the Doctors," The Oprah Winfrey Show, 2.
3. Ibid.
4. Block, *Bottom Line*, 15.
5. Schiebinger, "The History and Philosophy," 324.
6. Walker, *The Woman's Encyclopedia*, 1,078.
7. C. Christ, *Diving Deep and Surfacing*, xi.
8. Ibid.
9. Gilligan, *In A Different Voice*, 8.
10. van Gelder, "Carol Gilligan," 37.
11. Chodorow, "Family Structure and Feminine Personality," 43–44.
12. Ibid., 44.

13. Gilligan, *In A Different Voice*, 8.
14. Ibid., 9.
15. Wagner, *The Search for Signs*, 191.
16. van Gelder, "Carol Gilligan," 38.
17. Pogrebin, "Do Americans Hate Children?" 50.
18. Baruch, Beiner, and Barrett, "Women and Gender," 13.
19. Gilligan, *In A Different Voice*, 10.
20. van Gelder, "Carol Gilligan," 38.
21. Fiske, "People's Reactions to Nuclear War," 209.
22. C. Christ, *Diving Deep and Surfacing*, 5.
23. Ibid., 4.
24. Silko, "Running On the Edge," 4.
25. Allen, "The Sacred Hoop," 223.
26. Starhawk, "Consciousness, Politics, and Magic," 183.
27. Phyllis Chesler, quoted in Weigle, *Spiders & Spinsters*, 116.
28. Plato, *The Collected Dialogues*, 901.

Chapter 18
A Philosophy of Comprehensive Healing

1. van Gelder, "Carol Gilligan," 37. See also Rich, "Disloyal to Civilization," 279; Muina, "To Make Whole," 4; Lewis, "Woman Is Medicine," 8.
2. Gilligan, *In A Different Voice*, 124.
3. van Gelder, "Carol Gilligan," 37.
4. C. Christ, *Diving Deep and Surfacing*, 22.
5. Rich, *Dream of a Common Language*, 8.
6. Goldenberg, *Changing of the Gods*, 5–7.
7. Dossey, *Space, Time & Medicine*, viii.
8. Christ and Plaskow, *Womanspirit Rising*, 144.
9. Turner, "Ritual As Communication and Potency," 59.
10. Jastrow, *The Psychology of Conviction*, 5.
11. Norman, "Sex, Roles and Sexism," 13.
12. Easterbrook, "The Revolution in Medicine," 40–74.
13. Ibid.

Chapter 19
Reflections

1. *The Santa Fe Mexican*, June 10, 1988.
2. Easterbrook, "The Revolution in Medicine," 52–53.

BIBLIOGRAPHY

Books

Allen, Paula Gunn. "The Sacred Hoop: A Contemporary Indian Perspective on American Indian Literature." In *The Remembered Earth*, edited by Geary Hobson. Albuquerque: University of New Mexico Press, 1980.

Ball, Eve. *In The Days of Victorio*. Tucson: University of Arizona Press, 1970.

Brewer, E. Cobham. *A Dictionary of Miracles: Imitative, Realistic, Dogmatic.* Philadelphia: J. B. Lippincott. Reissue. Detroit: Gale Research, 1966.

Campa, Arthur L. *Hispanic Culture in the Southwest*. Norman: University of Oklahoma Press, 1979.

Chesler, Phyllis. *Women and Madness*. New York: Doubleday, 1972.

Chodorow, Nancy. "Family Structure and Feminine Personality." In *Woman, Culture, and Society*, edited by M. Z. Rosaldo and L. Lamphere. Stanford: Stanford University Press, 1974.

Christ, Carol P. *Diving Deep and Surfacing*. Boston: Beacon Press, 1980.

————., and Judith Plaskow, eds. *Womanspirit Rising: A Feminist Reader in Religion*. San Francisco: Harper & Row, 1979.

Cobos, Ruben. *A Dictionary of New Mexico and Southern Colorado Spanish.* Santa Fe: Museum of New Mexico Press, 1983.

Cox, David. *Modern Psychology: The Teachings of Carl Gustav Jung*. New York: Barnes & Noble, 1968.

Daly, Mary. *Gyn/Ecology*. Boston: Beacon Press, 1976.

Dea, Kay. *The Instructional Module*. New York: Council on Social Work Education, 1971.

Debo, Angie. *Geronimo: The Man, His Time, His Place*. Norman: University of Oklahoma Press, 1976.

Dossey, Larry, M.D. *Space, Time, and Medicine*. Boulder, Colo., and London: Shambhala, 1982.

French, Marilyn. *Beyond Power: On Women, Men and Morals*. New York: Ballantine Books, 1985.

Fromm, Erich. *The Anatomy of Human Destructiveness*. London: Jonathan Cape, 1974.

239

Gilligan, Carol. *In A Different Voice: Psychological Theory and Women's Development.* Cambridge, Mass.: Harvard University Press, 1982.

Goldenberg, Naomi R. *Changing of the Gods: Feminism and the End of Traditional Religions.* Boston: Beacon Press, 1979.

Grahn, Judy. *Another Mother Tongue.* Boston: Beacon Press, 1984.

Haley, James L. *Apaches: A History and Culture Portrait.* New York: Doubleday, 1981.

Hill, W. W. *An Ethnography of Santa Clara Pueblo, New Mexico,* edited and annotated by Charles H. Lange. Albuquerque: University of New Mexico Press, 1983.

Holy Bible, King James Version, Exodus 22:18.

Jastrow, Joseph. *The Psychology of Conviction: A Study of Beliefs and Attitudes.* Boston and New York: Houghton Mifflin, 1918.

Karolevitz, Robert F. *Doctors of the Old West.* Seattle: Superior Publishing, 1967.

Kelsey, Morton. *Discernment: A Study in Ecstasy and Evil.* New York/Ramsey/Toronto: Paulist Press, 1978.

Kiev, Ari, M.D. *Curanderismo.* New York: The Free Press (Macmillan), 1968.

Kluckholn, Clyde. *Navajo Witchcraft.* Boston: Beacon Press, 1944.

————, and Dorothea Leighton. *The Navajo.* Rev. ed., New York: Doubleday, 1962.

Lange, Charles H. *Cochiti: A New Mexico Pueblo Past and Present.* Austin: University of Texas Press, 1959.

Larner, Christina. *Witchcraft and Religion: The Politics of Popular Belief.* Oxford: Basil Blackwell, 1984.

Leek, Sybil. *The Complete Art of Witchcraft.* New York: Signet Books, 1971.

Luce, Clare Booth, ed. *Saints for Now.* New York: Sheed and Ward, 1952.

Major, Ralph H., M.D. *Faiths That Healed.* New York: D. Appleton-Century, 1940.

Moody, Edward J. "Magical Therapy: An Anthropological Investigation of Contemporary Satanism." In *Religious Movements in Contemporary America,* edited by Irving L. Zaretsky and Mark P. Leone. Princeton, N.J.: Princeton University Press, 1974.

Niethammer, Carolyn. *Daughters of the Earth: The Lives and Legends of American Indian Women.* New York: Collier Books, 1977.

Norman, Elaine. "Sex Roles and Sexism." In *Women's Issues and Social Work Practice,* by Elaine Norman and Arlene Mancuso. Itasca, Ill.: F. E. Peacock, 1980.

Patterson, Jane, M.D., and Lynda Madaras. *Woman/Doctor: The Education of Jane Patterson, M.D.* New York: Avon Books, 1983.

Peck, M. Scott, M.D. *People of the Lie: The Hope for Healing Human Evil.* New York: Simon and Schuster, 1983.

Plato. *The Collected Dialogues of Plato Including the Lectures,* edited by Edith

Hamilton and Huntington Cairns (Bollingen Series LXXI). New York: Pantheon Books, 1961.

Potter, Carole. *Knock on Wood and Other Superstitions.* n.p.: Bonanza Books, 1984.

Rich, Adrienne. *Dream of a Common Language.* New York: W. W. Norton, 1978.

———. "Disloyal to Civilization: Feminism, Racism, Gynephobia." (1978). In *On Lies, Secrets, and Silence: Prose 1966–1978.* New York: W. W. Norton, 1979.

Sanford, Nevitt, and Craig Comstock and Associates. *Sanctions for Evil.* San Francisco: Jossey-Bass, 1971.

Scott, Sir Walter, Bard. *Letters on Demonology and Witchcraft Addressed to J. G. Lockhart, Esq.* New York: A. L. Fowle, 1900.

Simmons, Marc. *Witchcraft in the Southwest.* Lincoln: University of Nebraska Press, 1974.

Starhawk. *Dreaming in the Dark: Magic, Sex, and Politics.* Boston: Beacon Press, 1982.

———. "Consciousness, Politics, and Magic." In *The Politics of Women's Spirituality,* edited by Charlene Spretnak. New York: Anchor Press, 1982.

Szaz, Thomas S., M.D. *The Manufacture of Madness.* New York: Harper & Row, 1970.

Tarvis, Carol, and Carole Offir. *The Longest War: Sex Differences in Perspective.* New York: Harcourt Brace Jovanovich, 1977.

Wagner, Jane. *The Search for Signs of Intelligent Life in the Universe. Starring Lily Tomlin.* New York: Harper & Row, 1986.

Walker, Barbara. *The Woman's Encyclopedia of Myths and Secrets.* San Francisco: Harper & Row, 1983.

Walsh, Mary Roth. *Doctors Wanted: No Women Need Apply.* New Haven: Yale University Press, 1977.

Ward, Molly Radford. *Molly Radford, M.D.* New York: Vantage Press, 1975.

Weigle, Marta. *Spiders and Spinsters.* Albuquerque: University of New Mexico Press, 1982.

Articles

Arenas, Silverio, Herbert Cross, and William Willard. "Curanderos and Mental Health Professionals: A Comparative Study on Perceptions of Psychopathology." *Hispanic Journal of Behavioral Sciences* 2, no. 4 (December 1980): 407–20.

Baruch, Grace K., Lois Beiner, and Rosalind C. Barrett. "Women and Gender in Research on Work and Family Stress." *American Psychologist* 42, no. 2 (February 1987).

Block, Dr. Susan. *Bottom Line* 8, no. 2 (January 30, 1987).

Brussel, James A., M.D. "Pants, Politics, Postage, and Psychic." *Psychiatric Quarterly Supplement* 35, pt. 1 (1961).

Cherry, Laurence. "The Power of the Pill." *Science Digest* (September 1981): 67.

Easterbrook, Gregg. "The Revolution in Medicine." *Newsweek* (January 26, 1987): 40–74.

Fiske, Susan T. "People's Reactions to Nuclear War: Implications for Psychologists." *American Psychologist* 42, no. 3 (March 3, 1987).

Garrett, Clarke. "Women and Witches: Patterns of Analysis." *SIGNS: Journal of Women in Culture and Society* 7, no. 22: 461–70.

Gray, Lynn. "Rediscovering Native American Medicine." *EastWest* (November 1986).

———. "Making The Spirit Whole: An Interview with Clara Sue Kidwell." *EastWest* (November 1986).

Hager, Mary. "The Myth of Objectivity." *American Psychologist* 37 (May 1982).

Hoffman, M. "Sex Differences in Empathy and Related Behaviors." *Psychology Bulletin* (1977).

Hŕdlicka, Alex. "Psychological and Medical Observations of Indians In The Southwest." *Bureau of American Ethnology Bulletin* 34. Washington, D.C. (1980).

Hurt, Wesley R., Jr. "Witchcraft in New Mexico." *El Palacio* 47 (1940): 78–79.

Lewis, Dale. "Woman Is Medicine: An Interview With CheQweesh Auh-Ho-Oh." *Woman of Power* (Winter 1987).

Lister, John, M.D. "Occasional Notes." *New England Journal of Medicine* 309, no. 24 (December 15, 1983).

McNamara, David. "Ancient Wisdom For A Re-Awakening World." *One Earth Magazine* 2, no. 6.

Morgan, William. "Human Wolves Among the Navajo." *Yale University Publications in Anthropology*, no. 11. New Haven: Yale University Press (1936).

Muina, Natalia. "To Make Whole." *Woman of Power* (Winter 1987).

Pogrebin, Letty Cottin. "Do Americans Hate Children?" *MS. Magazine* (November 1983).

———. "Work Friendships Are Very Difficult." *Bottom Line* 8, no. 3 (February 15, 1987).

Puck, Stirling, M.D. "Absence of H-Y antigen in an XY female with Campomelic dysplasia." *Human Genetics* 57 (1981): 23–27.

———. "Trisomy 22 mosaicism: another differential in the diagnosis of Turner-Noonan stigmata." In preparation.

———. Review of *Penetrance and Variability in Malformation Syndromes*, edited by J. J. O'Donnell and B. D. Hall. *Yale Journal of Biology and Medicine* 53 (1980): 571–72.

————. Review of *Diagnostic Approaches to the Malformed Fetus, Abortus, and Deceased Newborn*, edited by M. S. Golbus and B. D. Hall. *Yale Journal of Biology and Medicine* 53 (1980): 572–73.

————, and Jeanie Puleston. "Genetics, Environment, and Your Baby: A Workbook for Parents-to-be." Vivigen, Inc. (1987).

Rosenthal, Robert, et al. "Body Talk and The Tone of Voice: The Language Without Words." *Psychology Today* (September 8, 1984).

Schiebinger, Londa. "The History and Philosophy of Women In Science: A Review Essay." *SIGNS: Journal of Women in Culture and Society* 12, no. 2. Chicago: The University of Chicago Press (Winter 1987).

Scholes, France V. "The First Decade of the Inquisition In New Mexico." *New Mexico Historical Review* 10 (1935): 208–22.

Schwatka, Frederick. "Among the Apaches." *Century Magazine* (1887). Reissue. Palmer, Colo.: The Filter Press, 1974.

Skallman, Nathan, and Chella Herrera. "A Conversation With Juanita Sedillo." *New Mexico Magazine* (April 1982).

Swartz, Jacqueline. "Development of Self in Women Explored at Ortho Conference." *American Psychological Association Monitor* 15, no. 7 (July 1984).

Toufexis, Anastasia. "Why Mothers Kill Their Babies." *Time* (June 20, 1988).

Turner, Victor W. "Ritual As Communication and Potency: An Ndembu Case Study." *Southern Anthropological Society Proceedings* 9 (1975).

van Gelder, Lindsy. "Carol Gilligan: Leader for a Different Kind of Future." *MS. Magazine* (January 1984): 37–40, 101.

Wallis, Claudia. "Medical School, Heal Thyself." *Time* (May 23, 1983).

WMJ 6 (1889 p. 249; Emily Blackwell, "The New York Infirmary and College,") *Transactions of the Women's Medical College of Pennsylvania* (1900).

Women & Health 6-1/2, Spring/Summer 1981. The Haworth Press, Inc. (1982).

Interviews

Aragon, Jesusita. Interviews with authors. September 1982–December 1985.

Fairchild, Louise d'A. Interview with authors. January 1983.

Herrera, Sabinita. Interviews with authors. September 1982–May 1986.

Jaramillo, James, M.D. Interview with authors. September 28, 1983.

Kahn, Annie. Telephone conversations and interviews with authors. December 18, 1982, and January 8, 1983.

Kahn, Annie. Interviews with authors. February 1983–September 1986.

Lujan, Eileen, M.D. Interview with authors. September 27, 1982.

Martinez, Beatrice R. Interview with authors. August 1982.

Moonwalker, Tu. Interviews with authors. August 1982–August 1984.
Mondanaro, Josette, M.D. Telephone conversations and interview with authors. August 4, 1983 and September, 1983.
Ortiz y Pino, José III. Interview with authors. October 7, 1982.
Patterson, Jane, M.D. Interview with authors. August 23, 1983.
Pineda, Arturo. Interview with authors. January 2, 1987.
Puck, Stirling, M.D. Interviews with authors. November 30, 1983 and December 3, 1983.
Rodriguez, Gregorita. Interviews with authors. September 1982–September 1984.
Ward, Molly Radford, M.D. Interview with authors. July 29, 1982.
Ywahoo, Dhyani. Interviews with authors. December 1982–December 1983.

Newspapers

Albuquerque Journal Impact Magazine, August 21, 1984 and April 30, 1985.
Movement Newspaper, The, November 1980.
Dallas Times Herald, October 10–13, 1982.
Santa Fe Daily New Mexican, October 2, 1882.
Santa Fe New Mexican, June 17, 1982, June 10 and 27, 1988.
Santa Fe Reporter, April 24, 1985, December 3, 1986 and February 4, 1987.

Observations

Observations by Victoria Krueger, Ph.D., Clinical Psychologist, of former colleague Stirling Puck, M.D., at the State of New Mexico's Health and Environment Department's Children's Medical Services Agency, Santa Fe.

Television Transcripts

Silko, Leslie Marmon. "Running on the Edge of the Rainbow." In *Words and Place.* New York: Clearwater Publishing Co., Inc., 1981. Video Tape Transcript.
"Talk Back to the Doctors." The Oprah Winfrey Show. WLS-TV, Chicago. Transcript #82 (January 13, 1987).

INDEX

Abel: 194

Acne, Sabinita Herrera and: 104

Acupressure, as *curandera* technique: 91

Acupuncture: 221; among Cherokee medicine people, 59

Adam: 9

AIDS: 165, 206

Alchise, Bonito: 49

Alchise, Chino: 48

Allen, Paula Gunn: 208

Altamisa de la sierra: 101

AMA (American Medical Association): 3, 124; members of (*see* AMA medicine)

AMA medicine: 3–4; assumptions of, 6; coldness of, 13–14, 124–25, 202, 203, 215; negligibility of psychospiritual factors to, 14; Annie Kahn and, 40; Dhyani Ywahoo and, 74; Jesusita Aragon and, 116–18; and obstetrics, 117; procedures of, 124–26; and specialization, 125, 126; "For Men Only" aspects of, 126, 129–30, 203, 204, 215 (*see also* Hunt, Harriet K.; Patterson, Jane; Regensburger, A. E.; Walker, Mary); and money, 126, 203, 227–28; public perception of, 156; spirituality and, 218

American Hospital Association: 124

American Medical Association: *see* AMA

Amole: 104

Amulets: 12, 181, 183, 186, 187; see also *monos y muñecos*

Andrews, Lynn: 24

Anesthesia: 123

Anesthesiology: 138; as female specialization, 213

Angawi: 80

Ani Gadoah clan: 63, 74–75, 79, 81

Anil del muerto: 101

Antibiotics: 123

Apache Indians: last surrender of, 48; medicine women of, 49 (*see also* Moonwalker, Tu; Naiche, Dorothy); spirits of, 50; group orientation of, 53; religion of, 184; witchcraft among, 184–86; *see also* Moonwalker, Tu

Aragon, Jesusita: 96, 115–19, 200; childhood apprenticeship of, 115–16; and Western doctors, 116–18; spirituality of, 118–19, 218

Arbularias: 92, 179–81

Aristotle: 203

Asthma, Sabinita Herrera remedy for: 104

Basketmaking, Apache: 49–50; spiritual aspects of (*see* Moonwalker, Tu)

Bear Societies: 187

Bellido, Juan Diego: 177

Bennet oxygen machines: 139

Bible, witchcraft in: 169

Bioenergetics: 221

Birth control pill, Native American medicine and: 21

Birthrate, among adolescents: 221

Black Mass: 193

Blackwell, Elizabeth: 128

Blackwell, Emily: 129

Bleeding, as medical treatment: 22

Blessingway: 33, 34–36, 40

Block, Susan: 203

Hunt, Harriet K.: 128
Huntington's chorea: 149
Hydrotherapy: 221
Hymns, Cherokee: 59, 62

Ibuprofen, as Navajo drug: 43
Illness: Biblical explanation of, 9; as divine punishment, 15; stress and, 163; iatrogenic, 193; bewitchment and, 196
Immortal (herb): 101, 104
Incest, as Native American taboo: 189
Indian Market, of Santa Fe: 52, 54
Indians: *see* Native Americans
Innocent III (pope): 169
Insulin, Native American medicine and: 21

Jacobs, Sue-Ellen: 202
James I (England): 170
Jaramillo, James: 89–93
Jesus: 147; Dhyani Ywahoo on, 79
Jordan, Judith: 4, 5
Jung, C. G.: 73, 75, 173–74

Kahn, Annie: 25–26, 29–44, 201, 202, 225–26; spiritual pantheon of, 26; infancy of, 33–34; children of, 35; girlhood of, 35; healing technique/philosophy of, 36–44; and consciousness raising, 37, 38, 39; and AMA medicine, 40; prayers of, 40–41; spirituality of, 40, 218; as community college consultant, 43
Kahn, Charlotte: 30, 34
Kahn, Nez Bah: 30, 32
Kali: 174
Keeper of the Lineage: 62
Kelsey, Morton: 193
Kennedy, John F.: 119
Kent State University, National Guard massacre at: 193
Kidwell, Clara Sue: 25
Kiev, Ari: 96
Kluckholn, Clyde: 191
Koshare: 174
Kraemer, Henry: 169, 172
Krueger, Victoria: 225–29

Lamaze method: 144
Larner, Christina: 193
Laser beams, medicinal: 123

Leek, Sybil: 192
Levine, John: 11
Long Walk: 29
Looking Horse, Stanley: 24
Lujan, Eileen: 179

Madrid, Felipe: 178
Malleus Malleficarum (Kraemer/Sprenger): 169, 172–73
Mangas Coloradas: 48
Manson, Charles: 193
Martin, Bill: 137, 138, 139–40
Massage: 221; as *curandera* technique, 91; Gregorita Rodriguez and, 108, 109, 111, 112; see also *sobardoras*
Measles: 123
Medicaid: 126, 221
Medical school(s): and anatomy class, 160; dehumanizing character of, 160, 161–62; "For Men Only" aspects of, 203, 204, 213; women and, 126, 129–30, 203, 204, 213
Medicare: 126
Medicas: see *curanderas*
Medicine: changes in, 16; allopathic, 74; modern revolutions in, 123–24; witchcraft and, 170; in U.S. (*see* AMA medicine)
Medicine bundles: 64, 65–66
Medicine men: social, 51; and medicine women contrasted, 80–81; Apache, 185; Pueblo, 186–87; Navajo, 190; as temperamentally distinct from AMA doctors, 214; *see also* Cochise
Medicine women: 21–82; Navajo, 6; spirituality of, 9, 216; payment of, 31; Apache, 49; and medicine men contrasted, 80–81; perspective of, 125; tribal respect for, 213; as generous with time, 228; *see also* Kahn, Annie; Moonwalker, Tu; Ywahoo, Dhyani
Mendelsohn, Robert: 9, 202
Merlin: 73
Midwives: 128, 170; Apache, 51; see also *parteras*
Miller, Albert E.: 127
Millikan, Dr. (Jesusita Aragon mentor): 116–17